SHARP

THE EXCELSIOR

# PLANET LED
By Teddy Lo

Published by
ORO Editions
Publishers of Architecture, Art, and Design
Gordon Goff: Publisher
www.oroeditions.com
info@oroeditions.com

Copyright © 2014 by Demiurge Unit Intellectual Properties
ISBN: 978-1-935935-51-3
10 09 08 07 06 5 4 3 2 1  First edition

Graphic Design:  C Plus C Workshop Ltd.
Edited by: James Moore
Color Separations and Printing: ORO Group Ltd.
Printed in China.

This book was printed and bound using a variety of sustainable manufacturing
processes and materials including soy-based inks, acqueous-based varnish,
VOC- and formaldehyde-free glues, and phthalate-free laminations. The text
is printed using offset sheetfed lithographic printing process in (book specific)
color on 157gsm premium matte art paper  with an off-line gloss acqueous
spot varnish applied to all photographs.

ORO Editions makes a continuous effort to minimize the overall carbon
footprint of its publications. As part of this goal, ORO Editions, in association
with Global ReLeaf, arranges to plant trees to replace those used in the
manufacturing of the paper produced for its books. Global ReLeaf is an
international campaign run by American Forests, one of the world's oldest
nonprofit conservation organizations. Global ReLeaf is American Forests'
education and action program that helps individuals, organizations, agencies,
and corporations improve the local and global environment by planting and
caring for trees.

Library of Congress data:

For information on our distribution, please visit our website
www.oroeditions.com

# Teddy Lo

-
Author
Art Director

Teddy@planetledbook.com

Teddy Lo is a Hong Kong-based LED artist known for his work in the "tech-art" scene. He has held exhibitions in the United States, Europe, and Asia. Lo studied advertising design at the Art Center College of Design in Pasadena, California, where he began exploring the use of light-emitting diodes in art; he relocated to New York City after his graduation in 2002. He began his career in the advertising industry, and at the same time pursued art using LED as his medium. In 2003, Lo held his first solo art exhibition, *Morphology*, in New York City. He was named in *Lighting Magazine*'s "Who's Who of Lighting 2004," for his contribution to the lighting industry. Since then, Lo has held solo exhibitions in various locations, including Russell Simmons' Art for Life in NYC, Luminale in Frankfurt, the 2006 National Day Singapore Expo at The Esplanade and Microwave's "A-Glow-Glow" outdoor Media Art Exhibition at Hong Kong Museum of Art, Miaimi Art Basel and Burning Man Festival in Nevada.

As of 2008, Lo received a master's degree in lighting offered by the Queensland University of Technology in Australia. In addition to continuing his artistic pursuits, Lo is the founder and Chief Vision Officer of LEDARTIST, an LED experience design company in Hong Kong, New York and Shanghai. In addition, he founded Input Output Gallery, a new media art gallery in Central, Hong Kong.

# James Moore

-
Editor

James@planetledbook.com

Like many of this book's contributors, James' first LED memory was inside a school laboratory watching a red light flash on and off. Now, as a writer and editor living in between Hong Kong's skyscrapers, he's able to witness how far the technology has come.

# Christine Yuen

-
Project Manager

Christine@planetledbook.com

When not managing publishing projects like PLANET LED, Christine is the founder of Tree Translations Ltd., a simultaneous interpretation and translation service located in Hong Kong. They are not as different as they seem! Both roles require good organizational and multitasking skills, and the ability to think quickly. During the project there were many "lightbulb moments" and Christine counts herself incredibly privileged and proud to have been a part of this amazing journey.

First and foremost, I would like to dedicate this project to my dad, Paul-san, for his entrepreneurial aspirations, innovative inspirations and tremendous support on this project.

I wanted to make PLANET LED as resourceful and impactful as possible, which took us a while, but I think all the work has been well and truly worth it.

Special thanks to the contributors to the book's forewords. To Mr. Nakamura, Mr. Swoboda, Ms. Wu and Professor Cowling, your words are truly inspiring and it is my honour to have your inclusions in this volume.

I want to give a heartfelt thanks to all the interviewees for this book. I am much obliged to you all for taking the time to go through the interview process and I do hope we have done you and your work justice.

I want to give my project manager Christine a huge thank you for assisting me in this project throughout the years. You have great patience with my demanding schedules and have helped tremendously in all facets of the project. I could not have done it without you.

This also goes to James for editing all the book's material with a greater voice and consistency. Cindy, thank you for helping us with all the legal issues that arise when putting together an international project. As always, I can sleep better knowing that you're on board.

An acknowledgement, too, of Simon Grendene for his great collage artwork. You are one of the best artists that I have ever known; everything from our thumbnail sketches came out perfectly. Also, a special thanks to our photographer James Gabbard, as well as NASA, the graphic design studio C+C, and LEDARTIST for supporting the graphical and technical production.

I'm deeply indebted to the following for all their support and help critiquing content during the final stages: my brother Ron and his wife Phoebe, Howard M, Richard and Simon-san, Peter C, Joel K and Joshua G. I'm also grateful to have been able to call upon Andora and Catherine to help with the coordination with numerous parties.

Nicolai W – I hope that you know that all of your contributions to PLANET LED are hugely appreciated. Likewise, I'd like to say a big thank you to Light Engine, LPI, e:cue and all of Cree's engineers who consulted me about in-depth theories and technicality of the luminous technologies.

Mr. Crestejo – I'm indebted to you for introducing the publishing house ORO Editions to us. We realized that we'd finally seen the light at the end of a very long tunnel when we agreed to work together. They have a great distribution network and, as readers can see, superb quality in both printing and e-publishing. We have learned a great deal from this collaboration and the outcome of the book is immaculate. They make every effort that everyone on this page put in completely worth it.

Lastly, I want to thank the two most important and beautiful women in my life: my mom, Kathy, and my wife, Margi, for their unswerving love and emotional support. I can't wait for my next challenge.

Teddy Lo
Author and Art Director

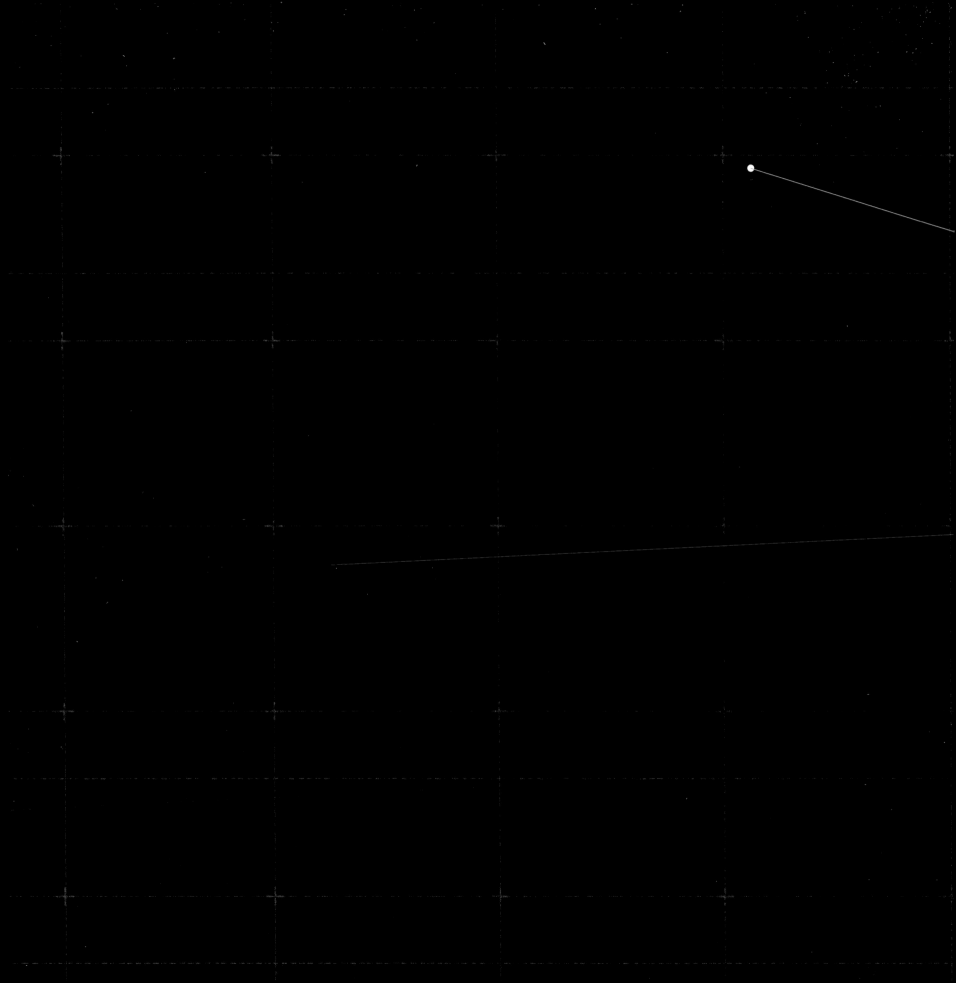

# CONTENTS

# CONTENTS

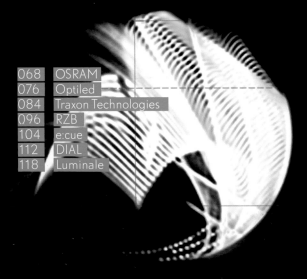

# FOREWORDS

# Shuji Nakamura

Professor,
Millennium Technology Prize winner,
Materials Department
of the College of Engineering,
University of California,
Santa Barbara

PLANET LED will educate and help many people know more about LEDs - the ultimate source of lighting. Most people don't understand much about these special light sources, but there's no doubting their importance.

Not long after I moved to Santa Barbara in 2000, about three months later, someone came in to my office and told me that I had saved his life. My first thought was that he was joking.

He said he was climbing a very high mountain, but that when he got to the top and tried to descend, it had become pitch black and he'd lost his way. The only light source he had was an LED light keychain that lit his way back down to safety.

He told me that he wanted to find its inventor and so he checked the internet, and came all the way to see me to say thank you.

Back in the 1990s, I was so surprised at the speed at which LEDs spread all around the world. When I invented the first bright LED in 1993, I never expected the technology to be such a huge market. It was so fast.

The discovery of blue LEDs was obviously an important milestone in my career. Before blue LEDs, the only available LEDs were red, yellow and green LEDs by using gallium phosphide — and they are very dim and the green wasn't pure green.

By using indium gallium nitride, I invented blue LFDs and pure green in 1996. Now green also has gallium nitride. And with these LEDs, people can make any kind of colours, including white.

Eventually all traditional lighting will be replaced with LEDs. This is a big "yes" especially in Japan, where many lighting companies are setting up LED branches.

In 2009 the price was still relatively high but in 2012 the price was cut in half to a more comparable price. In Japan, a compact fluorescent lamp was on average US$10 and an LED light was US$20. This price gap will be even more competitive in the future.

From a social context, the advantages of LEDs are their longer lifetime and use of safe manufacturing materials.

At University of California, Santa Barbara, our next step is to produce white LEDs able to achieve a brightness of 250lm/Watt within five years. We also are developing green and blue laser diodes for project applications such as laser displays and laser projectors.

Right now, projectors use LCD or traditional lamps, or for laser projectors we can use red and blue laser diodes. However, we are developing green diodes at 511nm for new projectors.

Research is like solving a puzzle. If there are problems or hurdles during the course of a research project, I've always found it fun to be able to solve them — just like a quiz.

I'm positive that PLANET LED will help more people know the importance of LEDs and their energy-saving abilities.

# Chuck Swoboda

-

President,
Chief Executive Officer
and Chairman, CREE

The core technology used in the lighting industry has remained relatively static over the past half century. However, right now, there is a revolution taking place, a revolution based on the light-emitting diode.

LED lighting technology has progressed from early uses in small, dim indicator lights in electronic appliances and equipment — such as VCRs, clocks and calculators — to today's uses in an increasing number of lighting applications. As the performance of the technology has improved, it has been employed in accent and decorative lights, signs and displays, flashlights, automotive applications and traffic signals.

Since the second half of the first decade of this millennium, LEDs have increasingly been used for white light applications for indoor and outdoor general lighting. This includes the street lights and ceiling fixtures that we depend on every day. This progression has been made possible by technology breakthroughs and continuous incremental improvements in LED performance — brightness and efficiency — as well as by cost reductions due to high-volume manufacturing and increased performance.

LEDs are becoming attractive for many lighting applications because of their reduced electricity consumption, long life and durability when compared to traditional lighting sources, i.e., light bulbs.

As the technology has improved and more applications are deployed, the visibility of LED lighting has increased. Recent notable installations are the color-changing lighting that accented the "Water Cube" and the "Bird's Nest" at the 2008 Beijing Olympics, as well as LED video screens and decorative displays now in use worldwide. Other high-profile projects include the city of Los Angeles' plans to replace over 150,000 streetlights with LED lights and the deployment of LED lights in the renovation of the US Pentagon in Washington, D.C.

LED lighting will have one the most significant impacts on the world's energy usage over the next several decades. Estimates are that up to 20 percent of the world's electricity is used for lighting and LEDs can reduce this by over 50 percent.

Although LED lighting has made great progress over the past few years, the vast majority of the world's lighting still uses traditional technology. The market opportunity to replace traditional lighting is large, and many of the world's leading industrial organizations are focused on capturing a share of this.

The companies that are able to harness this technology to produce cost-effective, high-performance and high-quality LED lighting products stand to benefit greatly. At the same time, the companies that cling to the old technology face a bleak future.

A generation from now, this old technology is likely to be nothing more than a curiosity relegated to museum shelves next to phonographs and film cameras.

# FOREWORDS

## Wu Ling

-

General Secretary,
China Solid State Lighting
Director,
China's SSL Program Office

Besides the excellent achievements made by many athletes, Beijing's beautiful Olympic stadiums, illuminated by LED light, also wowed spectators from around the world.

During the Games, LED technology lit up China's capital city and created a modern and artistic environment perfectly suited for the Olympics. The color-changing Bird's Nest (National Stadium) and crystal Water Cube (National Aquatics Centre) were simply stunning.

Technology has become an inseparable necessity for every human. We live by it, with it and are surrounded by it. With every new innovation, technology has broadened and fascinated our perspectives and ideals on so many levels.

Using LED as a medium to make art channels feelings, passion and renews designers' creative vision. To date, LED lighting technology has been extensively applied to outdoor displays, architectural lighting and stage lighting.

The combination of LED technology and art enables a greater aesthetic presence and lends vitality to otherwise "cold" constructions.

In this book, Teddy Lo, a young versatile artist, offers his vision of this promising combination.

# Ian Cowling

-

Professor,
Queensland University
of Technology

LEDs are the future of most lighting applications that we know of today. And, very likely, they are also the future of the applications that we don't yet know about.

While it is still a developing industry, LED lighting promises to deliver efficiency in a world where energy usage dominates our decision making. LED lights also have the advantage of being compact, and the ability to provide almost any color and sensation.

With all these positives, the future of LEDs is exciting, and for this reason I am proud to be asked to write the foreword for this book. Light-emitting diodes are complicated semiconductor devices. While people using them may not be interested in the science behind their production and control, the information contained within this book will help people understand many of the other fascinating issues surrounding LED lighting and its applications.

The book commences with a history of LEDs and then discusses the practical issues of lamps and devices using LEDs. It also covers the exciting world of design. But of particular interest are the interviews recorded with people who are leading the development and application of LEDs today — the same people who will continue to lead LEDs into the future.

This is a unique book which will give everyday people an insight into the future of lighting. I congratulate Teddy Lo on the production of PLANET LED.

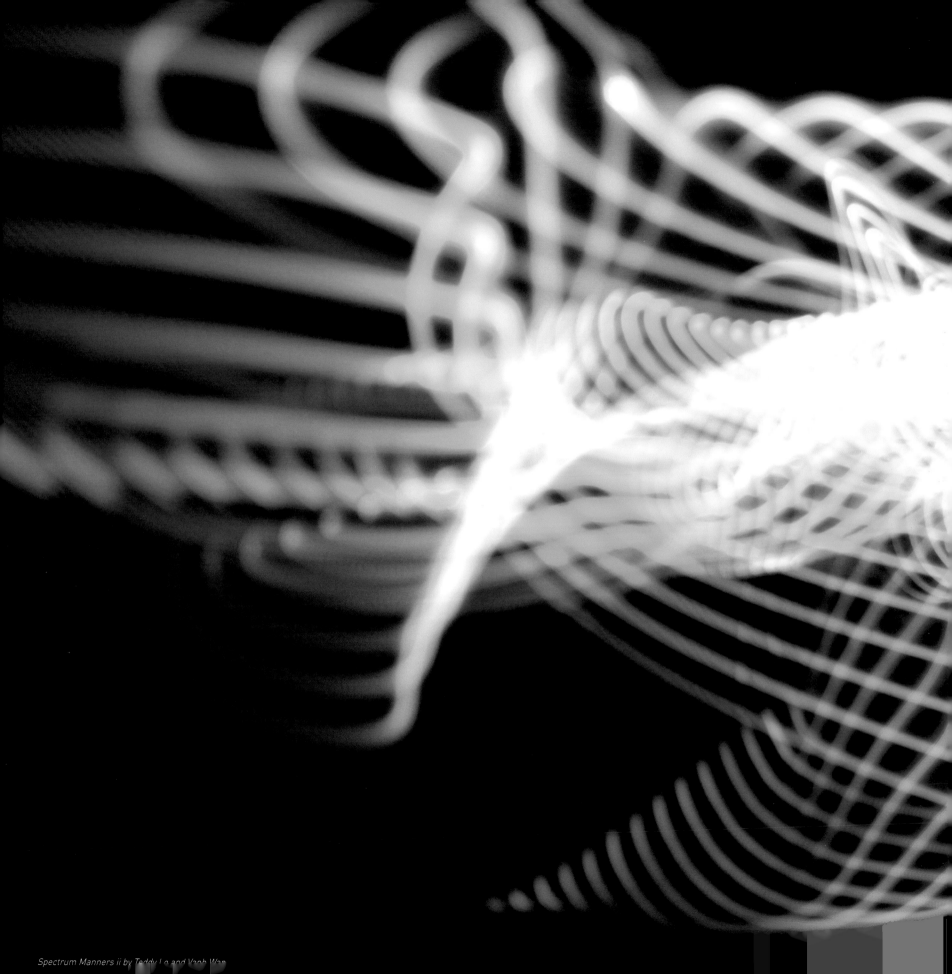

Spectrum Manners ii by Teddy Lo and Vanh Wee

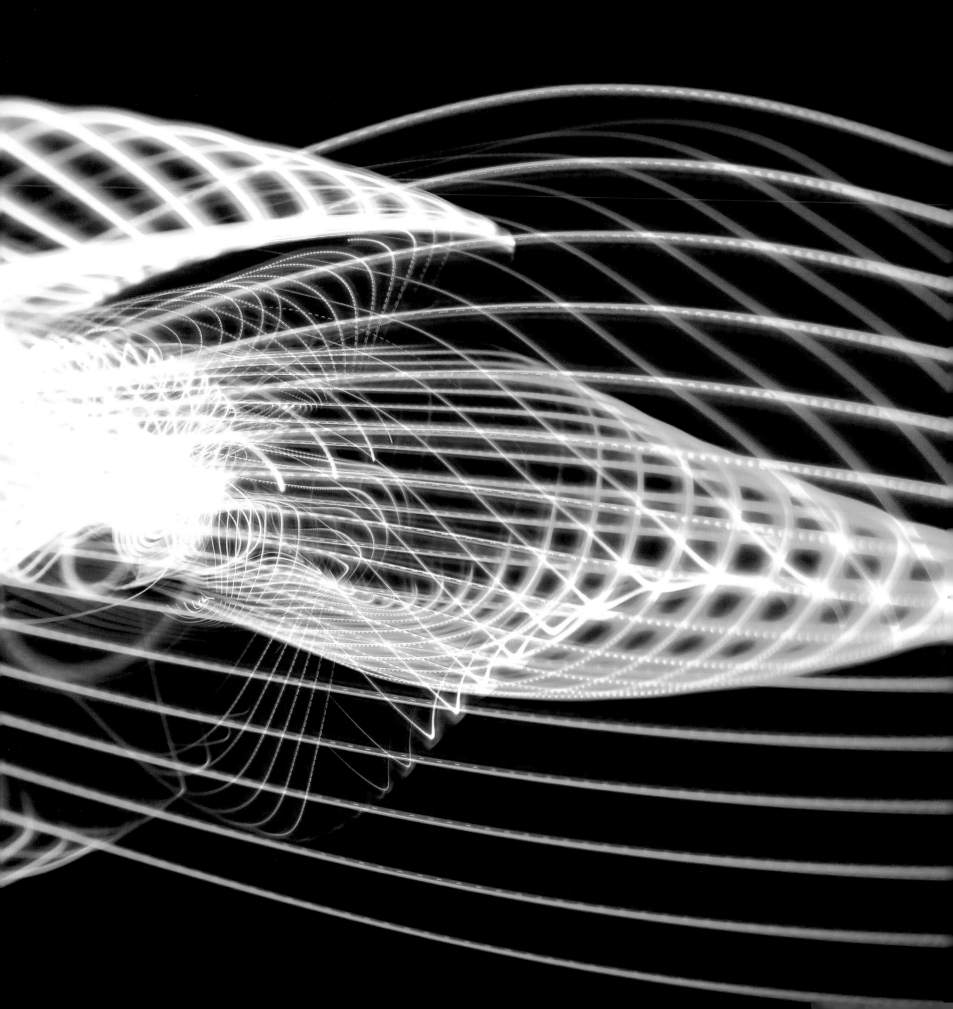

# DISCOVERY

CREE
United Luminous International
Wu Ling
Tsunemasa Taguchi
Light Prescriptions Innovators
LED Museum

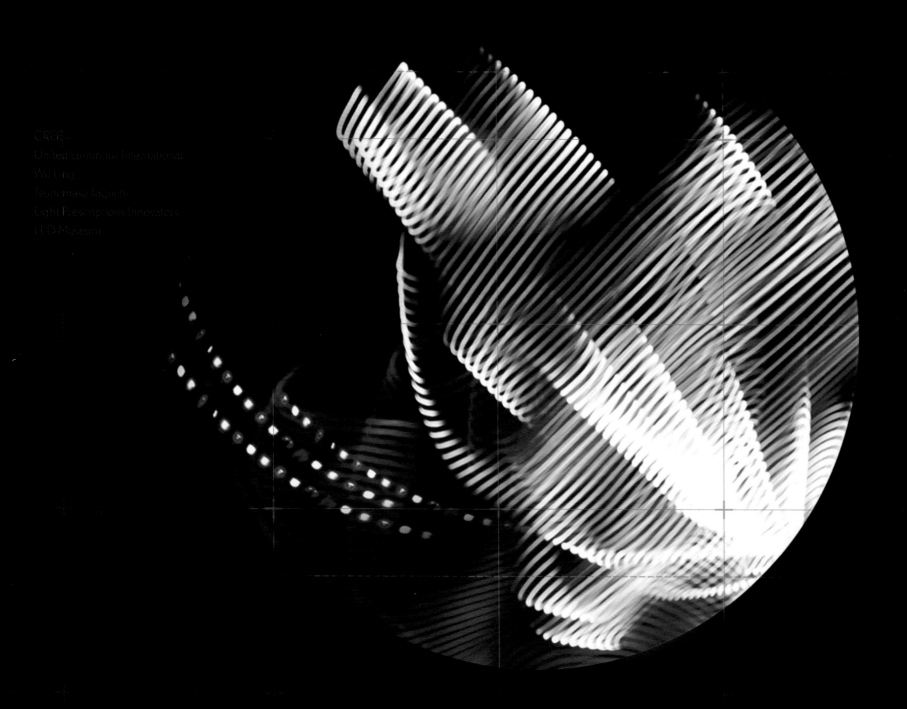

The story of the evolution of LEDs begins with the invention of the first LED by Russian scientist and inventor Oleg Vladimirovich Losev in 1927. However, the first visible LED was created in 1962 by Nick Holonyak Jr. of the General Electric Company. Red LEDs were used in most of the electrical appliances as the indicator lights, nothing more. They were on the clocks, VCR, Walkman and TVs just to name a few.

Since then, the wider spectra of red, green and yellow have been developed using various material implementations within the diode itself in the '70s and '80s. There are inorganic semiconductor materials like aluminium Gallium Arsenide (ALGaAs), Indium Gallium Aluminum Phosphide (InGaAlP) and indium Gallium Nitride (InGaN). The major turning point arrived in the '90s with the creation of the blue diode. The complete color spectrum was now possible to the world with the availability of all three primary color diodes (Red, Green, and Blue) in light.

There are other kinds of environmental lighting products now available in the marketplace. However, the use of high-power LEDs in lighting fixtures is currently the fastest growing application. The realization of environmental factors, the increase of LED's efficacy and the decrease in price all enable the expansion of this sector.

Lighting is responsible for 19% of total global electricity use and 6% of greenhouse gas emission. With the development of white "super bright" LEDs, demand from city planners to consumers has created a wave of LED evolution and revolution. Manufacturers are eying promising global sales forecasts of more than $4,317 million for high-brightness LEDs in 2014. It has a potential of 45% of CAGR from 2008-2014.

LED is a game changing technology. It is now widely used as integral components of architectural lighting, entertainment lighting, retail lighting, outdoor area lighting, commercial and industrial lighting, residential lighting, consumer portable, off-grid lighting, safety and security, channel letters, machine vision, LED backlit TVs and LED video screens. Curious observers have noticed LED's impact and how its aspects are making our world a more efficient, brighter and more interesting place.

But how are they made and why are they so special? Put simply, a light-emitting diode uses semiconductor technology to emit narrow-spectrum light diode when an electrical current flows through it. The diode charges electrons and holes, causing a p-n junction that releases energy in the form of a photon.

Not all LEDs are created equal. The manufacture of diodes is the key to creating a successful luminaire product. A top-end LED needs to be packaged with the right chemical and physical balance, so that its color falls in the right nanometre of the color spectrum. This balance also ensures an advanced level of brightness and lifespan.

For LEDs, a die and its packaging are its soul and, in order to create one, a "wafer" is required. The manufacturer needs a sophisticated Metalorganic Vapour Phase Epitaxy (MOCVD) facility to ensure the process of depositing the molecules in the wafer is done correctly. In addition, the applications of substrates and the categorization (binning) of LEDs into different nanometres of spectrum and burn-in for durability are vital to the whole process.

It is important to check an LED's origin and choose the components stringently — a strong foundation is always needed for a well-made luminaire or luminous product. A well-designed LED product system is a quantum leap beyond anything else in the market.

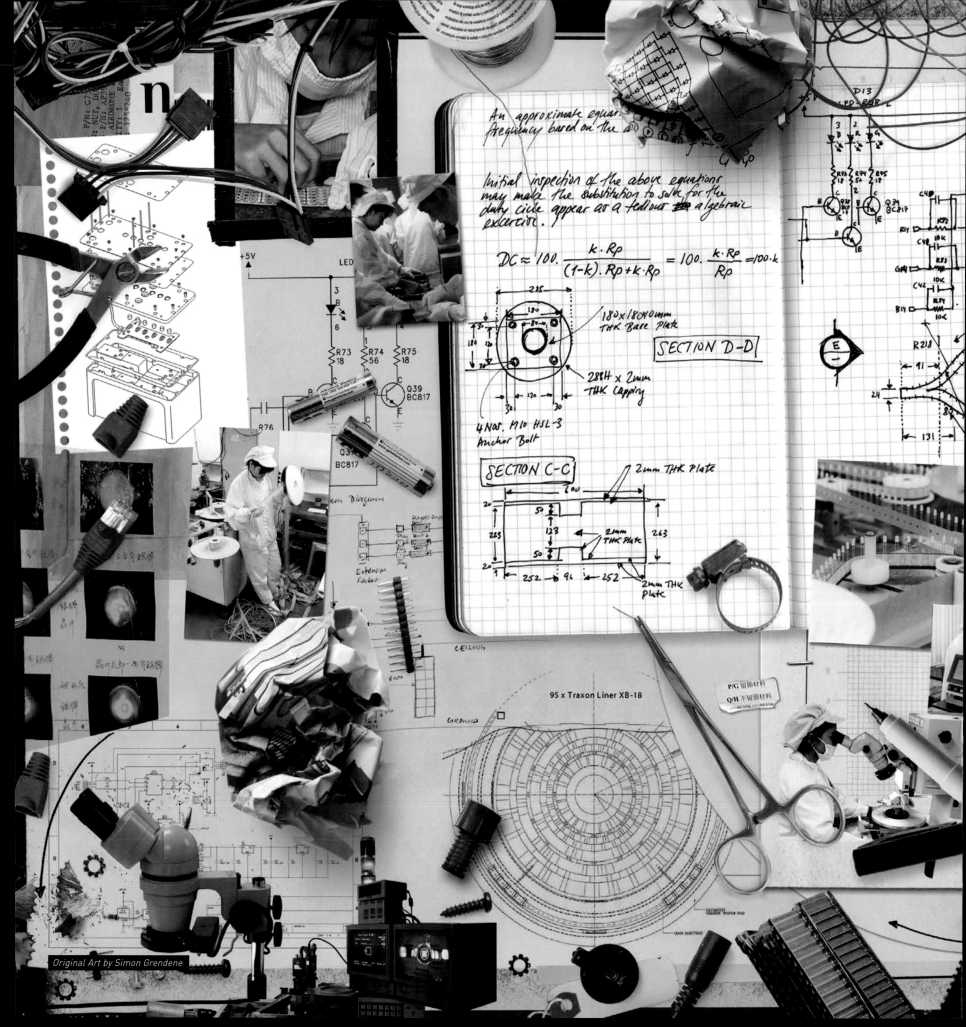

**DISCOVERY**

# CREE

Chuck Swoboda, President,
Chief Executive Officer and Chairman

**CREE◆**

United Luminous International
Wu Ling
Tsunemasa Taguchi
Light Prescriptions Innovators
LED Museum

**DISCOVERY**
-
**CREE**

CREE IS AN INNOVATOR IN THE FIELD OF LIGHTING-CLASS LEDS, LED LIGHTING, AND SEMICONDUCTOR SOLUTIONS FOR WIRELESS AND POWER APPLICATIONS.

CREE'S PRODUCT FAMILIES INCLUDE LED FIXTURES AND BULBS, BLUE AND GREEN LED CHIPS, HIGH-BRIGHTNESS LEDS, LIGHTING-CLASS POWER LEDS, POWER-SWITCHING DEVICES AND RADIO-FREQUENCY AND WIRELESS DEVICES.

ITS SOLUTIONS ARE DRIVING IMPROVEMENTS IN APPLICATIONS SUCH AS GENERAL ILLUMINATION, BACKLIGHTING, ELECTRONIC SIGNS AND SIGNALS, VARIABLE-SPEED MOTORS, AND WIRELESS COMMUNICATIONS.

Caroline Pines

Fayette Street

Beijing's Water Cube

**In what way would you say that LEDs are now essential to modern life?**

-

LED lighting offers unmatched energy efficiency, a long lifetime and contain no hazardous materials, all of which are essential as we strive to protect our planet for future generations.

**CREE claims that it can improve the quality of people's lives. In what ways does Cree do this?**

-

CREE's products can improve the quality of people's lives by helping to reduce the emission of greenhouse gases, reduce the resources consumed to light our world and by reducing the hazardous materials we introduce into our environment.

**How has the development of new materials and technologies aided the growth in the LED sector?**

-

New developments in any of the components of our LEDs can help by improving the performance of the product, reducing the cost to manufacture the product, simplifying the manufacturing or improving the reliability and lifetime.

**What is the ultimate potential of LED lighting?**

-

LEDs have the potential to replace all existing traditional lighting sources, thereby greatly reducing energy usage.

## DISCOVERY
-
**Cree**

LEDs light up this colorful multimedia fountain

Aesthetics and practicalities meet in San Jose, USA, where LEDs on these palm trees brighten up the highway for road users

**Are there still obstacles to face?**
-

The biggest obstacle is not technology, but increasing the end-customer's awareness of the benefits of LED lighting — convincing the market that the technology is ready and creating channels to deliver the product.

**What is your company philosophy?**
-

We are working to make energy-inefficient light bulbs obsolete. We aim to do this through a constant focus on innovation and velocity.

**How do you foresee LED technology influencing people's lives in the near future?**
-

People will no longer need to worry about changing light bulbs, and will commit fewer resources in lighting their homes and businesses.

The Golden Arches have never been so prominent

**DISCOVERY**

CREE

# United Luminous International

Paul Lo,
Founder
-

-
Wu Ling
Tsunemasa Taguchi
Light Prescriptions Innovators
LED Museum

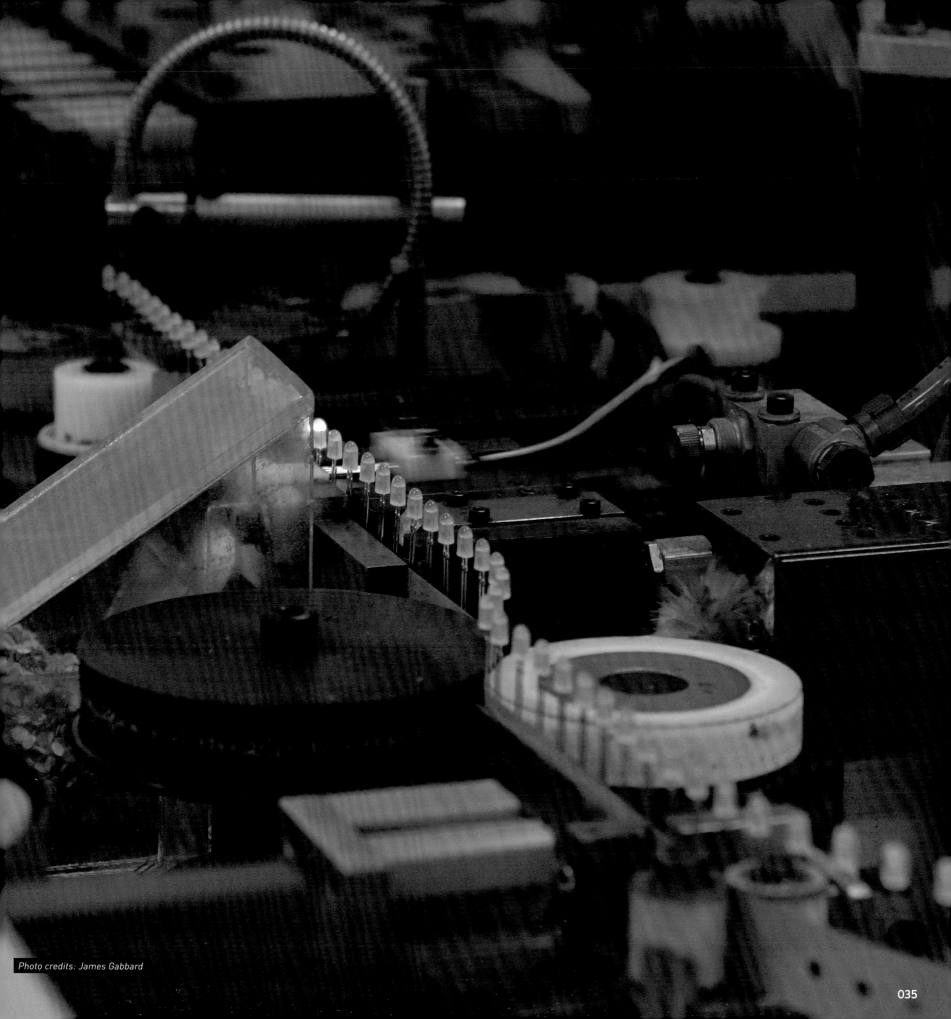

## DISCOVERY
-
**United Luminous International**

UNITED LUMINOUS INTERNATIONAL (ULI) GROUP HAS AN EXTENSIVE INVOLVEMENT WITHIN ALL SEGMENTS OF THE LED VALUE CHAIN. THIS INCLUDES RESEARCH AND DEVELOPMENT, PRODUCT DESIGN, THERMAL MANAGEMENT, OPTICS, POWER MANAGEMENT, PACKAGING AND PRECISION MANUFACTURING. IT IS A GENUINE PIONEER IN THE INDUSTRY.

PRODUCTS RANGE FROM HIGHLY SPECIALIZED LIGHTING SUCH AS FOR MEDICAL EQUIPMENT AND AUTOMOTIVE HEADLAMPS, TO GENERAL LIGHTING APPLICATIONS SUCH AS INTERIOR AND EXTERIOR LIGHTING, SIGNAGE, LARGE FULL-COLOR VIDEO DISPLAYS FOR STADIUMS, ROAD SIGNALS AND SPECIALITY LIGHTING.

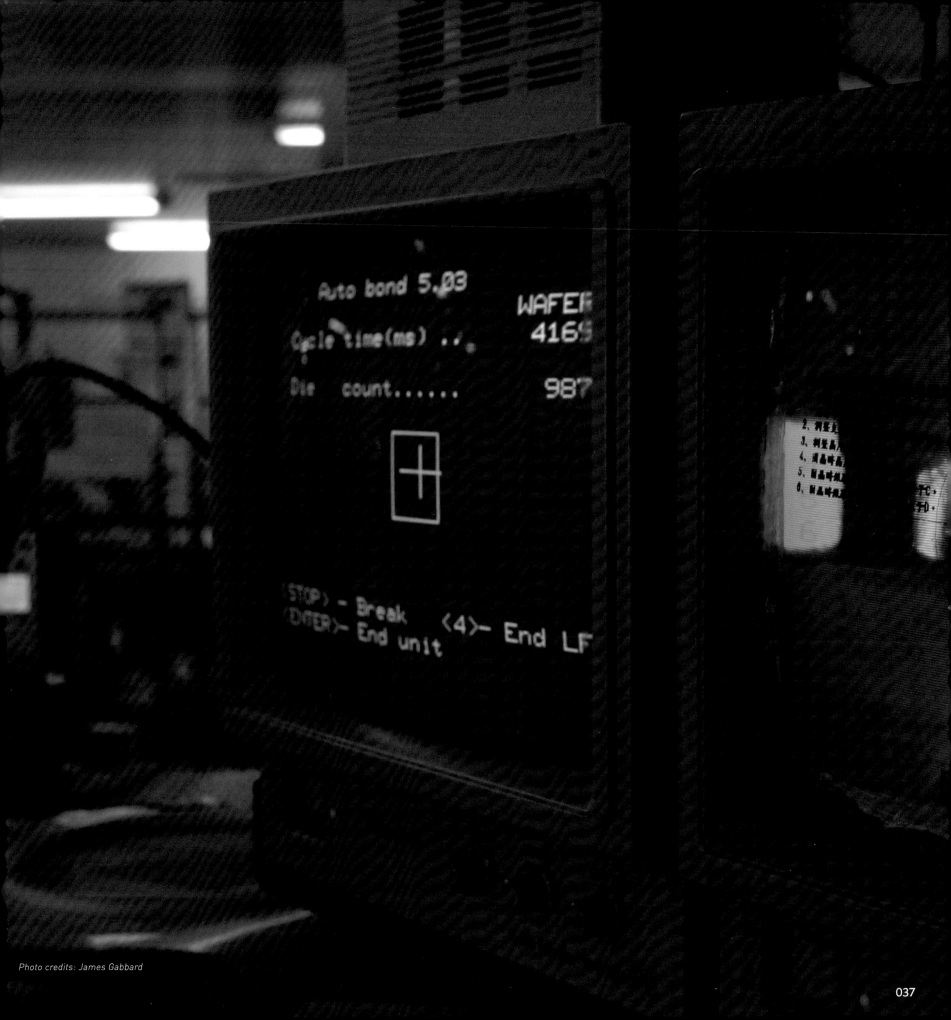

# DISCOVERY
-
**United Luminous
International**

**What is ULI's ultimate goal?**
-

LED lighting is a disruptive technology that is evolving extremely rapidly. Consequently, our goal, as our name "United Luminous International" implies, is to be able to leverage our extensive expertise within all aspects of the LED value chain, as well as our wide exposure through key joint ventures, in order to be, and to always continue to be, a top level player in this emerging industry.

Our unique positioning in China will assist us greatly in helping our international partners in the LED industry benefit from this vast emerging market.

**What obstacles do you believe still exist before LEDs are found everywhere?**
-

Firstly, I believe that this revolutionary light source will lead to big changes. Changes always present challenges. All conventional lighting will eventually be converted to digital technologies but those changes are no more radical than having replaced a cassette deck or a radio with an iPod.

Nevertheless, these changes are substantial and it will take more than one company, even an industry giant like Philips or OSRAM, to complete the transition to LED lighting.

Secondly, in order for small- and medium-sized companies to lead the way, they need to collaborate and work together with specialists who have the same confidence in the same path of the lighting evolution.

I believe that there will be thousands, perhaps millions, of engineers, scientists and manufacturers who will be working towards the same goal, particularly in the development of new materials.

**What about possible challenges to this technology?**
-

There are issues at the moment in maximizing lumen-per-watt as well as dollar-per-watt efficiency. One of the best transmittable heat-saturating materials is carbon fibre mixed with gold, however, its cost is prohibitive and there are complications with its processing.

Although this seems very remotely commercial, we are already studying this material very seriously with Mitsubishi Chemicals. We also hope to also secure the participation of an American company.

**What do you feel is the ultimate potential of LED technology?**
-

Once LED efficiency increases to its maximum potential, the issues related to thermal management won't be as significant as they are now. Furthermore, we will see cost reductions in all components related to LEDs to the point where we will also be able to enjoy affordable light automation.

In fact, LED circuits will not only change the way in which we light our homes, they will be equipped with sensors that will detect the number of persons who are at home and adjust lighting scenarios accordingly, as well as our air-conditioning systems to match our requirements.

People still think that lighting fixtures must be round or tubular, but this is not so. These designs were introduced because of the limitations of tungsten and glass materials that were available when my father founded Guangzhou's light bulb industry in 1942.

**Despite the challenges, do you feel that the acceptance of LEDs in our homes and business is essential from an environmental standpoint?**

-

I believe so, especially because global warming has now become a real threat. On top of that, the high cost of fuel is making energy saving even more important than before. At the moment, people have no choice but to use the current technology. We are working hard at changing this.

**Would you say that your company culture echoes these sentiments?**

-

Yes. Our aim is for the ULI group to remain a successful global light source provider, particularly in China. But I want all of our staff to come to work with the understanding that we are not only focused on making great products but also on contributing to a greener world.

**Is there a particular trend that you have noticed recently in the lighting manufacturing industry?**

-

In general, manufacturers are simply trying to make LEDs brighter and brighter. Very few companies are truly attempting to create "comfortable" lighting systems that enables users to convert from their incandescent lighting to LEDs. We are one of them.

**It seems as if there are hundreds of companies working with LEDs, particularly in China and in Asia. How will those markets develop?**

-

We are a very experienced player in the China market, therefore we are accustomed to such competition. The key to our success is, and will continue to be, our ability to be ahead of everyone else and to produce reliable products that really live up to the public's expectation.

At the moment, there are many small manufacturers in China who are making cheap, sub-standard LED products and they unfortunately spoil the reputation of the LED industry as a whole. On the positive side, they are pushing down prices which is good for the consumer and eventually for our industry as well.

We believe that as the market in China becomes more knowledgeable about LEDs, the demand for quality products with a good value-for-money ratio will ultimately increase.

**Will we see significant changes in the LED market when China and Asia set a standard for LED lighting products?**

-

Absolutely. In a country with a population of 1.3 billion and elsewhere in Asia — a region which is fast becoming the economic engine of the world — LED lighting standards will benefit not only governments but also consumers.

As a group, we are dedicated to high-quality products. We welcome any mechanism that can benchmark a certain quality standard.

**DISCOVERY**

CREE
United Luminous International

# Wu Ling

General Secretary,
China Solid State Lighting
Director,
China's SSL Program Office
-

Tsunemasa Taguchi
Light Prescriptions Innovators
LED Museum

MS. WU LING IS THE GENERAL SECRETARY OF CHINA SOLID STATE LIGHTING AND DIRECTOR OF CHINA'S SSL PROGRAM OFFICE. HER MISSION IS TO CREATE AN ENVIRONMENTALLY FRIENDLY AND ENERGY-EFFICIENT CHINA USING SOLID-STATE LIGHTING TECHNOLOGY. THIS IS HER VIEW ON LED DEVELOPMENT AND INFLUENCE IN CHINA.

**How do you view the development of LED lighting and how will it influence China?**

-

LED is a new generation of light source. Its features including a longer operational lifespan and environmentally friendly features will greatly benefit the sustainable development of China, as well as the rest of the world.

**What kind of LED research do you conduct?**

-

China Solid State Lighting Alliance conducts strategy research, standards development, project management and alliance construction.

**Who is the biggest player in China SSL industry to date?**

-

After years of development, seven national industrial parks have been established. There are now more than 2,200 LED companies and research institutions across China's entire industrial supply chain.

However, we have noticed that many of the entities are not very sizeable. Most of them are small- to medium-sized enterprises. We have to work harder to make the China SSL industry much more competitive.

**You host LED conferences in China every year. What is the goal of these events?**

-

China International Exhibition and Forum on Solid State Lighting (CHINASSL) has been running since 2004. CHINASSL is organized in order to provide a platform to facilitate communication to the industry worldwide. The quality of the event's presentations has become much better and attracts speakers and attendees from around the world.

**Where in China is SSL technology implemented?**

-

SSL technology is being used in architectural lighting, display, traffic lighting, signage, speciality lighting, functional lighting, automotive lighting, backlighting and so on. Seven national industrial parks have been established in Dalian, Shijiazhuang, Yangzhou, Shanghai, Nanchang, Xiamen and Shenzhen.

**Do you foresee LED changing the nightscape of cities?**

-

LED lighting technology was extensively applied during the 2008 Beijing Olympics. The capital's nightscape was truly gorgeous and amazing. LED applications, such as outdoor displays, architectural lighting and street lighting beautify cities and create a much more environmentally friendly urban space.

**What is the future of RGB (Red Green Blue) and white LED technology?**

-

RGB and white LED technology will greatly mature in the near future and be applied to broader scope of markets.

**Do you work with any R&D institutions?**

-

To date, China Solid State Lighting Alliance (CSA) includes 117 leading Chinese LED companies and research institutes. CSA members engage in a wide range of R&D projects involving LED.

**What is the alliance's ultimate goal?**

-

Our mission is to facilitate the development of the SSL industry in China and make it much more competitive.

**DISCOVERY**

CREE
United Luminous International
Wu Ling

# Tsunemasa Taguchi

LED Consultant,
Former Professor of Science & Technology,
Yamaguchi University
-
Light Prescriptions Innovators
LED Museum

Left: violet chips
Right: white light (4800 K)
–
High flux (→500 lm) and high-Ra (→98)
White LED: 121 n-UV LED chips (at 220 mA)
bonded on AlN ceramic substrate
( a size of 35mm x 35mm)

DISCOVERY
-
Tsunemasa
Taguchi

PROFESSOR TAGUCHI IS AN LED CONSULTANT AND A FORMER PROFESSOR OF SCIENCE & TECHNOLOGY, YAMAGUCHI UNIVERSITY.

HE HAS CONCENTRATED ON RESEARCH INTO WIDE-GAP SEMICONDUCTOR MATERIALS SUCH AS ZNS AND GAN, SEEKING NEW APPLICATIONS IN THE FORM OF SHORT-WAVELENGTH LIGHT-EMITTING DEVICES AND WHITE LED LIGHTING SYSTEMS. HE IS THE INVENTOR OF SUPER HIGH-COLOR RENDERING INDEX WHITE LEDS BASED ON VIOLET (N-UV) CHIP AND MULTI-PHOSPHOR TECHNOLOGY.

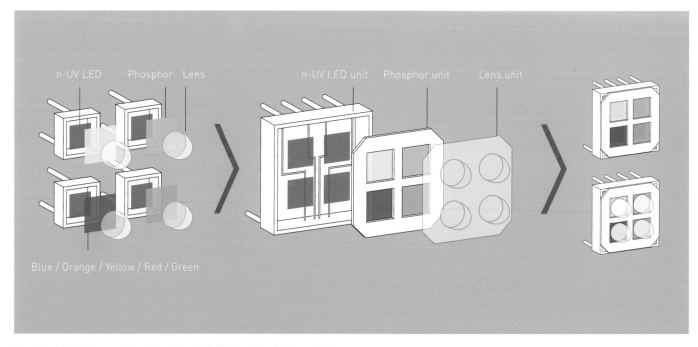

Tunable white light generation using primary R/O/Y, G and B multicolour lighting

**What are the main differences between traditional LEDs and the type that you work with?**

-

Traditional white LEDs are composed of blue LED and yellow phosphor, which originates from binary-complimented color LEDs.

The disadvantage of this is not the homogeneous distribution of light intensity. Right now, many companies around the world are working to improve the quality and characteristics of this type.

A decade ago, I developed a different kind of LED with better light distribution and high color rendering. With these kinds of LEDs, it's much easier to fabricate the type of light you'd get from an incandescent source.

These LEDs produce the kind of correlated color temperature that's a more "natural" at a temperature of about 5,000K.

**The Nichia LEDs from Shuji Nakamura are blue. Yours seem to be more red and green; UVs as well?**

-

Yes, mine are different from the blue diodes because of the use of violet LEDs, as well as red, green and blue phosphor materials. They are capable of covering a full spectrum of color. The natural light distribution for the white LEDs is similar to that of sunlight.

**Are there many companies using this kind of technology?**

-

The main companies using them are Mitsubishi Chemical Corporation, which works with Koizumi lighting, Olympus and CCS. CCS in Kyoto is a pioneering company that works on microscope apparatus that uses LEDs. But there are also many other Japanese companies that are interested in knowing more about our products.

**What do you think about the current popularity of LEDs?**

-

The structure and fabrication technology to create high-powered LED is advancing. Today we have to consider new types of light source and demand is driving supply.

For me, creative lighting is also very important — but I understand that opinions about this vary among others in different countries.

**In many cities in Asia, creative lighting using LEDs is increasingly common. What about in Japan?**

-

In Shanghai and other big cities in China, the lighting designs are very different from Japan. In Japan, designers are concerned about brightness and over illumination and so they use less LEDs in most buildings. But they do appreciate soft color LEDs.

## DISCOVERY
-
Tsunemasa
Taguchi

Sunlight includes the entire spectrum so people are fine with that. But even though we've had fluorescents for 30-40 years, the use of mercury is still a major problem. Fluorescent lighting can also change people's internal clocks. That's not healthy…
-

That's a very important point. Right now the world is looking to LED technology to save energy. In Japan, the reduction target of $CO_2$ emissions is 25 percent, which is a big problem for Japanese people. Replacing incandescent bulbs with LEDs seems to be a real solution.

LEDs are probably just one part of the solution…
-

Yes, and the priority on LEDs to replace traditional lighting is high. In a similar way, in Japan, we talk a lot about nuclear energy — is it the solution to our emissions problems? Regardless of the answer, we should also try to develop new systems of power generation, like solar.

The cost of electricity is very high compared with Taiwan and China. The savings from alternative energy and power reduction is enough motivation.

What is the ultimate potential of LED technology?
-

My personal objective is to create a "tuneable" type of LED — something that's impossible with traditional light sources. These LEDs would be able to display all colors, including white and different color temperatures of white light quality.

What obstacles are still out there to stop this from happening?
-

Philips refers to LEDs as intelligent light sources and dynamic white technology. We can already change the color temperature but it's hard to improve the Color Rendering Index (CRI) from 70 to 100.

We need a score of CRI of 85 for general lighting. Basically, we still need more improvements to quality to achieve a "tuneable" LED.

What impact will LEDs have in the future?
-

From a Japanese point of view, LEDs will definitely have an environmental impact and save electricity. Even now the government and the cabinet have announced the social and ecological importance of using white LEDs.

I think in the next two to three years, the replacement from traditional incandescent sources to LED lighting may be as high as 100 percent. Certainly, there is a lot of talk about LEDs here — in the media and from the government.

The next challenge will be to replace fluorescent lighting. There are still many issues preventing us from replacing this type of lighting overnight.

What is your most interesting project at the moment?
-

For the past five years, I've been looking at the implementation of LEDs in digestive endoscope and medical apparatus, which doctors use check cancer. We've been collaborating with the medical school at Yamaguchi University.

In the past, we usually used halogen and xenon 800W lamps. These have a very high-power consumption, and are large and expensive when using with fiber optics.

My hope is to replace these with white LEDs. Using only several watts, you can achieve the same brightness with a much smaller unit.

Medical LED light is a new type of illumination and a real advantage for doctors, engineers, students and artists.

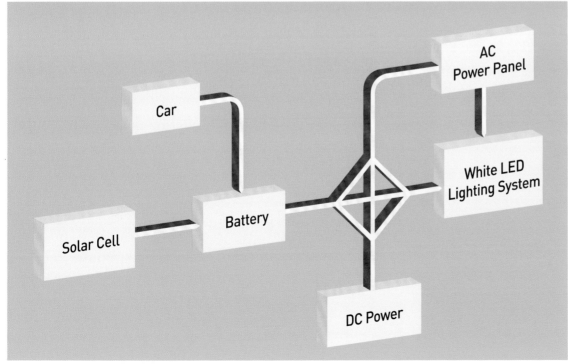

Smart-grid transmission and supply of electricity liked with white led street lamps

CREE
United Luminous International
Wu Ling
Tsunemasa Taguchi

# Light Prescriptions Innovators

Oliver Dross
Technology Director,
Europe
-

-

LED Museum

RIR lens for advanced projection optics
*Photo credits: Courtesy of Light Prescriptions Innovators*

**DISCOVERY**
-
**Light
Prescriptions
Innovators**

LIGHT PRESCRIPTIONS INNOVATORS (LPI) IS AN OPTICAL DESIGN, PROTOTYPING AND MANUFACTURING FIRM THAT SPECIALIZES IN PROVIDING ADVANCED OPTICAL SOLUTIONS FOR A WIDE RANGE OF APPLICATIONS.

IT SPECIALIZES IN STATE-OF-THE-ART OPTICAL SOLUTIONS IN THE NON-IMAGING AND IMAGING DESIGN SPACE FOR COMPANIES IN THE FIELDS OF SOLID STATE LIGHTING (LED SOURCES) AND IN CONCENTRATED PHOTOVOLTAICS SOLAR (CPV). THESE USE OPTICS TO CONCENTRATE 1,000-PLUS SUNS ON TO MULTI-JUNCTION PHOTOVOLTAIC SOLAR CELLS TO UTILIZE NOT ONLY THE VISIBLE LIGHT BUT ALMOST THE WHOLE SOLAR SPECTRUM.

**Why are optics so important to lighting?**

Up to now, the cost of fossil fuels has been so inexpensive that lighting companies could afford to utilize incandescent sources. They only boasted about two percent luminous efficiency as more than 75 percent of a light's energy was wasted as a thermal energy — a by-product in the creation of visible light. These days, oil prices are back to more than US$100 per barrel and that has changed everything.

Although Compact Fluorescent Lights (CFLs) are hailed around the world as a solution — with 50-72 lumens/Watt efficacies (versus 8-17 lumens/Watt for incandescent) — they are surpassed by LEDs with 65-100 lumens/Watt. Other problems that could spell the demise of CFLs demise are mercury content and their inability to be dimmed.

LED light sources do not have these problems. They do not have poisonous by-products and they utilize about one tenth of the energy of incandescents. Also, LEDs are very long-lasting.

However, their lighting pattern is Lambertian — i.e. they emit light in a hemispherical pattern away from the LED and therefore need optics in order to efficiently direct the light to where it is needed. Optics can help direct the proper beam pattern and emit general lighting in a spherical way, similar to that of an incandescent bulb.

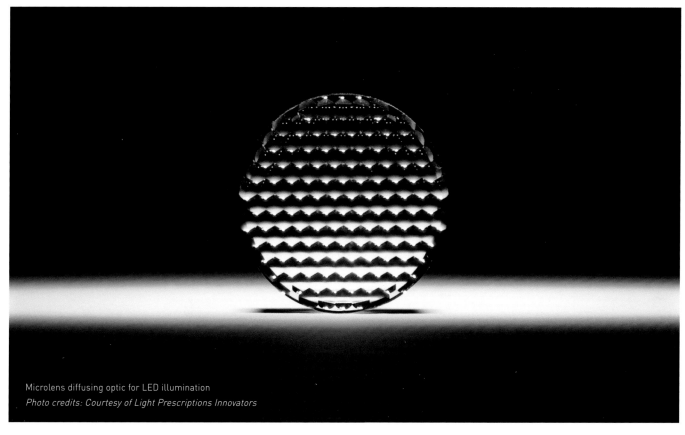

Microlens diffusing optic for LED illumination
*Photo credits: Courtesy of Light Prescriptions Innovators*

## DISCOVERY
-
**Light
Prescriptions
Innovators**

### So are LEDs the way forward?
-
LEDs are presently the light source technology that has the best chance of taking over the world's lighting needs in the short- to mid- term.

There are a number of applications (such as traffic lights, street lights and LCD displays) that make sense before others are implemented. However, as efficacies of LED light sources continue to increase (in lm/Watt) and the cost of utilizing LEDs for general illumination continues to fall, we will enter a time when even the common light bulb will be powered by LED technology.

Already, using today's costs, LED light bulbs in the household make sense when measured over their operating lifetime of approximately 50,000 hours.

### What kind of LED projects does LPI design?
-
LPI has been engaged in projects with varied applications in different fields such as:

| | |
|---|---|
| Automotive: | Taillights and headlights |
| Medical: | Surgical lamps and canulas that emit light where outside lighting is difficult |
| General Lighting: | Directed and non-directed lighting such as projector lighting, light bulbs and cove lighting |
| Backlighting: | Optics for LCD backlights |
| Projection: | Short-throw projector optics and theatre lighting optics |

LED collimator array
*Photo credits: Courtesy of Light Prescript Innovators*

A down light LED array
*Photo credits: Courtesy of Light Prescriptions Innovators*

### What are your main technical challenges?
-

The design challenges are usually sourcing proper LEDs to satisfy parameters such as luminance (brightness) and flux needed for the solution; to place all the available rays from the LED source exactly at the target and in the appropriate beam pattern; and to do it in a way that makes manufacturing and economic sense.

### What is the typical workflow of one of your projects?
-

We have recently been asked to design a solution for a high-bay light utilizing LEDs. The attributes of LEDs in this application have to do with long operating life and a higher efficacy to HID light sources.

In this case, the customer gives us the requirements needed, such as: luminance, flux, and pattern or angular spread of the beam. LPI then proposes one or two solutions, estimates the number of research and/or design hours to find and develop a solution and makes a proposal, including a design phase, a prototyping phase and a testing phase to prove the concept and the design.

After the project is initiated, LPI assigns one or more optical scientists to the task. Once the design is finished, LPI performs "ray tracing" that uses commercial packages that work out the solution virtually.

If the results are within the expected parameters, a CAD (computer assisted design) file is completed for the optics and the prototype is cut from a solid piece of optical acrylic. The optic is then tested utilizing the chosen light source. If the results are acceptable, the CAD is used to diamond-turn a mold insert, from which the optics can be injection-molded.

### What are your future plans for the LED market?
-

LPI plans to team up with manufacturing companies in order to develop luminaries, such as LED light bulbs. They will use the new LED light sources and other technologies where LPI has special intellectual property rights and they will begin to supplant incandescent lamps and CFLs.

**DISCOVERY**
-
**Light
Prescriptions
Innovators**

**How do you foresee LED technology developing?**
-
In 10 years, LED technology should be poised to take over a
substantial part of new construction general-illumination market
share and an important part of the existing lighting market.
In particular, for automotive, medical and street lighting the
application of LEDs will eventually surpass some of the speciality
lighting sources now being used.

**What is LPI's vision for the future?**
-
The lighting of the future will not be monopolized by one
particular technology but will be tailored by the most
appropriate technology for the particular application.

In all respects, lighting will be efficacious (lm/W) and efficient
and will deliver lighting for long periods of operation. This will
contrast markedly with the incandescent lighting past where
luminaire costs were important and energy was wasted to
achieve visible light.

**Can you name one of your most important upcoming projects?**
-
We are about to develop a "remote phosphor" light bulb with
a Japanese manufacturer that will use an LPI-proprietary
technology. It allows the phosphor, usually used to convert blue
LED light into white light, to be removed from the LED chip.

This allows the chip to operate at a hotter temperature and the
phosphor to last longer because it runs at a cooler temperature.
The light bulb emits the lumens equivalent to a 60W light bulb
and costs under US$50.

TIR LED collimation lens
*Photo credits: Courtesy of Light Prescriptions Innovators*

**DISCOVERY**

CREE
United Luminous International
Wu Ling
Tsunemasa Taguchi
Light Prescriptions Innovators

# LED Museum

Craig Johnson,
Founder

-

-

# THE LED MUSEUM IS AN AWARD-WINNING SITE MADE BY AN LED NUT, FOR LED NUTS. IT CONTAINS REAL-WORLD TEST RESULTS OF ALL KINDS OF DIFFERENT LED PRODUCTS.

# IT SERVES AS A PLATFORM TO DISPLAY MILESTONE LED TECHNOLOGY. BUT IT IS ALSO HOME TO THE WORLD-FAMOUS "PUNISHMENT ZONE" WHERE LESS FORTUNATE LED PRODUCTS COME TO DIE.

**What is the purpose of your website?**
-

My website was started on October 18, 1999, mainly out of curiosity. It originally consisted of just a single page with a smattering of photographs and hand-drawn images of the visible portion of various LED dice.

I got into reviewing LED flashlights when CMG (Course Made Good) sent me their Infinity LED torches in red and yellow in April 2000. My website has since evolved into a gigantic (over 1 gigabyte of viewable content!) source of reviews and information about flashlights.

**What kind of products do you feature?**
-

They are lasers (mostly diode and DPSS diode-pumped solid state), and all manner of other things that flash, glow, or otherwise generate EM radiation at wavelengths ranging from ~380nm to ~740nm and are generally considered as "visible light."

But there are mainly LED products and include clocks, reading lights, nightlights, scrolling message products, wristwatches, solar-rechargeable "garden globes," and even novelty items that use LEDs as a primary functional component.

**What do you think about LEDs in general?**
-

I think they're quite cool, actually. I mean, think about it. A source of light that utilizes a bit of strange quantum behaviour to generate light (in some cases, LOTS of it too!) instead of having a hot, fragile, short-lived filament.

**Do you think that LEDs are shifting our culture and creative landscape?**
-

I really do think so. Things that have been impractical or simply impossible to do with incandescent lamps are rather easily accomplished with LEDs.

Color Kinetics, based in Boston, Massachusetts, has been making some rather amazing color-changing lights using a combination of red, green, and blue LEDs for quite a number of years now.

No longer are you limited to a hot, short-lived incandescent bulb, color filter gels, and motors to achieve color-shifting effects; with LEDs running the show here, you can have color-shifting effects with no filter gels or motors; plus the available effects can be so much greater in quantity and quality with the LEDs controlled by microprocessors.

**Are LEDs going to change the world?**

-

I believe so, primarily in the field of household lighting. Say goodbye to the incandescent light bulb that was invented more than 100 years ago and has changed very little since.

With LEDs, the colour rendering can be just about as good, they save loads of electric power, and their lifespan is many, many times that of conventional household lamps.

**Who are the key players in the industry now and who will be in the future?**

-

The blue LED was invented by Shuji Nakumura; this "led" the way to the white LED as we know it today. So we have Shuji to thank for that.

Companies that appear poised to capture most of the market for LEDs used in household, portable, and automotive lighting right now would probably be Lumileds, CREE, and Seoul Semiconductor.

I'm just not at all certain what the future holds though, so I could not even begin to speculate future industry players.

**How did you get into LED technology?**

-

I got into LED technology sometime in 1975 at my home in Juneau in Alaska when I went to an electronics store and saw something called an "LED" on a pegboard display.

I was curious as to how something with no filament could generate light, so I purchased it. I believe it cost me US$6 - a lot of money for a preteen child at the time. Not only did it emit a pure red light when connected properly, it emitted a faint WHITE light when it was connected backward to the terminals of a nine-volt volt transistor radio battery.

I dabbled with LEDs on and off for several more years; then I purchased a "simulated laser kit" in 1980 from a company called Information Unlimited.

It consisted of two telescoping metal tubes, a long focal length positive (magnifying) lens at one end, and a pulsing circuit at the other - its light source was a Fairchild FLV-104 red LED...and let me just say that this LED was BY FAR he most intense LED I'd ever seen as of this time. I've been "hooked" ever since.

**What is the biggest challenge of predicting which LED appeals to a consumer?**

-

I'm honestly not that qualified to furnish a direct answer to this question. But in my experience (speaking of portable LED products such as flashlights), people generally want it all - high intensity plus extra-long battery life...you simply cannot have both simultaneously, regardless of the light source.

**Where do you see LED industry in 10 years?**

-

I think that the two primary foci regarding LEDs will be on the home and on automotive industry; with cellular telephone, computer monitor, and LED television backlighting (for LCDs) taking a smaller piece of the pie.

**If you wanted to share a truth that you've learned about LED lighting, what would it be?**

-

It will always be a fundamental to keep making LEDs brighter and brighter, and to improve the CRI (color rendering index) of white LEDs in order to make them more favourable to the consumer for home lighting applications.

Most consumers tend to prefer the warmer colors generated by household incandescent lamps, primarily because they're accustomed to it.

The phosphors used in current phosphor-type white LEDs (both cool white and warm white) run very low in several of regions of the spectrum — in particular, violet-blue, blue-green, and deep red. This can be somewhat noticeable, especially in a color-rich environment.

Dubai at Night
*Photo credits: Nasa*

# COLOR
# AND
# WHITE

OSRAM
Optiled
Traxon Technologies
RZB
e:cue
DIAL
Luminale

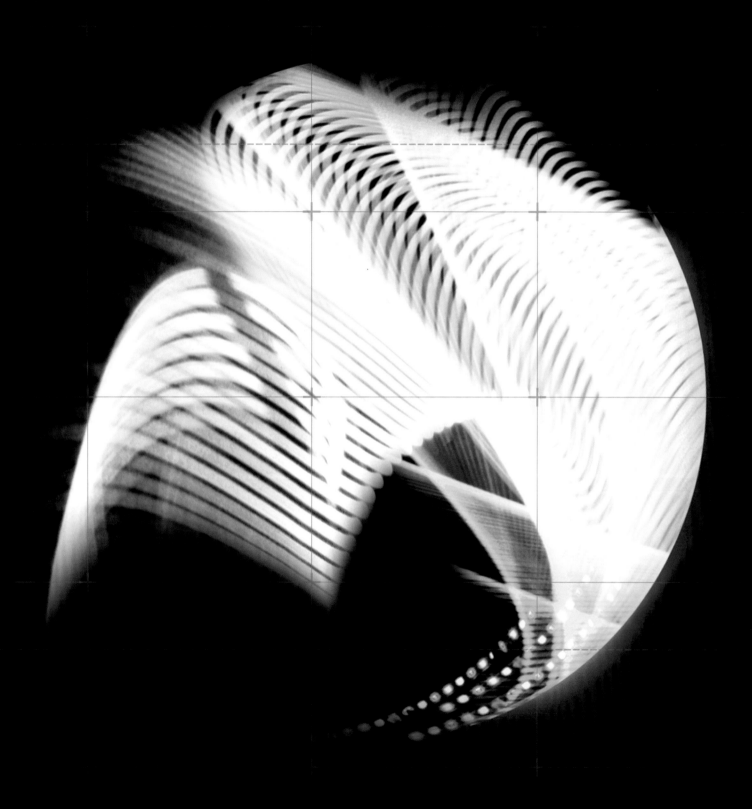

The quantum leap in this evolutionary process took place when the first high-brightness blue LED was created by Shuji Nakamura in 1993. This invention from the Millennium Prize winner has since made numerous contributions to the world such as blue laser and blue ray.

Huge scale full color spectrum video displays were made available because of the available high-brightness RGB (red, green and blue) LEDs. The creation of an RGB and blue LED also led to the development of white LEDs — general lighting applications were finally made possible.

Since man first discovered fire, we have been trying to stave off the nightly darkness. Now our night times are the more interesting, compelling and humane than they have ever been. This achievement in our age of information has made the world an even more dynamic and colorful one. An example of this is that we can now witness buildings draped in different kinds of light. Unlike in the past when our urban landscape died down after sunset, now many of the landmarks and monumental buildings can be transformed at night.

The compact and colorful diode graces building façades through different settings and sequences via sophisticated lighting designs and programming. Buildings can even demonstrate different emotions during different times of the night. We are at the stage now where the value of real estate can dramatically increase because of a good lighting design plan.

Color lighting and communications have also found its way to other structures in our urban setting. Thanks to new urban planning visionaries, we see colorful bridges guiding traffic and the skylines around the world are lit up by innovative color sequences. What's more, the energy expenditure of LED is a the fraction of the cost of traditional lighting.

It is a designer's and an artist's dream to have color LEDs at one's disposal. Many in the industry talk about them as having access to a whole new set of paints and tools in their design palettes. The compact size of LEDs allows more intricate designs and there are more than 16 million colors to experience in most standard products. Trillions in some advanced systems. For some, it is overwhelming when they master the programming side of this technology because of the seemingly endless possibilities of visual effects that are created and precisely controlled. Be ready for a new and alluring world.

Even with all this excitement, color lighting only represents about five percent of lighting in the industry. The focus is squarely on white lighting technologies. Most general outdoor and interior fixtures which including decorative lighting, floodlights, wall washers, accent lights, cove lighting, downlights, street lamp and various landscape fixtures.

If you consider that the market for replacement Edison-type standard socket lamps or retrofit lamps alone is valued at USD$21 billion; you can easily see the potential of the whole lighting market. There are more than 4 billion incandescent sockets in the U.S. alone, and 12 billion worldwide. This figure only represents less than 1% of the total market for all lamp types in the world.

This is the reason why every manufacturer is scrambling to invent the most efficient, affordable and energy efficient fixtures in this new green market. The biggest challenge for all the manufacturing giants as well as smaller newcomers is integrating a high-quality LED with good optical design, efficient thermal management, industrial design and developing electronic components with flexible programmable capabilities. Even the runners-up will get a lucrative piece of the market in this environmentally and economically aware society. With the aim of saving the planet, energy efficiency can be achieved at the same time as production of better and more comfortable lighting. Studies have shown that there is only less than 3% of total conversion to LEDs to date. LEDs definitely has a lucrative blue ocean market to conquer.

The continuing price and performance improvements, the ban on incandescent bulbs and various government stimulus packages to favouring LED technology are the needed development that will cause the tipping point for the vast public reception to this technology. Hence, LEDs have become a subject of social, political and environmental debate around the globe. The world is definitely going through a change, and with this new lighting technology, the future will only be brighter.

ON LIGHT AND PERCEPTION

$$x = \frac{X}{X+Y+Z} \qquad y = \frac{Y}{X+Y+Z} \qquad \frac{Z}{X+Y+Z}$$

i. Spectrally, a "white" LED's light comprises a blue peak from the diode junction and a spread of red and green from phosphors inside the package. The trick is to mix the red and green to produce a yellow that complements the blue. Different phosphor systems shift in the "cool" and "warm" directions.

LED

Red

*Original Art by Simon Grendene*

**COLOR**
**AND**
**WHITE**

# OSRAM

Klaus-Günter Vennemann
CEO OSRAM General Lighting

## OSRAM

Optiled
Traxon Technologies
RZB
e:cue
DIAL
Luminale

Lighting is a critical aspect of all interior design. At the Gelateria Fanny in Italy

**COLOR
AND
WHITE**
-
**OSRAM**

THIS GLOBAL PLAYER HAS ITS HEADQUARTERS
IN MUNICH AND EMPLOYS MORE THAN 41,000
PEOPLE. OSRAM AG IS ONE OF THE TWO LARGEST
LIGHTING MANUFACTURERS IN THE WORLD AND
HAS 44 FACTORIES IN 16 COUNTRIES. IN 2010
SALES AMOUNTED TO €5 BILLION. SIEMENS AG
IS THE SOLE SHAREHOLDER IN OSRAM GMBH.

THE COMPANY IS A TOP SUPPLIER OF
AUTOMOTIVE LAMPS AND LED FOR VEHICLES,
BUT ITS HIGHEST SALES ARE STILL ACHIEVED BY
ITS GENERAL LIGHTING DIVISION. THE OPTICAL
SEMICONDUCTORS BUSINESS IS ALSO GROWING
RAPIDLY AND HAS TAKEN ON MAJOR STRATEGIC
IMPORTANCE.

In the Expo Center energy-efficient lighting solutions of Osram show sustainability

## COLOR
## AND
## WHITE
-
## OSRAM

**What changes have you observed in the field of LED technology during your time in the industry?**
-
Since the 1970s, Osram has been a player in the LED industry with extensive expertise in Research and Development, chip production and packaging — everything under one roof.

In the entire spectrum of semiconductor technologies, OSRAM Opto Semiconductors — a subsidiary of OSRAM — holds several thousand patents and patent applications. A large portion of these cover technologies for industrial production of LEDs and lasers based on Indium Gallium Nitride and Indium Gallium Aluminium Phosphide.

OSRAM Opto Semiconductors is one of the pioneers of outstanding chip and packaging technologies that set standards in the industry.

Without the immense innovations in chip technology, the high-brightness LEDs that we know today would not have been possible. White LEDs, the basis for the energy-efficient light sources, had not been possible with these performance levels before 2002.

In the past, LED luminous efficacy more or less doubled every two years. This is still increasing but not as quickly because we are getting closer to the physical limits of the technology. But there are still some milestones to be achieved.

We are especially proud that we had been awarded over the years with various awards, for example the German Future Prize 2007 for the Thinfilm chip technology.

Due to these kinds of achievements, LEDs have become a serious lighting technology for the mass market. You can now find high-efficiency light source in everyday life — even in applications that had previously been dominated by conventional light sources.

Automotive headlamps, projection, TV backlighting, signage and general illumination are the segments where LED are entering or have entered already.

The famous arch is illuminated at the 80,000-seater Moses Mabhida Stadium stadium in Durban, South Africa
*Photo credits - Design: gmp; Architects: Gerkan, Marg and Partner; Rendering: Macina*

**How have these changes resonated through your company?**
-
OSRAM is driving the changeover to new technologies and is a leading manufacturer at all stages in the SSL (solid state lighting) value-added chain.

We are our customers' preferred partner thanks to an integrated range of LED products, systems and solutions. And the power of innovation, a first-rate IP portfolio and standardization are the pillars on which our LED business is built.

The individual segments of the value-added chain are no longer as clear-cut as before. The combination of technical know-how and market access will be crucial to long-term success on the market.

This means that we should not only maintain and improve our leading position in the classic lighting part of the business but also defend and extend our lead at all stages of the LED value-added chain.

**What are your thoughts about the current popularity of LED as a medium and method of lighting?**

-

LEDs will increasingly become the standard light sources for general lighting and gradually supplement or replace conventional sources. The driving forces for market penetration are energy savings and quality of light.

LEDs within the SSL sector (general illumination) are already well established in some market segments such as architectural lighting, decoration/beautification and signage. In other segments the breakthrough will take place step by step, notably in outdoor lighting, professional shop lighting and residential lighting.

The China pavilion at Expo 2010 Shanghai was illuminated by Osram LED in Gugong Red

**LEDs have a number of fundamental advantages over conventional technologies:**

✦ They are extremely small and robust and give designers enormous freedom in creating lighting applications. In addition, LEDs are extremely efficient at creating colored light without having to filter it from white light with the resultant losses.

✦ In contrast to the situation with incandescent lamps, light and heat are separate entities. LEDs have no IR and nearly no UV components in their light.

✦ The benefits in applications include low maintenance costs based on long life and predictable service intervals.

✦ A white LED with a life of more than 50,000 hours lasts about two to seven times as long as a fluorescent or a compact fluorescent lamp, and 20 to 50 times as long as an incandescent lamp.

✦ LEDs do not contain any substances that might harm the environment.

✦ LEDs have very high energy efficiency. With OSRAM LED retrofit lamps it is now possible to achieve energy savings of 80 percent compared with classic incandescent lamps. In the future, LEDs will even outperform energy-saving lamps.

# COLOR
# AND
# WHITE
-
# OSRAM

At the Gelateria Fanny bar in Venice, its architects, interior designers and lighting engineers decided to use modern LED lighting throughout.

### How important is LED technology to OSRAM?
-

In front of our headquarters in Munich we have an LED installation with seven LED screens with a height of six meters each. These artistic light steles form a lighting platform for temporary digital art projects.

The steles are equipped with LED systems on both sides. Their design as well as their vertical separation corresponds with the façade design of the OSRAM building, which was built by Walter Henn in 1965.

Static or moving pictures can be shown on the steles in a classic or interactive scenario. Up to twice a year OSRAM invites artists to develop site-specific works of art.

More generally, our company is constantly looking for new innovations. LED and OLED are in the main focus and offer completely new opportunities as a light source.

### How are the needs and priorities of the world changing, and how can LED lighting grow to meet them?
-

Future market success calls for: higher levels of efficiency (lumens per watt), higher lumen values, increased brightness that remains constant throughout the life of an LED and reduced costs.

On the product side, good color rendering and uniformity of the light are required and, in the case of white LEDs, it is particularly important for the white tone to be precisely matched within a color group (binning).

The growth segments are: exterior lights in the automotive sector, general lighting such as street and square lighting and lighting applications in retail outlets, hotels and restaurants; LED backlighting for LCD displays, projection applications, and sensors for mobile applications.

### What obstacles to market growth still exist?
-

We ourselves have to be the ones that drive this change in the direction where we want it to go. And we need to take into account of how this new business model will work.

In the past, if we lost an initial installation, we had various opportunities to convince customers to switch to us in subsequent replacement cycles.

But if we miss out on an SSL installation in the future that opportunity will probably be gone forever because LEDs last so long that there won't ever be a replacement. Therefore we have to be much better at getting that initial order.

We are building up the know-how and the resources to support our customers as they themselves make the transition. Our customers are examining the future technology very closely and trying to understand what it means for them and how they can be part of this future. And we have to help them because it's not always obvious how they can do this.

**What is your company philosophy?**

-

Light is life. Our philosophy is: passion for light, solutions for life.

**Can you tell us about your collaboration with Traxon Technologies?**

-

The joint venture with Traxon has strengthened our position in the architainment segment. The know-how that we have gained as a result relates not only to applications but also to the technology behind them.

We are talking here, not just about luminaires, but also controllers and light management systems. Traxon is one of the world's top players in this market. We have made excellent progress in our cooperation and have already managed to secure a number of exciting projects. And we are tackling more and more new applications.

**What are your aims and aspirations for the future of LED technology and, via extension, your company?**

-

We have a presence at all stages of the value chain, including single LEDs, modules, ballasts, light management systems and luminaires, and we continue to push our R&D activities into new technologies.

We shall ensure that the leading role that we have played in classic technologies will continue into LEDs so that we shape the future of light. As a result, we are strengthening our resources and know-how in solid state lighting at an even faster pace.

LED systems are increasingly establishing themselves in illuminated advertising as an innovative alternative to conventional lamps, such as neon tubes.

**COLOR
AND
WHITE**

OSRAM

# Optiled

Anthony Wong
General Manager,
Optiled Asia Pacific

-

# OPTILED

-

Traxon Technologies
RZB
e:cue
DIAL
Luminale

Lights that purr - a different kind of illumination

OPTILED IS A CHINESE LEADING-EDGE LED LIGHTING COMPANY WITH AN EXTENSIVE INTERNATIONAL PRESENCE, KNOWN FOR THE DEVELOPMENT AND DESIGN OF NEW LED GENERAL LIGHTING PRODUCTS.  IT PROVIDES ONE-STOP LED LIGHTING SOLUTIONS THAT UTILIZE HIGH-QUALITY, ULTRA-BRIGHTNESS LEDS WITH WORLD-CLASS OPTICS, EFFICIENT THERMAL, CONTROL AND POWER MANAGEMENT DESIGNS.  OPTILED'S LED FIXTURES ARE TECHNOLOGICALLY SUPERIOR AND AESTHETICALLY ADVANCED AMONG THE COMPETITION.

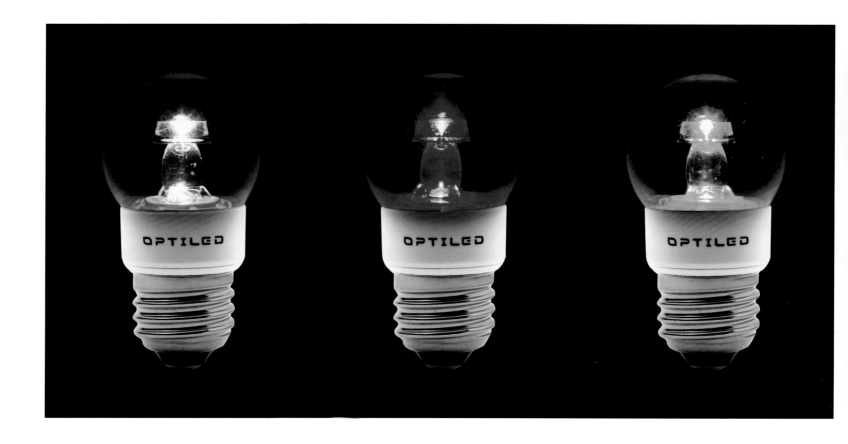

Optiled won the Circle of Excellence – Real Estate Industry Award in 2012 as one of the top five lighting providers and installers in Singapore. This project was in the city's New Majestic Hotel

079

## COLOR
## AND
## WHITE
-
**Optiled**

One of Optiled's cube application projects at
a Lyndhurst Terrace building in Hong Kong

**You are one of the industry leaders in LED lighting in China. How can you achieve this at a time when modern world is changing as fast as it does?**
-
The Optiled group forms strategic partnerships with key companies. We help them foster their own product innovation by integrating their visions with our group's expertise. Our technological expertise is thus helping our customers realize their visions and innovations.

By implementing this strategy, Optiled has been able to work in close cooperation with some of the biggest players in our industry and to earn the respect of some of the most highly regarded multi-national companies in the lighting industry.

**Why is that partnering strategy so successful?**
-
Because finding the right mix of technological expertise and mutual understanding is difficult.

Some manufacturers have the technological know-how but they cannot grasp the expectations of their customers. Others do comprehend those expectations but they do not have sufficient expertise to be able to deliver what is required. Customers want the products that they want, when they want them and how they want them.

**How did the development of new materials and technologies help growth in the LED sector?**

-

Technological developments within the entire industry are mutually beneficial to all players within it. For instance, new designs, new optic lenses and thermo-conductive plastics help us develop better LED products faster.

We design LED products that focus on practical design and high-performance for the present and the future, by leveraging on technological expertise from various engineering and manufacturing disciplines related to LED applications.

**What is the ultimate potential of LED technology?**

-

The potential is vast because the benefits of LEDs are significant. One of the most important ones is in bringing us a brighter and cleaner future. LED is the most environmentally friendly lighting technology available, because it is non-toxic and highly efficient.

Unlike compact fluorescent lighting (CFL), LEDs do not produce any ultraviolet or infrared light and they do not contain any toxic substances, such as mercury, therefore they are safer to handle and easier to dispose of without harming the environment. Furthermore, LED lights produce no heat. This can represent significant reductions in the use of air-conditioners.

The advantages of LEDs go beyond simply improving lighting power consumption and being environmentally friendly in their own right. For instance, because they consume so little energy they can easily be powered by eco-friendly solar panels and this means a cleaner source of power too.

Another exciting aspect of LED lighting is that the LED circuitry can be linked with sensors that can detect the number of persons in a room and therefore the amount of light required. This circuitry will also be able to detect strangers and automatically send warning messages to our mobile telephones.

I believe that all these technologies will eventually merge into a single system which will include: lighting, home automation, audio, security and energy saving.

LEDs are therefore more comfortable, safer and healthier for humans. With all those benefits, the future of LED lighting appears bright.

The candle effect. Another interior design project at The Palazzo, Hong Kong

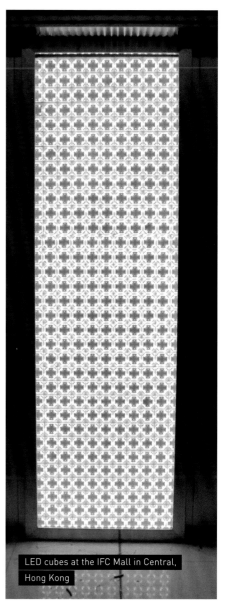

LED cubes at the IFC Mall in Central, Hong Kong

**COLOR
AND
WHITE**
-
**Optiled**

A high-profile residential project at the Spottiswoode Singapore

**What sort of product or technological innovations do you feel have particularly helped you achieve your goals?**
-
One of our important milestones, among many others, was the development of our virtual filament which has been patented worldwide. This device allows us to divert the light emanating from an LED and to convert it to a 360-degree light source in certain applications.

Another example is our uniquely designed AR 111, which was designed entirely in-house. It won several awards, including the Design Plus Award by the Messe Frankfurt Light + Building show. It features excellent heat dissipation. This is extremely important for the life of LEDs. Its special reflector design offers a non-glare and collimated beam control. Each lamp can be adjusted to a precise lighting angle.

I cannot possibly mention all our innovations here, but I should at least mention our waterproof CabLED light strip, which also won several awards including the Hong Kong Innovation & Creativity Award.

In addition, we've been considerably involved in the development of private label product innovations for our major customers.

**Are your efforts bearing fruits and are you seeing a change in the urban lighting landscape?**
-
Definitely yes. We have begun to witness a change in the lighting landscape of our cities and the trend is accelerating.

For instance, in Hong Kong, we've been granted one of the major local housing projects for LED conversion, and in Singapore, the Jurong Town Council replaced 100,000 fluorescent light fixtures with our LED fixtures, thus proving that there is a strong need to bring sustainable lighting to public housing. In Japan, we are one of the leading imported brands.

In China, we have been granted two prestigious awards from the China Technology Department. In Guangdong Province, we are one of 23 companies specifically selected by the Provincial Government as key strategic and innovative partners in LED development.

During this decade, we will witness a definite transformation in the lighting landscape of our cities and Optiled is proud to be a key player in this transformation.

LED or incandescent? Can you tell the difference?

083

OSRAM
Optiled

# Traxon Technologies

Mike Mastroyiannis
Chief Executive Officer

-

traxon | e:cue

-

RZB
e:cue
DIAL
Luminale

One of the host cities for the 2012 European Football
Championship: Warsaw's National Stadium

*Photo credits: OSRAM*

Dynamic LED Lighting Lantern, Lee Kum Kee Lantern Wonderland 2011
*Photo credits: LEDARTIST*

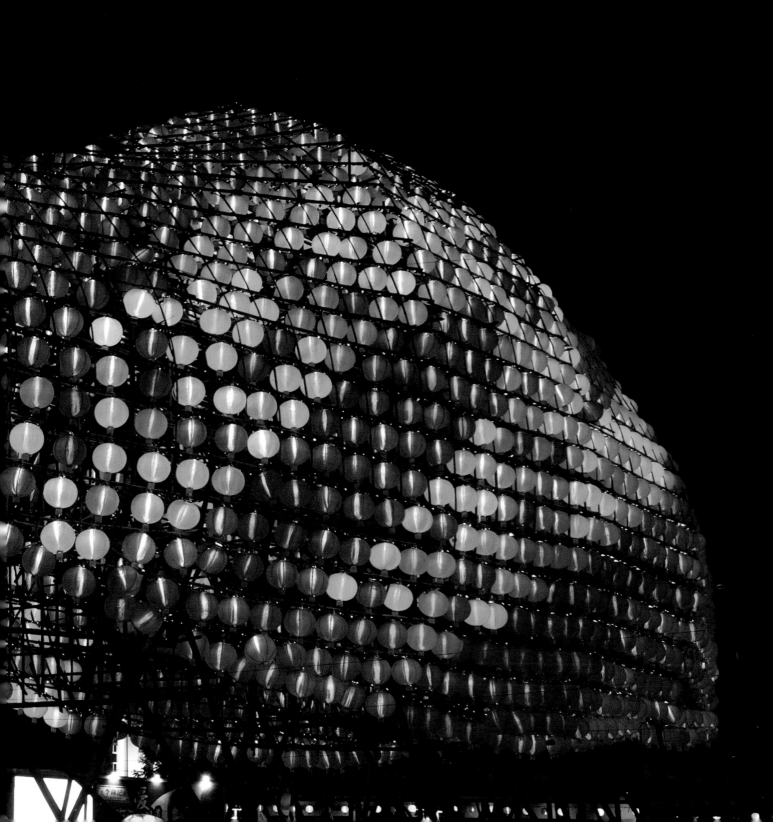

PLANET LED
-
Chapter 02

**COLOR
AND
WHITE**
-
**Traxon**

TRAXON TECHNOLOGIES, PAIRED WITH ITS CONTROL BRAND, E:CUE, IS A LEADER IN SOLID STATE LIGHTING AND CONTROL SYSTEMS. WORKING WITH AN EXTENSIVE PARTNER NETWORK, TRAXON AND E:CUE TRANSFORM CREATIVE VISIONS INTO UNFORGETTABLE LIGHTING EXPERIENCES — ELEVATING ARCHITECTURAL, ENTERTAINMENT, HOSPITALITY AND RETAIL ENVIRONMENTS AROUND THE WORLD.

FLEXIBILITY, SIMPLICITY AND INNOVATION. THESE COMPANIES' GUIDING PRINCIPLES DRIVE AND SHAPE IT WITHIN AN EVER-EVOLVING INDUSTRY. TRAXON'S CUSTOMERS AND PARTNERS ARE LIGHTING DESIGN, ARCHITECTURE AND ENGINEERING FIRMS, AS WELL AS THE WORLD'S PREMIER DEVELOPERS AND BRANDS.

IN 2011, OSRAM ACQUIRED TRAXON TECHNOLOGIES, STRENGTHENING ITS POSITION IN THE MARKET BY COMBINING KNOWLEDGE AND EXPERIENCE IN TECHNOLOGY AND MARKETING — BUILDING ON SYNERGIES WITH ITS PARENT'S GLOBAL PRESENCE.

Dynamic LED Lighting Lantern, Lee Kum Kee Lantern Wonderland 2011
*Photo credits: LEDARTIST*

**COLOR
AND
WHITE**
-
**Traxon**

This egg-shaped art structure concentrates, magnifies, and diffuses positive energies. The OVO in Lyon, France
Photo credits: Lucia Carretero

**What is your company's philosophy to business?**
-

Our mission is to achieve customer and partner success while developing people, through flexibility, simplicity and innovation. We maintain this by efficiently adapting to the changing demands of our clients, our partners, and our industry.

Traxon provides simple yet sophisticated, scalable LED lighting and control solutions. And we are committed to constant innovation as we strive to provide the most original, inventive, cutting-edge systems available to the market.

**What changes have you observed in the field of LED manufacturing during your time in the industry?**
-

We have certainly observed an acceleration of the product development cycles, significant industry consolidation, a growth of competition and increasing digitalization of the lighting industry. Systems are becoming more efficient while offering of an overwhelming array of possibilities, both in size and complex capability.

### And has Traxon changed since its become part of OSRAM?

-

In fact, very little has changed. We are happy to be part of a larger group, as it strengthens our position in the market. We have combined our knowledge and experience in technology and marketing, while building on synergies with OSRAM's global presence.

### In what ways has Traxon had to adapt to changes in the industry and demand for products?

-

We have expanded our global reach with geographic presence in over 25 countries. This has also enabled us to build the quality and number of our partners, increase our professionalism in business processes, and increase the skills and competencies of our team.

### How do you see LEDs affecting the creative lighting landscape?

-

LEDs are the present and future of lighting. From an environmental perspective, they are a sustainable solution. LED technology saves energy, requires little maintenance, does not produce dangerous emissions, and has a lifespan far exceeding of older, less efficient light sources, therefore resulting in less waste.

As a creative medium, LED simply cannot be beaten. Ultra flexible, customizable fixtures paired with intelligent control can typically achieve any desired aesthetic from elegant façade illumination to complex media façades for communication, entertainment and advertising.

### What exactly is e:cue and how does it fit in with your company structure?

-

It is a Traxon Technologies' lighting control brand. e:cue lighting control develops state of the art control and automation solutions. The brand is an industry leader with an integrated software and hardware portfolio and provides reliable solutions for any dynamic lighting project.

## COLOR
## AND
## WHITE
-
**Traxon**

**Are there any projects in particular that you feel you had to adapt to in terms of unique needs and requirements?**
-

The majority of projects have unique needs and requirements; it's a large part of what makes this industry so exciting.

To realize these projects we often customize unique lighting and control systems. Our solutions are scalable to fit a wide range of project sizes and requirements, including architectural, retail, hospitality and entertainment applications.

Here are some great examples:
Architectural: National Stadium, Warsaw, Poland.
We worked very closely with the architects and designers from the very beginning to understand their lighting vision and unique requirements, and to then discover a solution.

The main objective was to illuminate the stadium with equal light levels of white and red mesh panels of different sizes, mounted at different angles. The light sources needed to be hidden and each fixture had to be controlled separately (via DMX512).

The most critical technical requirement was to find the right mix of lenses, LED type, shutter, and fixture angle. Our solution had to be completely integrated into the façades with no unnecessary fixtures visible.

As such, Traxon developed the solution for the first 360° media façade stadium in the world with a dynamic lighting solution. By understanding the customer and lighting concept requirement, Traxon was able to support the concept realization with mock-ups and tests on different lenses to fulfil the customers' requests.

**Retail: Esprit flagship outlet, Frankfurt, Germany**
The main objective of this project was to achieve an intriguing storefront and exciting interior to attract guests, enhance the shopping experience, and further Esprit's unique worldwide brand.

Arranged behind a special glass diffusion material, each individually addressable dot was given a blurred effect. Traxon was able to customize the fixture's pixel pitches and cable lengths, down to differing pitches within a single string, for ultimate flexibility within the application.

Paired with an intelligent control system from e:cue, the installation is capable of complex color and graphic scenes via a simple user interface. Suitable for daylight viewing, the installation boldly furthers Esprit's cutting-edge branding by transforming the building's façade and interior ceiling into large LED palettes.

**Hospitality: Washington Hospital Center, Washington D.C., United States**
Healthcare facilities are reinventing themselves as they strive to focus on the patient experience, comfort level and healing process while taking into account what type of environment makes their staff as efficient as possible.

Washington Hospital Center held its patients and employees top of mind when it remodeled its emergency room lobby and waiting areas.

To create a comfortable, calm, and stress-reducing emergency room space, Traxon's 1 PXL Cove Light XR RGB, a slim profile fixture, was hidden easily in recessed areas of the ER ceiling. To add another dimension to the environment, customized Liner XB-9 RGB was installed discreetly between two etched Corian half-walls, illuminating them with a rich and even wash.

In addition, a control system, which enables gradual color-changing undulations and long timed fades from daytime to nighttimes, emulates the course of the sun throughout the day as triggered by an astronomical clock, thus putting visitors at ease with its the natural and relaxing mood that it sets.

### Entertainment: OVO, Lyon, France

OVO in an art installation and part of lighting art festivals in Lyon, Jerusalem, Frankfurt, and Istanbul. This egg-shaped art structure concentrates, magnifies, and diffuses positive energies while appealing to multiple senses.

Traxon delivered the illuminated portion of this artistic lighting concept through collaboration with the artist/lighting designer to make his vision a reality. Close cooperation ensured the intention of the artistic team is realized in detail as there were many unique requirements, including hiding the chosen Dot XL-6 RGB fixtures within in the wooden egg structure.

The patching and programming of the 3D structure was developed through well-planned RGB scenes and specific white CCTs, with adaptations to its geographical position; no simple video mapping was used. The intelligent e:cue control system was also able to synchronize and automate the sound and water portions of the feature to orchestrate with the illuminated elements.

The dynamic lighting and control system uses only about 700 watts of continuous power, making it a sustainable solution for this stunning art installation.

### Entertainment/Festive Lighting: Lantern Wonderland, Hong Kong, China

Lantern Wonderland was originally designed for a mid-autumn celebration in 2011 in Victoria Park hosted by the Hong Kong Tourism Board. The design concept was selected through a competition, of which CL3 was the winner. Their winning design and the centerpiece of the 2011 celebration, was a massive, fish-shaped lantern, sculpted out of more than 2,000 LED-lit Chinese lanterns. Every 15 minutes, the sculpture entertained festival attendees with a musical light show; between the shows, it subtly changed appearance. CL3 was able to orchestrate this brilliant, world record-setting display, while LEDARTIST implemented the advanced lighting fixtures and control products by Traxon & e:cue. With their high-intensity light, weather resistance, customizable pixel pitch, and ease of installation, Traxon's Dot XL was ideal for this project. 250 Dot XL-6 RGB fixtures were applied to the organic form of the sculpture. The lights were programmed to interact with different musical pieces, composed specially for the celebration. To control the display both on-demand and automatically, custom software was written, and e:cue's Video Micro Converters (VMCs) e:pix were added to manage all of the LED fixtures. Said Angus Yu, Business Development Director for LEDARTIST, "We were extremely happy with the results of Lantern Wonderland. Traxon's product reliability and system flexibility were crucial in making this project into the Guinness Book of World Records."

## COLOR
## AND
## WHITE
-
**Traxon**

**How do you foresee LED technology developing?**
-

It is expected that by 2020, LED technology will cover 70 percent of the lighting applications. We are already seeing a dramatic increase in LED systems replacing areas where solutions such as fluorescent, incandescent or metal halide would have originally been considered.

These applications range from small alcove illumination in patient rooms and waiting areas of medical facilities, to adding a prominent glow to the exterior of some of the world's tallest towers and skyscrapers. And more and more exterior advertising and branding is changing from backlit static images, to bold, dynamic LED media screens.

Even automobile headlamps and interior accent or safety lighting are making the switch as LED often exudes a cleaner, brighter, more focused light while remaining more efficient.

**Do you feel that this is an unavoidable trend because of environmental reasons?**
-

Lighting currently accounts for 19 percent of the world's energy consumption. If we can replace 50 percent of the world's lighting with LED, we will substantially reduce the world's energy consumption and contribute to the environmental sustainability.

In the near future, we envision even better integration between building materials and LED systems; we have already been investing in this segment.

We predict integration between solar technology and LED systems to create more sustainable outdoor and façade lighting solutions. We also visualize centrally-controlled content management systems through intelligent networks of lighting systems and solutions. With the digitalization of the lighting industry, we foresee that lighting services will become a very significant and sought after part of the industry.

**What excites you most about LED technology?**
-

LED technology is changing the way we light the world. The light-emitting diode has made measurable advancements throughout the years and has now become a leading element in intelligent illumination worldwide.

A reduced carbon footprint and human health safety are just a few of the many benefits of LEDs. LEDs boast longevity, lasting nearly 30 times longer than incandescent bulbs. They require minimal maintenance, therefore providing impressive returns on investment for the duration of their lifetime.

Innovative LED technology lighting solutions are highly flexible to tailor and transform different visions and create unique experiences for various needs.

We are excited to be part of a company that is at the forefront of this revolution. We look forward to the outstanding innovations and creative uses of this intelligent technology that are still to come.

LEDs up-close: Esprit's flagship retail outlet in Frankfurt, Germany
*Photo credits: Frank Alexander Rummele/LightLife GmbH*

**COLOR
AND
WHITE**

OSRAM
Optiled
Traxon Technologies

# RZB

Dr. Alexander Zimmermann
President and Chief Executive
-

-
e:cue
DIAL
Luminale

RZB's Coros range of fixtures

**COLOR
AND
WHITE
-
RZB**

RZB STANDS FOR "RUDOLF ZIMMERMANN BAMBERG," A COMPANY FOUNDED IN 1939. THE COMPANY FACILITATES, DEVELOPS AND PRODUCES A PRODUCT RANGE OF MORE THAN 10,000 ITEMS. OVER 20,000 LUMINAIRES LEAVE THE FACTORY EACH DAY.

THE COMPANY'S FOCUS IS ON LUMINAIRES FOR INDOOR AND OUTDOOR APPLICATIONS, AS WELL AS SPECIAL SAFETY LUMINAIRES AND LUMINAIRE SIGNS. INNOVATIVE LIGHT SOURCES SUCH AS LEDS PLAY A CENTRAL ROLE IN ITS PRODUCT POLICY. THE AIM OF RZB IS TO CREATE DISTINCTIVE PRODUCTS. THE ORIGINALITY OF THE BRAND LIES IN THE DESIGN AND LIGHTING TECHNOLOGY. CREATING A STRAIGHTFORWARD ASSEMBLY PROCEDURE AND PRODUCT CONVENIENCE ARE ALSO PRINCIPLES THAT THE COMPANY ASPIRES TO.

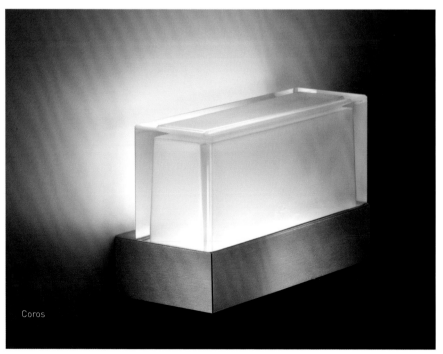

Coros

## COLOR
## AND
## WHITE
-
## RZB

Lavano

### Can you tell us about RZB's history?
-

When Rudolf Zimmermann started to produce electro-technical products more than 70 years ago in Bamberg, he wouldn't have known that RZB would develop into a luminaire manufacturer of today's dimensions.

Every day, more than 20,000 luminaires leave the factory in Bamberg and are shipped to customers all over the world — to Europe, Asia, the Middle East, Africa, Australia and America. Rudolf Zimmermann, Bamberg GmbH (RZB) is now among Europe's largest and leading manufacturers of interior and exterior lighting as well as specialized orientation and emergency lighting.

While the broad product range of highly specialized, but rather classical luminaires was focused mainly on functional features, RZB has developed as well into a manufacturer of technologically innovative luminaires with architectural design in the past two years.

### What is RZB's involvement with LED technology?
-

In order to strengthen our competence in light engineering — particularly in the LED sector — RZB entered into a strategic cooperation with Optiled Lighting International. The company is one of the leading companies in the lighting sector and is 100 percent focused on the development of LED products.

This partnership combines the core competencies of both companies. We are now focused on the development of luminaires and lamps that are technologically advanced, very high quality and based on LED technology for private and professional applications.

With Optiled, RZB has sided with a ground-breaking and competent partner in the field of LED technology. Through our common know-how, the speed of product development will significantly increase.

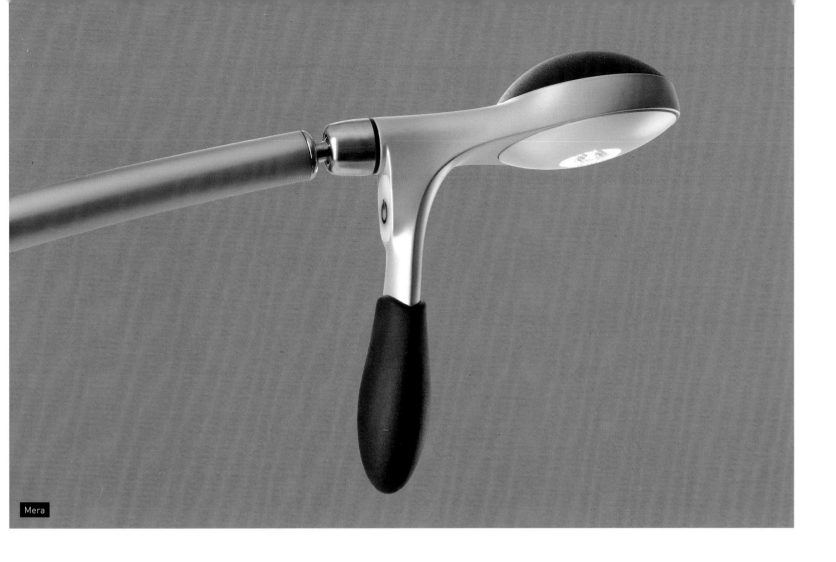

Mera

## How has the development of new materials and technologies aided the growth of the LED sector?

-

The main, but not sole, focus from a light engineering point of view lies on the use of energy-efficient LEDs. The construction principle of many new luminaires is based on a modular system, i.e. a constructive design made with high-quality materials and technical realization, and is used in several ways and gives every luminaire range an unique design.

Crucial components, such as glass covers, have a long life cycle and can be recycled. RZB's understanding of lighting is not only focused on pure cost and benefit aspects, which are of course closely tied to the fast developing LED technology. Central motives also contain ecological aspects, which are successfully included in new lighting systems and solutions.

Douala Kristall

COLOR
AND
WHITE
-
RZB

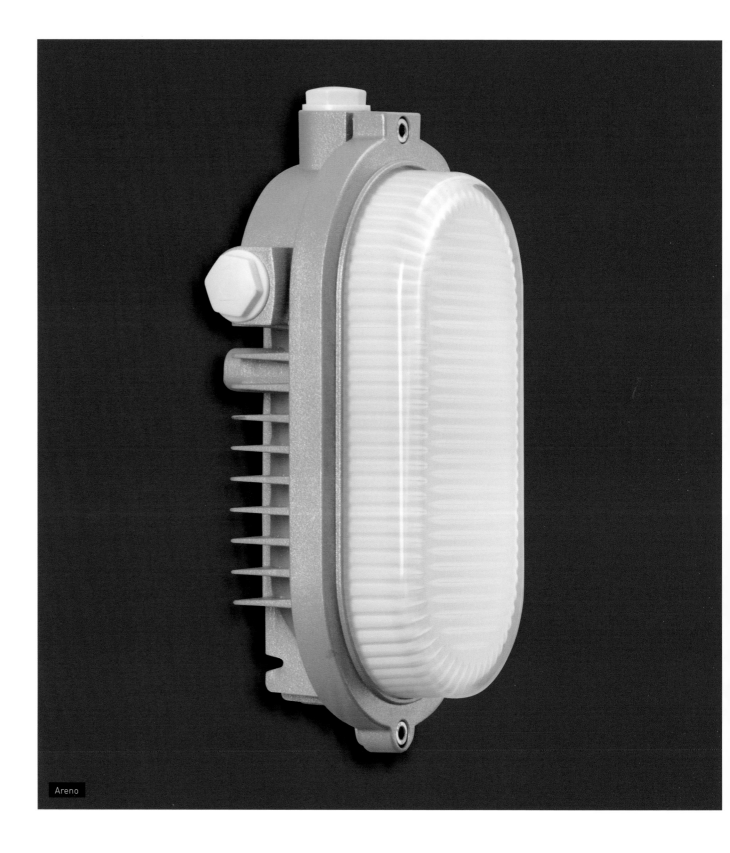

Areno

### What do you feel is LED's ultimate potential?

-

There have been few remarkable developments in the last 150 years of history of artificial lighting. The development of LEDs, however, represents a revolution, in which we actively participate. In order to shape this future of light, we joined our forces with Optiled, and are looking forward to a bright future.

We see LED technology as the main source of lighting for the future, and RZB has participated in this development from the start.

The improvement of LEDs' energy efficiency and ecological aspects are vital for the focus of new and further developments in RZB's product portfolio.

LED technology brings us all completely new lighting applications such as cove lighting or mobile lighting. But, in the future, we will use LEDs to replace existing light sources without even thinking about it.

### Do you feel that this is essential on a more socially related and ecological level?

-

Yes, absolutely. Man's consciousness influences his existence. Social and ecological aspects are influencing human actions in a growing degree.

### What obstacles do you think still exist out there?

-

Obstacles include LED's technical capabilities, especially the need for a cooling system in the light partition. The current costs also set limits to the uses of LEDs.

### How will the lighting industry and market develop in Europe?

-

The lighting market in Europe is changing and there is a growing connection between luminaires and lamps. The manufacturing of luminaires will change because luminaires play an important role for the longevity of LEDs. Like in many other branches, new technologies come with a lot of new protagonists.

Tenuo

Slopia Strahler

**COLOR
AND
WHITE**

OSRAM
Optiled
Traxon Technologies
RZB

# e:cue

e:cue lighting control Marketing

-

# e:cue

-

DIAL
Luminale

Star Place, Kaohsiung, Taiwan
*Photo credits: Christian Richters*

**COLOR
AND
WHITE**
-
**e:cue**

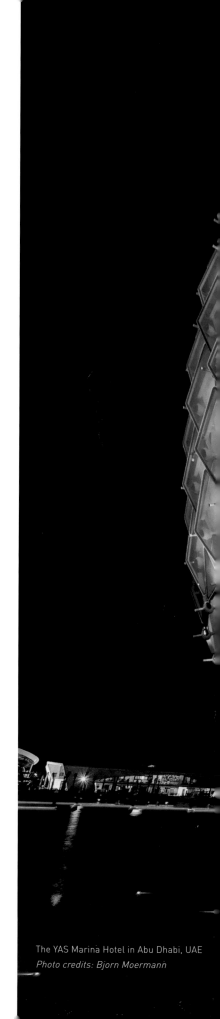

E:CUE LIGHTING CONTROL — AN OSRAM COMPANY — DEVELOPS STATE OF THE ART CONTROL AND AUTOMATION SOLUTIONS TO DELIVER SUSTAINABLE DYNAMIC LIGHTING EXPERIENCES.

E:CUE IS HEADQUARTERED IN PADERBORN, GERMANY, WITH REGIONAL OFFICES IN EUROPE, NORTH AMERICA, ASIA AND THE MIDDLE EAST. DISTRIBUTION AND SUPPORT IS ALSO MANAGED THROUGH E:CUE'S EXTENSIVE PARTNER NETWORK AROUND THE WORLD. INCORPORATING COMPANY VALUES OF INNOVATION, FLEXIBILITY AND SIMPLICITY, E:CUE PROVIDES RELIABLE SOFTWARE AND HARDWARE SOLUTIONS FOR ANY DYNAMIC LIGHTING PROJECT.

The YAS Marina Hotel in Abu Dhabi, UAE
*Photo credits: Bjorn Moermann*

## COLOR
## AND
## WHITE
-
**e:cue**

**What is your company philosophy?**
-
We always strive to develop the perfect lighting control products that enable unlimited capabilities to turn any lighting design idea into reality.

**What programming developments have you witnessed recently?**
-
When developing our software products we always look at our clients' needs. We observe an increasing demand for more advanced systems that are flexible to work with and various triggering systems that need to be programmed using the e:cue programmer. Using e:script, our advanced scripting language, many triggering systems are integrated in the e:cue lighting control solution.

**How important is training in this area?**
-
We put great importance into software and hardware training. e:cue has a dedicated team working on educating our clients and partners about our products, while at the same time we work on improving the simplicity of using our products.

There are many e:cue training options available in different languages in different locations throughout the year. We always try to facilitate any training need and interest from one-to-one trainings to group workshops.

**You have participated in many projects across the globe. What kind of cross-cultural communication are you involved with?**
-
We strive to communicate and adapt all our content to be understood locally. Some examples are support materials such as data sheets and manuals. We are currently working to translate more web and print content into more languages. Our projects are indeed becoming more global and this is not only relating to the project location itself, but also to the "chain of creation" of a project. For example, something can be designed in Europe and installed in the Middle East by a U.S. company.

Our global set-up and international team structure help us to answer these challenges.

**Are LEDs now flexible enough to fit almost any kind of assignment?**
-
LED technology is becoming increasingly more powerful and therefore suitable for a wider range of applications.

Especially in dynamic lighting control, which is our focus, LEDs have revolutionized design and interactivity opportunities. This is why for us, and the lighting control market in general, it is so important to match the needs of LED flexibility with a flexible system.

Our product development team works with project managers to follow trends in LED installation and get input for future developments to facilitate challenging LED assignments. However, conventional lighting technologies also remain important in the future and therefore our system also allows seamless integration of all kinds of conventional technologies and protocols.

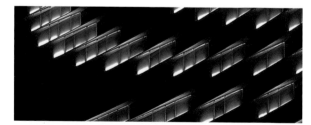

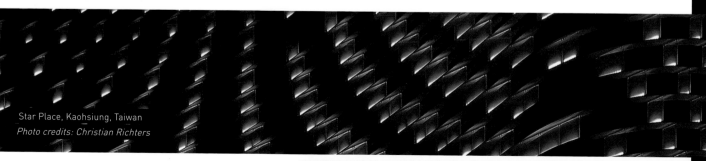

Star Place, Kaohsiung, Taiwan
*Photo credits: Christian Richters*

The LIV Club in Miami, United States
*Photo credits: Joshua Spitzig and Simon Hare*

## COLOR
## AND
## WHITE
-

**e:cue**

**What is your priority to achieve such a huge global presence?**
-

Our main priority still remains developing innovative products that make sense for our clients, that are easy to use and to understand, and at the same time flexible enough to solve any lighting control scenario while being easily modified for future ideas.

**Can you give an example of a mega-project you've worked on? What were the technical challenges and contributions?**
-

The New Year's Eve Ball in New York City is one of our most prominent projects. In 2009, the ball was three times bigger than in 2008 and required a custom programming patch by our software team to be used by the lighting design firm, Focus Lighting, for video pixel-mapping and 3D visualization.

Our CS-1 servers (main server plus one as backup) together with butlers ensured a reliable system, which is very important for this type of event. On the night of the event, e:cue's programmer enterprise software worked with time code to synchronize controlled light with audio and video, ensuring a simultaneous experience when the ball descended for all spectators watching the countdown.

Bring London's Spitalfields Market into the 21st century
with some colorful LED magic
*Photo credits: e:cue*

**What do advances in LED technology mean to your company and your company culture?**
-

The advances in LED technology bring more room for improvement for both our products and our company. We embrace new LED technology as it enables our developers to add more functionality that can be creatively used in lighting design projects.

**Generally speaking, do you see LED playing a greater role?**
-

LEDs are undoubtedly changing the way we live, by adding more capabilities that improve people's well-being and adding more interactivity with users and environment.

We are seeing many more applications that improve patient experience in healthcare projects, that customize an ambiance in the hospitality industry, and applications that use more color using sustainable lighting. Through LEDs, dynamic lighting is also becoming part of everyday life from office to entertainment environments.

**Will LEDs evolve to meet the changing needs of society?**
-

We believe that LEDs will be the preferred choice for all architectural, themed-entertainment, retail, museum and hospitality lighting installations.

The capabilities and flexibilities of LEDs will one day be unmatched when compared with other lighting options. Furthermore, solid-state lighting will become increasingly prevalent into every home and merge various applications of media, light, ambiance and entertainment.

**What about in the world as a whole?**
-

LED will obviously help the environment while satisfying more lighting needs.

Photo credits: Joshua Spitzig & Simon Hare

**What current projects are you currently involved in?**

-

We are working on numerous projects ranging from small and simple to complex large LED installations mainly in architectural/ architainment, hospitality, retail and residential projects.

One particularly interesting project is a major resort project in Dubai that involves sophisticated RDM communication to monitor LEDs.

We are also working on retail projects of famous clothing brands and many complex LED installations for hotel casinos.

**Do you have a message that you would like to convey to our readers – particularly those in the LED industry?**

-

We would invite those readers to go to our website and try our software for free, to experience our lighting control capabilities. LED lighting is increasingly demanding more sophisticated control and our software is a great tool to discover this.

The sparkling new shop-front of the Louis Vuitton outlet in Las Vegas, United States
Photo credits: Jens Freihoefer

OSRAM
Optiled
Traxon Technologies
RZB
e:cue

# DIAL

Jürgen Spitz
Team Leader
Light Team
-

# DIAL

-

Luminale

Planning the interior light in the comBOTS building in Karlsruhe, Germany

PLANET LED
-
Chapter 02

COLOR
AND
WHITE
-
DIAL

DIAL IS BASED IN LÜDENSCHEID, GERMANY, AND HAS BEEN A SERVICE-PROVIDER FOR THE LIGHT AND BUILDING TECHNOLOGY FOR MORE THAN 20 YEARS. DIAL WAS FOUNDED IN ORDER TO OFFER THE MARKET COMPLETELY NEUTRAL AND MANUFACTURER-INDEPENDENT PHOTOMETRIC AND LIGHTING DESIGN KNOW-HOW, ESPECIALLY WITH THEIR DIALUX SOFTWARE. THE BUILDING TECHNOLOGY DIVISION WITH ITS SEMINARS AND LABORATORIES WAS FOUNDED IN 1992 WITH THE LAUNCHING OF EIB (EUROPEAN INSTALLATION BUS, TODAY KNX).

JÜRGEN SPITZ, A GRADUATE IN ENGINEERING AND INTERIOR DESIGN, IS CURRENTLY A LECTURER FOR LIGHT PLANNING. HE HAS MANY YEARS OF EXPERIENCE IN THE FIELD OF LIGHTING DESIGN, PLANNING AND CONFIGURATION, AND IS ALSO TEAM LEADER AT DIAL.

At the BASF and Feierabendhaus building in Ludwigshafen, Germany

## COLOR
## AND
## WHITE
-
## DIAL

**What is the Expert in Lighting Design session?**

-

It is a five-day training seminar at our headquarters and explains the systematic way to develop lighting concepts. It follows our DIAL design philosophy and analyzes all the requirements the lighting design has to fulfill: psychological and human needs, architectural requirements and demands of the usage. If you want to know what I am talking about visit our training seminars at www.dial.de.

**What recent changes have you seen in your industry?**

-

One thing that I have noticed is a trend to minimize the dimensions of luminaire housings, influenced of course by smaller light sources.

More generally, I've observed that the main "impulses" always come from the lamp industry. A luminaire manufacturer usually only develops covers for existing lamps in the market.

**What are the key factors to a successful lighting design?**

-

The main issue is to achieve a feeling of well-being. To reach this you must know human needs very clearly. You have to understand how we see our environment, how to appeal to their emotional world and of course you should know about the physical aspects of visual perception.

**What are your thoughts about LED lighting?**

-

From our point of view, LEDs are a typical light source with plenty of advantages and plenty of disadvantages.

People who are not experts in lighting see only all the new applications of light. In furniture, clothes, shoes, decorative stuff, garden...everywhere you find LEDs. It seems to be a light source without limits. It fascinates and is a symbol of modernity and being up to date.

**What are the most important developments that you see emerging in the creative lighting landscape?**

-

I see a lot of new products, many of them with LEDs, a lot of colored light and many dynamic light effects.

However, many of these developments are used quite in contrast to our design philosophy. We do not need random RGB color changers – not at all! We prefer a perfect color that corresponds with the relevant material. Less is sometimes more.

**With that in mind, does LED technology have potential?**

-

Of course, the potential is huge. We are sure that the LED technology will replace the traditional lamps in almost all applications. But not in all!

**In the future, do you think LEDs will influence consumers, designers and manufacturers?**

-

This future is already here.

Impressions from the "Expert in Lighting Design" seminar

**Is this progression important given LED's environmental benefits over more traditional lighting?**
-

No, we think that the ecological aspects are not really important, although the marketing departments of the lighting industry use this argument. Saving energy for the purpose of saving money is the much more powerful point.

**If there was one additional insight that you would like to share with our readers, what would it be?**
-

Think about light and the distribution of brightness, not about lighting technology. The technology should be the slave of the lighting concept.

The most important part of working with light is the analyzing process. Unfortunately there are only a few people in the world who follow this workflow.

Jacob's Ladder: a lighting project for the 2010 Horticultural Exhibition in North Rhine-Westphalia, Germany

OSRAM
Optiled
Traxon Technologies
RZB
e:cue
DIAL

# Luminale
## Biennial of Lighting Culture

Helmut M Bien
Curator, Luminale
-

PLANET LED
-
Chapter 02

COLOR
AND
WHITE
-
Luminale

LUMINALE – BIENNIAL OF LIGHTING CULTURE HAS BEEN DESCRIBED AS A EUROPEAN CATWALK OF LIGHTING CREATIVITY. IT IS AN INTERNATIONAL FESTIVAL OF LIGHTING CULTURE THAT TAKES PLACE EVERY TWO YEARS IN FRANKFURT AND THE SURROUNDING RHINE-MAIN REGION.

OVER 160 LIGHT EVENTS PRESENTED IDEAS AND CONCEPTS TO 140,000 VISITORS WHO EXPERIENCED THE FASCINATION OF LIGHT. CURATOR HELMUT M. BIEN INTENDED THE FESTIVAL TO BE AN INTERNATIONAL CAMPUS FOR THE CREATIVE WORLD. FOR THE PAST FEW YEARS, LUMINALE HAS RUN ALONGSIDE FRANKFURT'S FAMOUS LIGHT+BUILDING TRADE FAIR.

PLANET LED
-
Chapter 02

COLOR
AND
WHITE
-
Luminale

**Luminale is already a well-established institution. Can you tell us about its origins?**
-

In 2000, Germany's lighting industry's major tradeshow moved from Hannover to Frankfurt. Organizer Messe Frankfurt asked me to design an event concept that could "connect" the city with the new tradeshow, Light+Building.

During the fair, we wanted Frankfurt to become a meeting place for everyone in the world who worked with light. Not only for industry specialists but also creatives, architects, designers and artists — even consumers and curious visitors.

The idea was to create a trans-disciplinary festival focused on lighting and energy, and the qualities of urban living. I want Frankfurt to become a laboratory that experiments with a wide range of lighting approaches.

Ten years later, I am very happy that artists from around the world display their installations at the festival.

**How did you get involved with light art and what motivates you to organize such a big event?**
-

In the late 1980s I worked in Berlin as a curator for the Berliner Festspiele. There I had my first professional experience with light and began to understand the power of lighting in scenography. Since then, the idea to realize a lighting exhibition has followed me.

Luminale was the chance to showcase that light has the power to change atmospheres and reorganize space. In the classical sense of the word, I am something of a romantic. And the poet Novalis explained the notion of romanticism was to give normal things a new and higher meaning. Lighting designs give us the opportunity to enchant the world.

**Compared to other light festivals, what do you think makes the Luminale a unique event?**
-

Since 2002, when we started the first edition of Luminale, it has been a great success. In fact, many people have tried to copy the concept.

Some festivals are important for local people, some are made to promote tourism. But the unique position of Luminale is its combination with the most important trade fair for the lighting industry, Light+Building. Luminale is a festival for everyone: specialists and non-industry people alike.

There are some festivals much bigger than Luminale, but ultimately you have to count the heads and not the legs. Luminale is well-known throughout the worldwide community of lighting enthusiasts and is already an important part of the careers of younger designers and artists.

The festival, although very popular, is not a mass-market event where colored buildings resemble something like sad clowns. Our unique positioning and combination with Light+Building provides the possibility to try out new technologies and approaches. It gives a chance to the unknown.

**Are there any themes that you would like Luminale to cover in future editions?**
-

The digitization of light is a fascinating subject and the storytelling is a never ending challenge.

LED façades, Vj-ing, projections are also great themes. On the other hand so are the issues of energy reduction, recycling and sustainability. Another dimension is the development of the urban life. Frankfurt's skyline and nightlife are also stages of Luminale.

**What are your biggest wishes and dreams for the long-term development of Luminale?**
-

The biggest wish is that the whole Frankfurt region accepts lighting as an important dimension of its identity. Then, we can realize projects not only for a short time during the festival.

My dream would be that the festival creates a masterplan for the whole region with landmarks and light art. Frankfurt would be a green "balancity" that produces and consumes energy in a way that enriches its inhabitants' quality of life.

# COLOR
# AND
# WHITE

-
**Luminale**

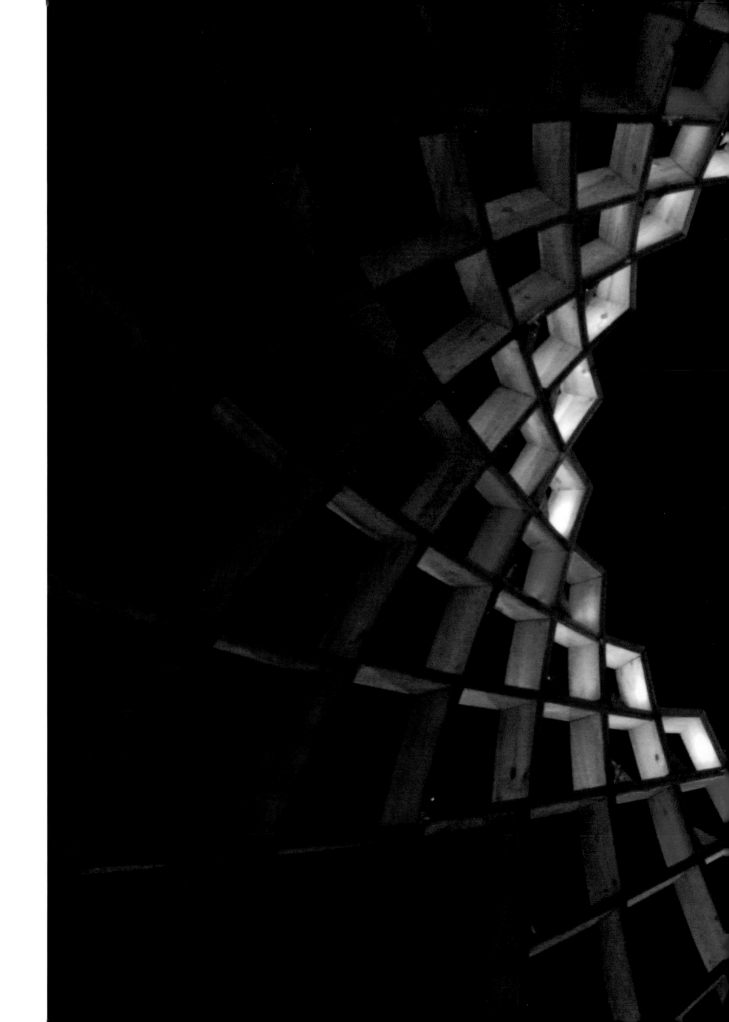

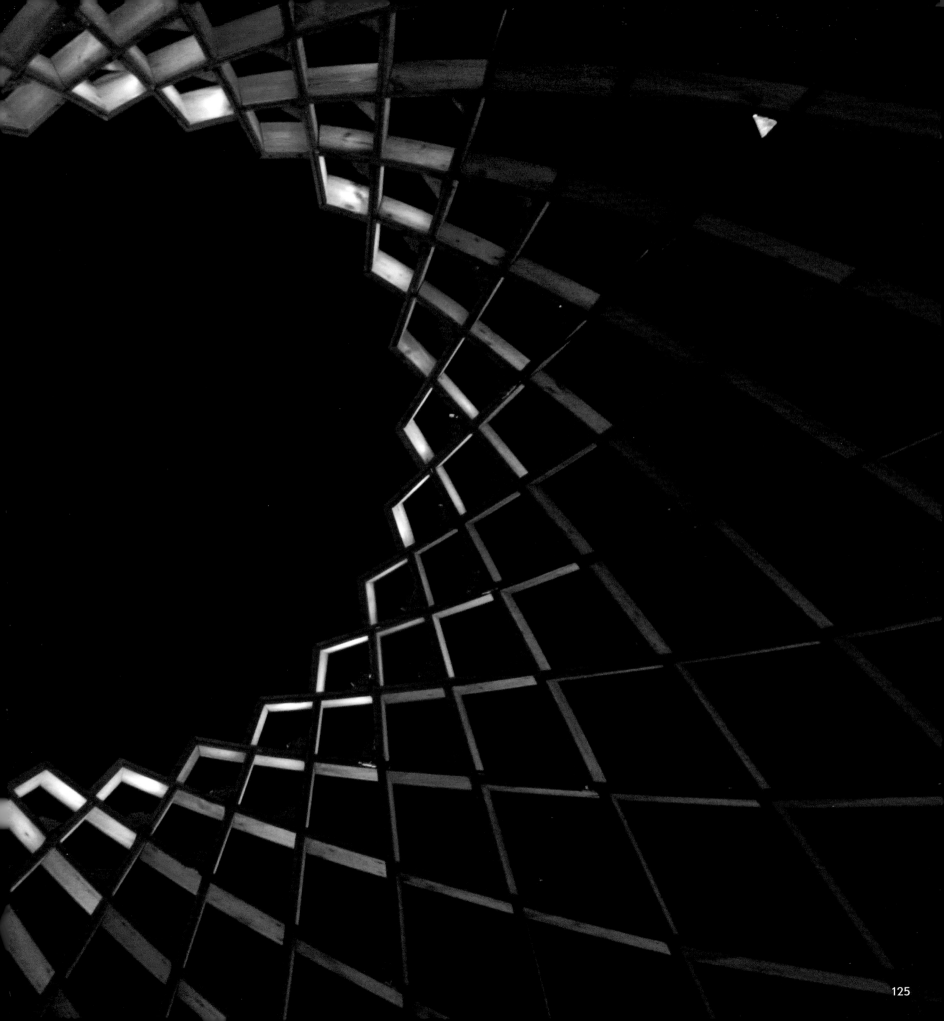

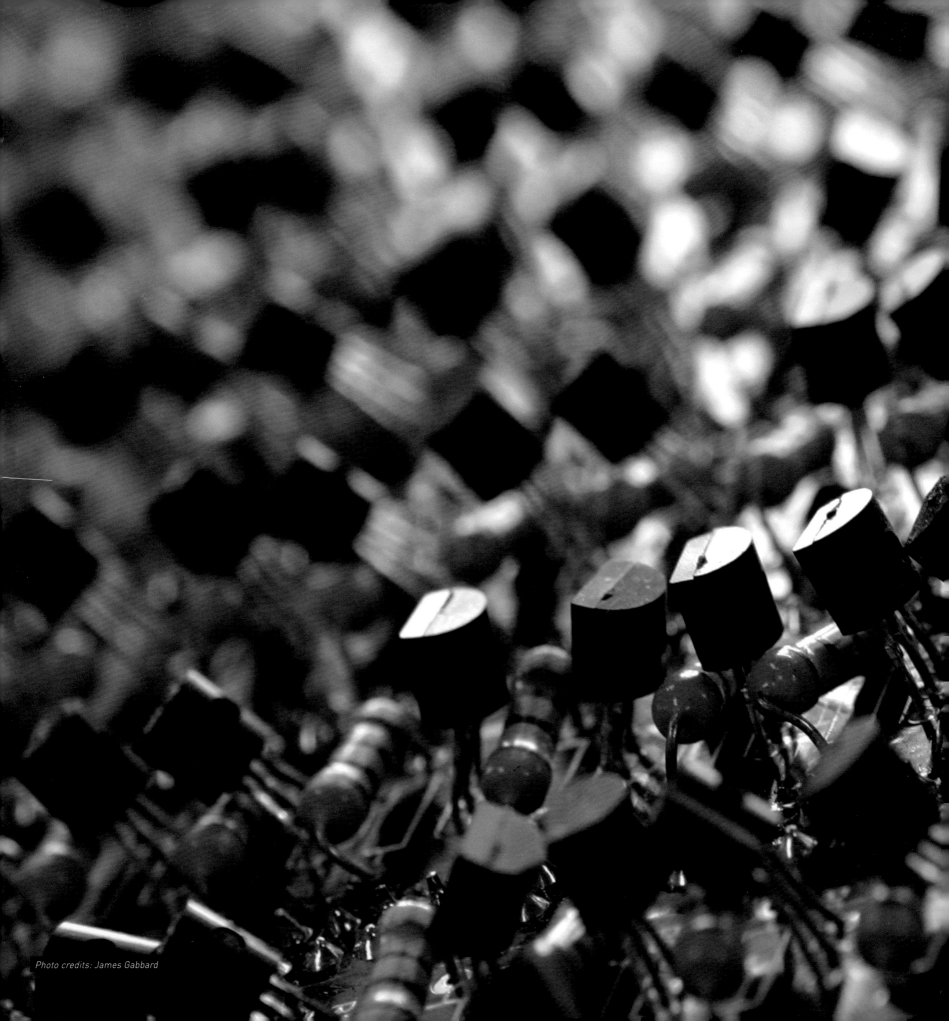

# NEW VISUAL CULTURE

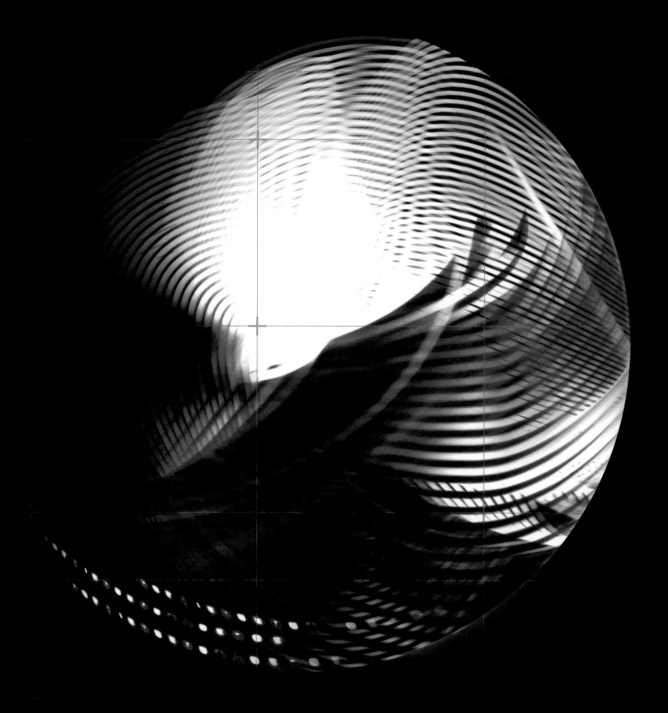

The birth of RGB LEDs has given way to a new era in indoor and outdoor display technology. The benefits of LED-based video are its flexibility in scale, physical design, color, contrast and brightness. It is also the only medium that shows clear digital content under bright daylight conditions.

Indoor events, such as trade shows or live performances, perfectly demonstrate dynamic and scalable video and branded advertising content. And at outdoor events like sporting occasions and large festivals, creative and flexible hardware configurations are invaluable.

LED solutions that utilize creative video content can be created anywhere that "eyeball count" is needed for brand or information projections. New York City's Times Square is the ultimate shrine for commercial and artistic media expression.

Let us examine the various facets on the mechanics behind the innovation. A truly great LED video screen consists of well-calibrated LED modules, advanced video processing control and attractive range of creative products to fit the client's needs. The modular electronic platform allows motion content to be displayed on a scale that's larger than life.

Commercial LED screens and modules have been installed on building façades to present a media surfaces for video display purposes and, in also many cases, for artistic expressions. The term "media façade" has been coined by the industry for exactly this type of installation.

Our urban landscape is evolving. It is turning into a communicative and interactive environment — a playing field in which a passerby can absorb information in a passive but engaging manner. With millions of static billboards belting out messages across the globe, motion content breaks through the clusters and steals our attention. No one can doubt that. Some observers have criticizes this development and dismissed it as "visual pollution." But on the other hand, many believe it represents a milestone in the development of our collective consciousness in an age of information.

From a designer's point of view, the use of LEDs in video enables a remarkable platform for creative expression. The modular and flexible qualities of new LED video products allow designers to manifest innovative structural configurations that compliment dynamic creative content. Many property owners and architects have embraced the technology.

Media installations act as the next level of lighting design. In addition, media façade innovations have added financial incentives. When implemented correctly, a building's video art can receive international recognition, substantially increasing the value of the property containing the luminous work. Hence, investors calculate an installation's return on investment and scout around for the right technology provider and designer.

The market is largely separated into permanent installation and rental, and while there are many suppliers, the majority of the screens to date are being manufactured in China. Besides pricing, LED screen manufacturers and rental companies fiercely compete for business on the basis of their products' color uniformity and reproduction, LED quality, power consumptions, industrial design flexibilities, pixel resolutions as well as weight.

Only a few "elite" companies have gone beyond a mediocre standard. It is their product creativity, environmental factors and technical awareness that have elevated them above the rest. This chapter is devoted to the astonishing progress made by these key market players.

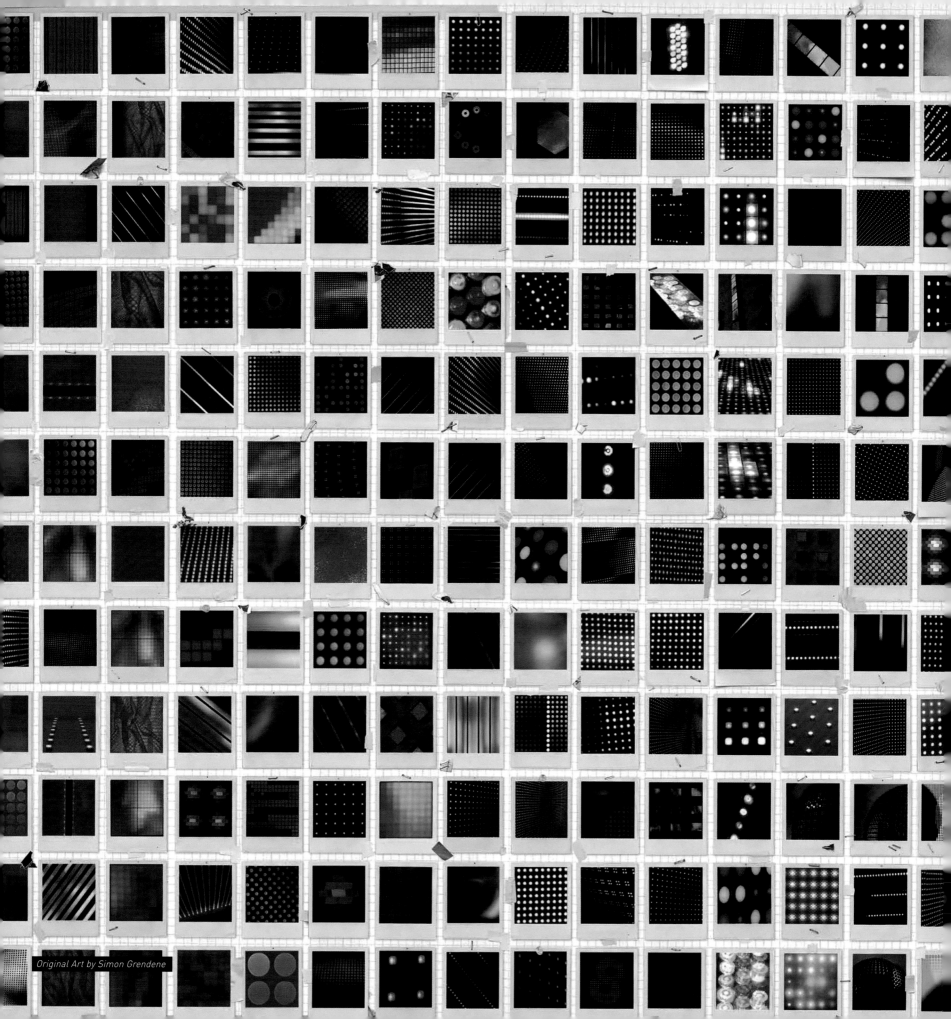

Original Art by Simon Grendene

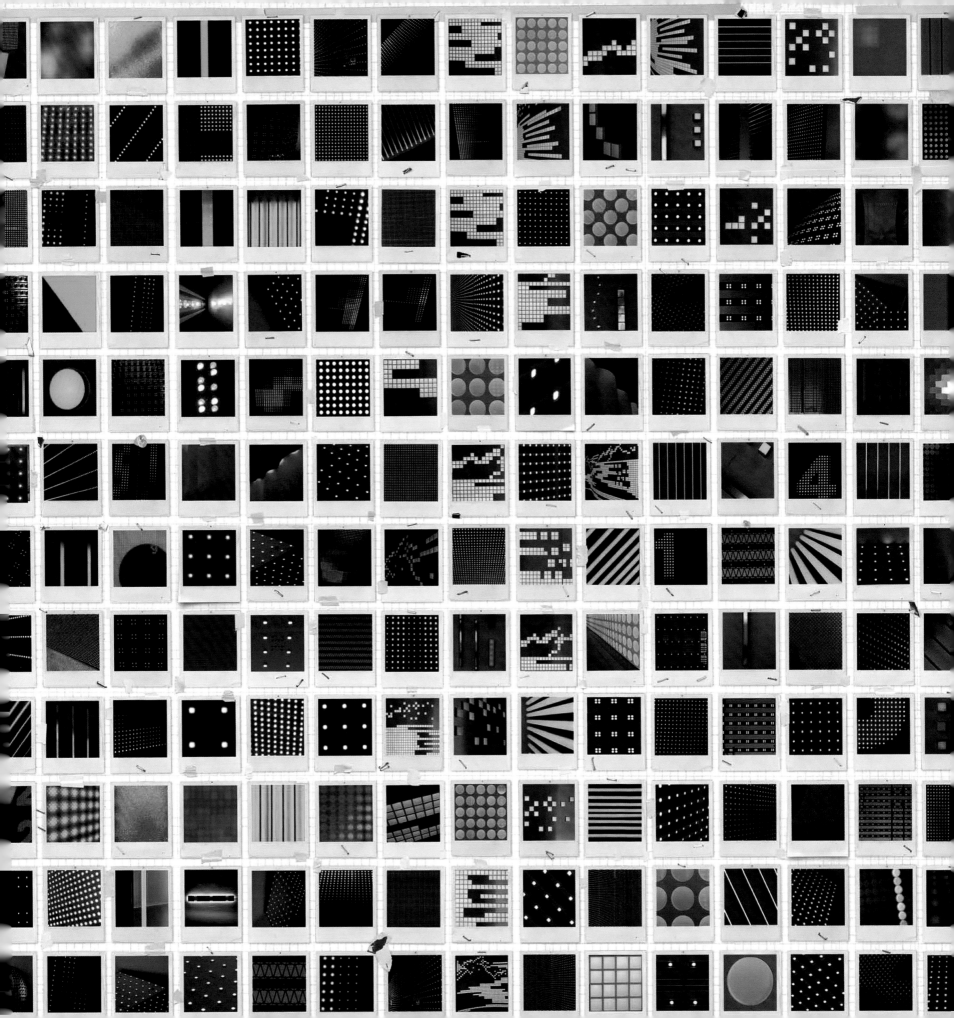

NEW VISUAL
CULTURE

# ag4
# mediatecture

Ralf Mueller
Managing Partner
-

**ag4** | media facade GmbH

-

Lighthouse
Hibino
Join Merit
Urban Media Research
Imago
Electric Signs

Balance Tower, 2009, Barcelona, Spain – Transparent Media Façade
*Photo credits: ag4*

NEW VISUAL
CULTURE
-
ag4

AG4 MEDIATECTURE COMPANY WAS FOUNDED IN 1991
AS A COOPERATION BETWEEN ARCHITECTS AND MEDIA
DESIGNERS. AG4 STANDS FOR "ARBEITSGEMEINSCHAFT
FÜR VIERDIMENSIONALES BAUEN" (WORKING GROUP
FOUR-DIMENSIONAL CONSTRUCTION) AND ESTABLISHED
"MEDIATECTURE" IN 1993.

AG4 DEVELOPS BOTH SYSTEMIC AND INDIVIDUAL PROJECT
SOLUTIONS, WHICH PROVIDES SUPPORT FOR ARCHITECTS IN
THE "MEDIALIZATION" OF THEIR PROJECTS.

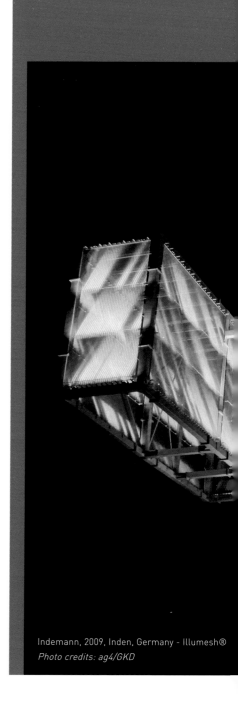

Indemann, 2009, Inden, Germany - Illumesh®
*Photo credits: ag4/GKD*

### What is a transparent media façade?
-

A transparent media façade allows for an unrestricted view from inside the building, as well as from outside looking in. Unlike conventional screens that are attached to building façades, media façades create a symbiosis between the media installation and the architecture. Every media façade is unique, custom-made and becomes an integral part of the building.

With the transparent media façade and its lamella structure, we have developed yet another medialization system that is highly transparent and perfectly suited for use in daylight.

The system is based on a frame construction: horizontal or vertical running lamellas fitted with light-emitting diodes are integrated in profiles. These are mounted onto a static frame hanging from the façade that is attached to the structure. The profiles accommodate the large part of the electronics required. This system offers a wide spectrum of visual installation possibilities using light, images, text and videos as well as live broadcasts that are even visible in daylight.

The image formats are specifically designed for use in architecture. The LED resolution can be freely selected — regardless of conventional 4:3 or 16:9 standards. The system also acts as an effective sunscreen — even at transparency values of up to 90 percent.

Wax modules with integrated LEDs. Merck Serono, 2006, Geneva, Switzerland
*Photo credits: ag4*

### Can you provide us an example?

-

ag4 created the first transparent media façade for T-Mobile, the telecommunications company. The client was looking for an innovative way to stage their brand directly at the main entrance of the building.

Set on a surface area of 300 square meters, the horizontal lamella construction is mounted in front of the glass façade of the building entrance. LEDs are integrated into the lamellas, making it possible to display visual installations on the architecture. The distance between the lamellas provides an unrestricted view of the campus square from inside the building.

Looking in from the square, the electronic media installation is superimposed on the view of the rooms inside the building. The transparency created from both inside and outside the building is what creates the special magic of the transparent media façade. The great potential of the media façade makes it not only possible to animate the company logo but also to present the entire brand using visual images.

### That sounds difficult to implement…

-

One of the challenges in this connection is to integrate the media technology into the façade in such a way that it generates a symbiosis with the architecture.

However, this does not mean that the visual media is simply adapted to the mere size of the architecture or to the urban design and development. A further central challenge is the conceptual design of the content that is to be communicated on the façade.

The conceptual design of a media façade installation is an individual process unique to each project that commences only after its completion and continues to be further developed. This can be likened to a paradigm shift in the history of the over 5,000-year-old discipline of architecture and it forms the basis of the discipline of Mediatecture.

**How does this new installation method and product change the face of the digital video landscape?**

-

Due to the increasing scarcity of urban space, the role of exterior façades is changing. In addition to its communicative function, a transparent media façade also makes it possible to use the space located behind it as an office space as it allows 90 percent of the daylight to fall through.

Architecture in the 21st century reflects, among other things, the mentality of our communication-influenced society. Ever-advancing technologies combined with major changes in the way we live and the way we see have placed different demands on architecture today. In particular the use of integrated media design in the overall design of an architectural façade can serve as an additional communication function.

**Does it allow for more creativity when designing architectural lighting installations?**

-

Every building has its own individual façade with different requirements and criteria, which not only must comply with architectural demands but also with economic and communication goals. This requires a high degree of creativity.

The transparent media façade permits deviations from the conventional standards of visual display. By making it possible to work outside the framework of 4:3 and 16:9 standards, the transparent media façade opens up new forms and formats of visual installations that can be customized according to the requirements of the architecture. The goal is always to create an emotional connection between the viewer and the architecture.

A computer-controlled installation on the façade creates a direct reference to its environment through interactivity or reactivity. Such a dynamic façade can enhance the value of an architectural structure with relatively little effort. The structure stands out in its environment and engages it in a continuous process of development. The process of designing media façades for buildings is both a creative and planning challenge.

## NEW VISUAL
## CULTURE
-
**ag4**

**Can you walk us through the creative and management process
for one of your installations?**
-

Merck Serono is a leading global pharmaceutical company
that wanted to expand the size of its headquarters. The architect
Helmut Jahn created the architectural design for the expansion
of the headquarters and integrated existing, older buildings
into the new company complex. One of the walls of the
existing building complex became a section of the newly built
company foyer.

To create this wall, Helmut Jahn asked ag4 media façade for
a media-tectonic concept that can visualize the conceptual
orientation of Merck Serono onto the surface area of the wall,
thereby organically integrating it into the entire ensemble. ag4's
creativity and experience gave birth to a media-tectonic concept
that convinced both Helmut Jahn and Merck Serono, which was
then implemented in 2006.

ag4 arranged 128 wax blocks according to an abstract form of a
genetic code on to a total surface of around 360 square meters
and spanning five floors. By using natural yellow beeswax, ag4
fell back on a material that has been in use for centuries and that
can be organically formed.

These wax blocks form the first level of the installation and,
through this natural, part-translucent part-opaque material
they act as an emotional antithesis to the glass architecture of
the building. Beeswax is a valuable resource in nature, which
bees use among other things for the flow of information within
the bee colony.

ag4 transferred the communicative function of this material
metaphorically onto the space installation by integrating light-
emitting diodes "or LEDs" into the wax modules. These form the
second layer of the installation.

The wax blocks are the transfer medium that acts as the
multimedia communication of Merck Serono's complex
identity. Images, videos and text fragments depict the themes of
company, people, products and science, and artistically stage
them on several superimposed layers. Images and videos shine
through the wax, creating the distinctive poetry of this visual
media installation.

ag4 specifically developed a software tool for the programming
of complex media content display for mediatecture: the
Interactive Media Pool Platform, or in short, IMPP. The
content, designed according to an individual personal profile
developed specifically for Serono and consisting of images,
videos and text fragments, is combined by IMPP according
to a complex principle to create a multidimensional media
presentation and display.

After the initial programming is done by ag4, the media content
of the installation composes itself continuously anew and can
be expanded with new content by Serono at any given time. The
company can thus specifically display time- and event-related
contents on demand.

Piazza Del Duomo, 2007, Mailand, Italy - Mediamesh®
Photo credits: ag4/ GKD

141

ag4

# Lighthouse

Peter Chan
Managing Director
-

## LIGHTHOUSE
-

Hibino
Join Merit
Urban Media Research
Imago
Electric Signs

Hammersmith Broadway, London, UK

NEW VISUAL
CULTURE
-
**Lighthouse**

LIGHTHOUSE DEVELOPS, MANUFACTURES AND MARKETS LED VIDEO SCREEN SOLUTIONS FOR MULTIPLE INDOOR AND OUTDOOR APPLICATIONS, INCLUDING DIGITAL SIGNAGE, MEDIA AND ENTERTAINMENT EVENTS, AND SPORTING ARENAS ACROSS THE GLOBE. WITH NUMEROUS TECHNOLOGICAL BREAKTHROUGHS TO ITS NAME, LIGHTHOUSE HAS ESTABLISHED ITSELF AS AN AWARD-WINNING LEADER IN THE LED VIDEO INDUSTRY THAT HOLDS ITSELF TO THE HIGHEST STANDARDS OF QUALITY.

FOUNDED IN 1998, LIGHTHOUSE HAS A STRONG GLOBAL PRESENCE, WITH REGIONAL OFFICES IN EUROPE, NORTH AND SOUTH AMERICA AND ASIA PACIFIC. LIGHTHOUSE EMPLOYS THE MOST ADVANCED TECHNOLOGY, THE HIGHEST QUALITY MANUFACTURING FACILITIES, AND WORLD-CLASS ROUND-THE-CLOCK TECHNICAL SUPPORT, TO ENSURE THAT ITS LED VIDEO SCREENS CONTINUE TO SATISFY DEMANDING CUSTOMERS ON EVERY MAJOR CONTINENT AND TO CAPTIVATE THE IMAGINATION OF MILLIONS.

Westfield car park in the UK

McCoy Stadium in the United States

### What does Lighthouse do?

-

Lighthouse is a global leader in LED video technology. We develop, manufacture, supply and support creative LED video solutions. These solutions make a significant impact on the viewers and they connect with the audience whatever the message, the venue or the budget.

### Have you had ever had to overcome any significant technical challenges in order to offer better products?

-

Yes. In fact, the most important challenges have been weight, versatility, waterproofing and energy consumption.

Video panels need to be light in order to facilitate installation and minimize structural costs. They need to be concave or convex so that they may be used in any architectural design. Waterproofing is obviously critical for outdoor applications and low-energy consumption is also important in our environmentally conscious market. Our engineers have overcome those challenges and all our products reflect this.

I should also add that today, our market demands true-color reproduction. Our advanced back-end control systems provide excellent control over brightness uniformity and color accuracy. This is critical to be able to reproduce natural and vivid colors on screen.

## NEW VISUAL CULTURE
-
### Lighthouse

**Do you think your products have changed the digital video landscape?**
-

Yes, certainly. Lighthouse's digital video screens are now creating an impact that was not possible until recently. The digital video landscape is changing because of our true-to-life image quality, high brightness, superior color correction, and flawless panel alignment. The result is an ultimate solution to flawlessly broadcast any message visually. That content could be a newscast, advertising, television coverage or anything else.

Another way in which our products are changing the industry is through the variety of screens now available. For instance, Lighthouse's "Impact" has the advantage of offering both front and rear access. This is important in places with difficult access or where screens are to be mounted on a wall. Another example is the versatile and transparent "Bar." It can be arranged in any form or configuration, therefore it is an ideal product for rooftop situations.

One of our products, "Tile," is an ultra slim, creative screen that can be installed where minimum thickness is required, for example on the side of a vehicle. Finally, the roll-up and detachable feature of our "VideoBlades" provides the ability to wrap uneven surfaces or building façades.

Its individual blades can be used singly or in groups as set-lighting fixtures. It can be raised or lowered extremely quickly. In addition, this system can be set up faster than any other system in the world.

Roll up! At the Hammersmith Tower in West London, UK

**How do these products allow for more creativity for architectural lighting installation designs?**

-

LED lighting and panels are no longer limited to traditional forms. Our products are excellent solutions for architects who are looking for creative lighting installation options that offer virtually unlimited flexibility in lighting design.

**Can you give us some real world examples of some of your most creative installations?**

-

The Wynn resort in Macau is a prime example of how Lighthouse's product can support creative designers. More than 1,000 10mm LED panels have been arranged to form a circular ceiling screen that can be split into halves. These halves are servo-powered.

They open and close in a tightly choreographed manner, in perfect synchronization with moving lights, a Golden Tree Fountain and the rhythm of the music. The result is a spectacular multimedia experience, which combines light, video and sound. It is a centerpiece of Wynn's daily showtime programme.

Lighthouse also designed several spectacular advertising solutions, including one for the Carphone Warehouse Group, Europe's largest independent mobile phone retailer. An 18.5-meter by 5.8-meter "Impact 12" indoor screen was built behind glass, on the side of a building on show to the London traffic.

This innovative solution has 6,000 nits of brightness and its novel installation makes it possible to view it effectively behind glass and in direct sunlight. Large panels were used, each measuring 768mm by 1,152mm. Their large size made the installation simple and servicing them will be quick and easy.

In Hong Kong, we completed the installation of an impressive LED display for one of Asia's most renowned fashion designers, Vivienne Tam. Located at her 1881 Heritage shop, in Tsim Sha Tsui, this screen, which consists of eight LED panels of 4mm pixel pitch, in a 1x8 configuration, forms an impressive floor-to-ceiling display. It attracts customers because of its vivid and rich visuals of Vivienne Tam's latest creations, from fashion shows from around the world.

The screen's 4mm pixel pitch delivers unbelievably sharp visuals. This is important for close-distance viewing. Furthermore, its 2,000 nits-brightness, 1000:1-contrast ratio, and its wide viewing angle guarantee crystal-clear visibility from any direction. The screen can be rotated to difference angles so that customers may see the screen from all angles.

Another example of our screens' versatility can be found in the USA, where we have installed 45 10mm LED panels in an unusual configuration in the lobby area of the Nokia Club. Our LED screens play a major role in displaying this mobile phone giant's corporate and promotional messages. Because of their unusual and creative configuration, they can show diverse contents in different format, thus resulting in a considerable amount of content flexibility.

Westfield, UK

At the Rose Bowl in California, United States

## NEW VISUAL CULTURE
-
**Lighthouse**

**Sports venues are now using LED displays. Is your new technology making a significant impact on sports fans' experience?**
-

There's no doubt about it. All the technological advantages that we have discussed so far can also be applied directly to the use of our LED screens in sports stadium. In fact, our screens have been part of both an installation with the largest number of pixels and one with the largest screen.

Our high-definition LED screens were part of a large scale technological renovation project at the NBA and NHL facility of the American Airlines Center in Dallas, Texas. These new digital screens increase video quality dramatically.

A total of 25 Lighthouse LED screens of various sizes and pixel arrangements were installed at that facility, including a centrally hung display, several scoring screens, an octagonal and a round-shape advertising screens. These screens offer spectators dramatic instant replays, scoring information and dynamic advertising content, all in bright, vivid color and with ultra-sharp details.

Two stadium-sized 20mm video screens were installed, one at each end of the arena. These are three times larger than the previous screens, therefore every fan will enjoy a stunning high-resolution view of the action and game statistics. In addition, two screens made of 10mm panels have been placed along the dasher boards. During hockey and basketball games, they display advertising content to both the arena and the TV audience.

Circling the entire perimeter of the arena is a huge 360-degree, 20mm fascia banner, which was installed on the Platinum level boards. Another 10 LED banners were added to the Flagship level boards. Each banner displays dynamic advertising content, which is clearly visible from any seat in the arena.

Another one of our most impressive projects can be found at BC Place, in Vancouver, Canada, which is home to the MLS' Vancouver Whitecaps and the CFL's BC Lions. It is also home to the world's second-largest centrally hung LED video system. Integrated with four-sided centrally hung structures, it features two gigantic main screens and two end screens, for a total of 325 square meters of full-color LED video.

**What do you foresee as the future of LED screens and their impact on the world?**
-
LED screens are already widely used in securities trading, finance, transport, sports, retail shops, shopping malls, casinos, corporate brands, advertising and other fields.

LED panels will improve our quality of life because they have less impact on our environment. LED screens have low energy requirements. They also need little maintenance and few parts' replacements. This leads to long life cycles.

**How have LED panels changed the face of the media and the advertising market?**
-

LED screens have already brought a lot of innovation to the media and advertising market. In particular, LED panel technology has added a renewed vitality to the outdoor advertising market.

Compared to traditional methods of outdoor advertising, LED panels' dynamic and continuous display not only easily attract audiences, but they can also show a large volume of information. This approach is favoured by both the general public and advertisers.

With innovative developments, our LED screens occupy an increasingly important role in the media and in advertising, especially in stadiums, on billboards, in transportation as well as in other related fields. Because of the advantages mentioned already, our LED screens offer greater flexibility than traditional billboards and therefore greater return on investment for advertisers.

They also have a much greater aesthetic appeal as well as a stronger visual impact. They can reproduce trillions of colors, therefore a far wider color range than any other display technology, such as LCD and plasma. Interactive displays also allow for more creativity in advertising campaigns.

**Are installation costs competitive and are financial returns attractive?**
-
Yes, but many consumers still make the mistake of simply looking at acquisition cost. In fact, the total cost of ownership over the lifetime of the product should be taken into consideration when evaluating LED screen options.

Our complete display solutions provide our customers with a significant return on their investment within a very reasonable period.

Dancing on the ceiling at the Wynn Resort in Macau

NEW VISUAL
CULTURE

ag4
Lighthouse

# Hibino

Takashi Nihongi
Managing Director,
Hibino Chromatek Division
-

**H!BINO**

-
Join Merit
Urban Media Research
Imago
Electric Signs

Hibino's on the big screen in Shibuya, Japan

151

NEW VISUAL
CULTURE
-
Hibino

HIBINO CHROMATEK DIVISION IS THE HIGH-END MANUFACTURING DEPARTMENT WITHIN HIBINO CORPORATION. IT STARTED MANUFACTURING AND SELLING LED PRODUCTS IN THE MIDDLE OF THE 1990S.

IT PIONEERED AND MANUFACTURED A 270-INCH PROTOTYPE LED DISPLAY CALLED QUANTUM WALL, WHICH WAS EXHIBITED AT INFOCOMM IN LOS ANGELES, AND PROVED TO THE WORLD THAT A NEW ERA OF LARGE, FLAT VIDEO SCREENS HAD BEGUN.

HIBINO CHROMATEK DIV.'S PROCESSING TECHNOLOGY BECAME WELL KNOWN AND WAS USED ACROSS THE WORLD IN A WIDE VARIETY OF LED SCREENS FROM FIXED INSTALLATIONS TO MOBILES AND RENTAL APPLICATIONS.

TV studio installation

**What exactly is Hibino and how does it operate?**

-

Hibino takes pride in being an audio and visual specialist. We are leaders in the field of professional A/V equipment, providing a total package of services including system design, construction, and installation, as well as equipment sales, operation and rental.

We handle many events and have had very good feedback from our clients and the market as a whole. In the years ahead, we want Chromatek Div. to contribute to society by becoming a total solution company.

We want to be able to provide the most professional A/V and IT equipment, acquire a vibrant management team and use a higher level of manufacturing techniques. We also want to be known for our reliability, professional skill, and international and multicultural focus.

**What are your biggest creative and technical challenges? For example, how difficult was it to make your 3mm LED panel?**

-

When we developed the ChromaLED 3, 3.0mm Pixel Pitch SMD-LED Display, our consultation process included spending as much as time as possible looking at many electrical and mechanical issues and technical tasks — especially the LED module, processor, mechanical chassis and countermeasures for heat generation.

The results of that process were implemented in the final design. And because of that, we were able to supply the broadcast-quality ChromaLED 3 display to television studios. We are very proud of that pioneering achievement.

NEW VISUAL
CULTURE
-
Hibino

**How are new installation methods and new products changing the face of the digital video landscape?**
-
We always focus on providing unique displays, and flat-screen units have become extremely popular recently.

We usually have quite unconventional ideas and innovative designs for display units. We have already supplied oval-shaped and even stairway-design screens to high-profile boutiques and shops.

**Do these developments allow for more creativity?**
-
Yes, they do. We anticipate the collaborative design work done on LED displays and LED lighting will increase. Despite this, we do acknowledge that until now, there have not been that many remarkable achievements.

We expect the designer's role to flourish. Successful designers should have a rich sense of originality and creativity for implementing innovative designs for both LED displays and lighting.

In our experimental installations, we have two LED displays: see-through types of displays and ordinary displays.

We are convinced that those collaborative designs will be effective when in use with lighting effects. We anticipate that the combination of LED display and lighting will increase the originality and creativity of the overall effects of imaging.

**Can you tell us about your creative and management processes?**
-
In Japan, installation and construction processes are divided and managed separately. In most cases, construction processes are managed by the project's owner or a management company.

Overall installation and construction processes are planned and scheduled after there is complete mutual understanding. Hibino, as a supplier of LED display systems, join the process as a supervisor for the design and installation.

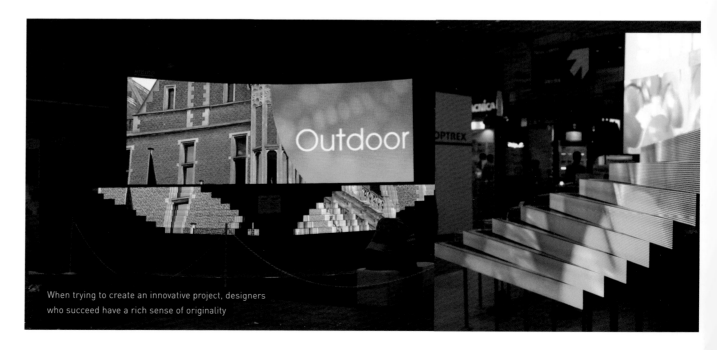

When trying to create an innovative project, designers who succeed have a rich sense of originality

Hibino's see-through display in action

155

# NEW VISUAL CULTURE
-
**Hibino**

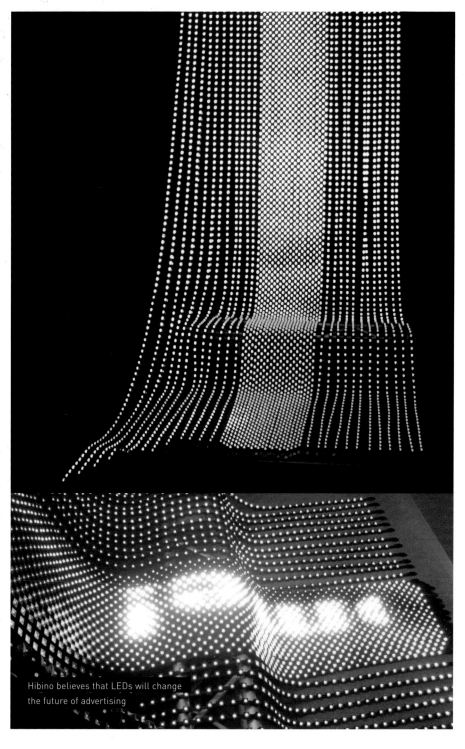

Hibino believes that LEDs will change the future of advertising

**What do you see as the future of LED and what will be its impact on the world?**
-

LED is one of the attractive light-emitting materials with the capability of a longer operating life and energy conservation. It may have positive influence on the world. For example, fewer power stations would be needed if traffic lights are replaced with LEDs.

But there are also other advantages too. LEDs have the possibility to initiate a new lighting culture that uses different kinds of light — such as flames, color shades and flashing. We realize that LED is a material that can be used for its colorful application, but also for the sheer number of potential uses.

**Do you see LEDs influencing the media and advertising market?**
-

Yes, we do. Concerning the advertising market, it has been quite a long time that the term "digital signage" has been in use. For some time now we have seen many flat-screen TVs used to display a digital advertisement.

LED display screens are capable of applying a digital message to an even larger size, over 100 inches in size. We expect the demand for this will grow in the future. LED displays have the potential to take over printed advertisements in a newspaper or on a standard poster or billboard. This is why we are convinced that LEDs will change the future of the advertising market.

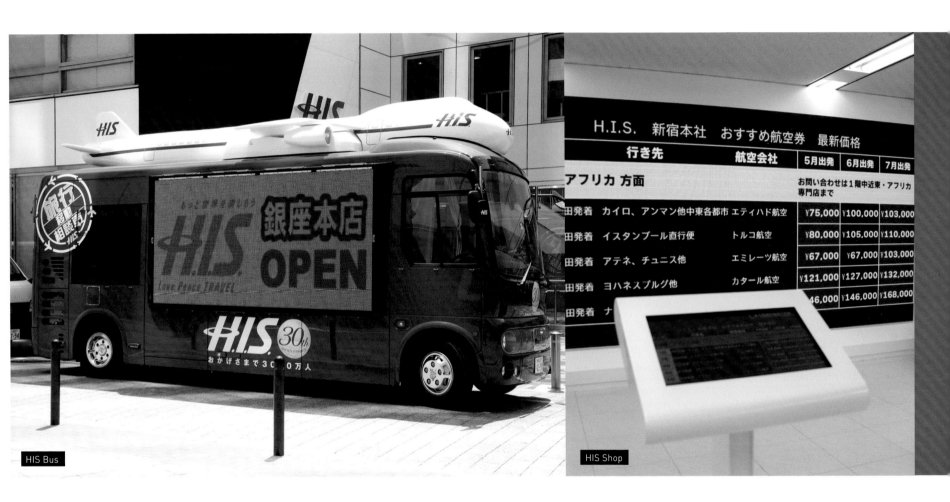

HIS Bus

HIS Shop

| H.I.S. 新宿本社　おすすめ航空券　最新価格 | | | | | |
|---|---|---|---|---|---|
| 行き先 | 航空会社 | 5月出発 | 6月出発 | 7月出発 | |
| アフリカ 方面 | | お問い合わせは1階中近東・アフリカ専門店まで | | | |
| 田発着 カイロ、アンマン他中東各都市 | エティハド航空 | ¥75,000 | ¥100,000 | ¥103,000 | |
| 田発着 イスタンブール直行便 | トルコ航空 | ¥80,000 | ¥105,000 | ¥110,000 | |
| 田発着 アテネ、チュニス他 | エミレーツ航空 | ¥67,000 | ¥67,000 | ¥103,000 | |
| 田発着 ヨハネスブルグ他 | カタール航空 | ¥121,000 | ¥127,000 | ¥132,000 | |
| | | 46,000 | ¥146,000 | ¥168,000 | |

**Why would someone use this kind of installation?**

-

A client may consider investing in an LED display as an advertising medium, which will help to enhance the value of their product or service.

Compared to an ordinary printed poster, which can by its very nature only show one image, an LED display can portray various scenes. This in itself can be considered as a cost-benefit application, and we expect this concept to appeal to advertising agencies and clients alike.

**What else can you say about the future of LEDs in your market?**

-

We strongly believe in the potential capacity and positive global influences of both LED displays and LED lighting. LED applications have a relatively low environmental impact and also have the potential to be wonderfully efficient.

We are looking forward to working together with many of the designers in this book — and also the readers. We look forward to combining the best hardware and software to establish a global network of LEDs, leading the world towards a more peaceful and prosperous society.

**NEW VISUAL
CULTURE**

ag4
Lighthouse
Hibino

# Join Merit

Ronald Lo
Chief Executive Officer

 **JM NETWORK**

-

Urban Media Research
Imago
Electric Signs

CommonSpace, Causeway Bay, Hong Kong

159

JOIN MERIT IS A MEDIA GROUP THAT IS HUGELY INFLUENCED BY LED TECHNOLOGY. ITS CORE BUSINESS INCLUDES GLOBAL LED VISUAL EQUIPMENT RENTAL AND OUT-OF-HOME DIGITAL MEDIA NETWORKS.

THE COMPANY SEEKS TO PROVIDE VALUE FOR ITS CLIENTS, STAFF, PARTNERS AND THE INDUSTRY AS A WHOLE. JOIN MERIT'S GOAL IS TO BECOME THE MOST COMPREHENSIVE VISUAL EQUIPMENT RENTAL COMPANY IN THE WORLD. IT SEEKS TO ACT AS A PLATFORM TO PROVIDE THE MOST UP-TO-DATE AND REALISTIC VISUAL SOLUTIONS FOR CREATORS TO PROJECT THEIR CREATIVE VISION.

ANOTHER OBJECTIVE IS TO PROVIDE THE MOST EFFECTIVE OUT-OF-HOME MEDIA PLATFORMS FOR ADVERTISING MESSAGES THAT ACT AS A BRIDGE BETWEEN AN AUDIENCE AND A BRAND.

A gigantic 3D screen at CES Las Vegas 2011

Leehom MUSIC MAN Tour

**How are you different from traditional media companies?**
-

The difference between us and a traditional media company is our ability to quickly adapt to change. The media landscape is changing every millisecond. We are a young start-up so we try to innovate and refine our ways to find a solution every time we confront an obstacle.

As a company, we try to create a close-to-zero political working environment to be as efficient as possible.

**What are the advantages of LEDs in your business?**
-

Currently, LEDs are the optimum solution for our media projects. They are bright under the sun, waterproof and LED solutions can be extremely versatile. We can create any shape or size of a digital media canvas for our clients to visualize their expression or message.

**How popular have LEDs become?**
-

LEDs are now widely known by the general public. You see them as features in cars, in TVs, and even in your rice cooker sales brochure!

In the realm of media and production, we use LED technology as our digital displays, we use them as colorful illumination backdrop, and even use them as special lighting for our video production. The application of LED technology is limitless.

Hong Kong Fashion Week

**NEW VISUAL
CULTURE**
-
**Join Merit**

**Do you think LEDs can change our way of life?**
-

LEDs are definitely one of the driving forces revolutionizing our lifestyles today. They can influence our mood with different lighting solutions, they display sporting events to millions of viewers worldwide, they offer us safety through a quicker braking system for motor vehicles, through our iPod dock alarm they even help wake us up in the morning...the application list goes on and on. The technology is definitely a game changer.

LEDs also represents the future of lighting. They have became a key component in every energy-efficient lighting design, as they are the ultimate, efficient way to save energy, save money and create a greener and healthier planet.

**What about the impact of LEDs on the world as a whole?**
-

LEDs have become an important inspiration for us all. They offer us all a better way to light up our homes, our workplace, our train stations, our airports...LEDs help us preserve our valuable resources.

Chung King TV in TST

80 outdoor screens network in Manhattan, NY is a collaboration between JM, MTA and Clear Channel

Commonspace in Causeway Bay

**What kind of effects do you feel this is having on our visual landscape? And how is the manufacturing process evolving?**

-

With more and more screens and media façades appearing in city skylines, LEDs are definitely becoming more dynamic and interesting.

With the increase of creative demands from clients, manufacturers react by investing their time and effort in R&D. They are currently focusing on more affordable solutions, smarter mechanical designs to save space and weight, optimizing energy consumption and better color uniformity in their visual solutions.

**How do you define "media façade"?**

-

The term, "media façade," is a gigantic communication platform created by lights. Through visual and interactive technologies, it connects our minds and emotions.

**What is the cost of a typical installation and how impressive is its return on investment?**

-

Currently, media façades are only affordable to the most premium real estate developers, as the cost of such technology remains prohibitive.

Return on investment has drastically improved through the availability of lower cost visual solutions. They also makes the most sense financially if an architect or lighting designer is involved earlier in the design stage.

In metropolitan cities such as New York, Hong Kong and London, the advertising value could potentially make up for the huge setup costs of gigantic media façades, but it is certainly not a solution for everyone.

## NEW VISUAL
## CULTURE
-
**Join Merit**

**Can you tell us about one of your "mega-projects" and its technical challenges?**
-
For IDEX 2011 (International Defense Expo), we erected three outdoor LED screens with 696 Lighthouse R7 panels. The dimension of the main display was 60 meters (wide) by six meters (high), with a resolution at 3,840 pixels by 384 pixels. It acted as the backdrop of this important event in the Middle East.

The technical challenges included safely packing and delivering these panels from our warehouse in Hong Kong to Abu Dhabi. We had eight 40-foot containers filled with screens and equipment. We also had to orchestrate technicians and local helpers to construct the screens within three days.

The power management of these panels was not the only issue we encountered; we also had to deal with the ultra-high-definition visuals. Then of course, we had to dismantle everything safely and ship them back to Hong Kong. Our achievement was nothing short of magnificent. It was an installation that was enormously challenging and we are very proud of what we achieved.

IDEX 2011

Bangkok International Motor Show 2010

**What is your vision for the future of outdoor digital media?**

-

In order for the out-of-home media industry to truly flourish and become a powerful advertising network, it needs consolidation. A centralized system that could provide micro- and macro-advertising solutions to clients would be key.

Wireless identification systems such as RFID and virtual reality technologies such as immersive technologies are examples of what should be integrated into the platform. Like in the film *Minority Report*, someone walks past an advertising system and targeted and relevant messaging is loaded onto multiple digital displays. Future advertising systems could also personally greet and interact.

**Do you have any predictions about how LEDs can evolve to meet society's changing needs?**

-

Five years ago I was asked a similar question. Back then I predicted that LEDs would one day become a construction material for all projects, just like paint or a brick.

They could be embedded within our walls at home and become an illuminative surface or a general illumination light source or an interactive display when we need it to be. I'm confident that we are still heading in this direction.

**What excites you about the LED industry right now?**

-

The last couple of years have been filled with excitement. The LED screen industry has seen advancements in color uniformity, lighter mechanical designs as well as a drastic drop in price.

One thing that is still lacking is the amount of attention to R&D in the area of application of screen technologies. We need to work with creative people to deliver more innovative uses of these LED systems. That would foster and encourage better content and increase interactivity between a screen and an audience.

This kind of development is something we should all be contributing towards in order to create a flourishing industry.

**NEW VISUAL
CULTURE**

ag4
Lighthouse
Hibino
Join Merit

# Urban Media Research

Mirjam Struppek
Urbanist, Researcher and Creator
-

-
Imago
Electric Signs

Measuring gas supplies has never been so entertaining.
The Moodgasometer in Berlin, Germany

NEW VISUAL
CULTURE
-
Urban
Media Research

MIRJAM STRUPPEK WORKS AROUND THE WORLD AS AN URBAN
MEDIA RESEARCHER. HER FOCUS IS ON THE "LIVEABILITY" OF
URBAN SPACE, THE PUBLIC SPHERE AND ITS TRANSFORMATION
AND ACQUISITION THROUGH NEW MEDIA.  MS. STRUPPEK
HAS DEVELOPED THE CONCEPT OF "URBAN SCREENS," THE
REDEFINITION OF THE GROWING INFRASTRUCTURE OF DIGITAL
MOVING IMAGES AS A NEW COMMUNICATION FORMAT IN
PUBLIC SPACES. THESE SCREENS CONTRIBUTE TO A CREATIVE
AND HEALTHY URBAN SOCIETY SUPPORTING THE EXCHANGE
OF CULTURE.

TO SUPPORT URBAN SCREENS EVENT SERIES AND WORLDWIDE
RELATED INITIATIVES, SHE CO-FOUNDED THE INTERNATIONAL
URBAN SCREENS ASSOCIATION WITH GLENN HARDING.
TOGETHER WITH SUSA POP FROM PUBLIC ART LAB, SHE HAS
ALSO DEVELOPED THE MEDIA FAÇADES FESTIVAL, ESTABLISHING
URBAN SCREENS AS A NEW EXHIBITION FORMAT FOR MEDIA ART.

Dream O₂ World

**Describe what the term "media façade" means to you?**
-

As a trained urban and environmental planner I see an urgent
need of the sustainable and aesthetic integration of the urban
screens infrastructure into our cityscape.

Media façades should inspire new thinking how to creatively
integrate this new visual technology into the architectural face of
our cities.

Making use of its potential as a new artistic communication tool,
media façades as well are a chance for the corporate world to
contribute to an inclusive, high-quality urban environment.

## NEW VISUAL CULTURE
-
**Urban
Media Research**
-

**What are some of the more compelling design trends right now?**
-

New installation methods that allow a more invisible integration of LED lights into architectural elements allow a more creative play with the relationship of the light as well as the moving image and architecture.

Architecturally well-incorporated and purpose-built screens can provide interesting aesthetic experiences with space and structure. An interesting example is the new $O_2$ World in Berlin. During daytime, LEDs that are incorporated into the curvilinear window frames of the arena are not visible, but provide interesting perspectives into interior and exterior space at night when the building is lit inside.

Depending on the light's intensity, the interior either outshines the message or is eclipsed by it. A temporary use is becoming possible without the aesthetic problem of a "black screen."

Looking at the issue of energy consumption, a combination of LED lights with a direct source of energy through solar technology is a new interesting trend and a challenge for aesthetic constructions.

Outdoor screens have the ability to easily adjust to their surroundings which is important — not only to help to save energy, but also to prevent light pollution.

Another trend is that more and more flexible, lightweight and easy to install, LED "net-constructions" have started to transform scaffolding on construction sites and turn them into temporary digital façades. This is a trend that needs to be critically observed, bearing in mind the danger of neglecting their integration into our urban surroundings.

Paradise Panorama Katrin Schoof

**How does media façade affect society generally?**
-
This is hard to generalize. It depends on the general attitude of a particular society towards the concept of their urban space.

Media façades combine three unique aspects: light radiation, flexible and strategic programming of content, and the movement of images. A fourth possible feature is audience interaction.

If strategically situated in the urban environment, this combination makes a media façade a powerful medium in our information-saturated modern cities — the next step in the evolution of a façade becoming a communication tool.

To create real social benefits from this medium, content is the key. We have to ask who is responsible for the content and if it is relevant to citizens. Can media façades express the creativity of a city by showing urban gestures, telling public stories, illustrating political iconography or even thought-provoking graffiti?

Content is the key to the acceptance of this attention-grabbing medium. Meaningful content can change the experience of place or create affective and strong shared experiences among strangers and enhance social cohesion, for example lucid interactive experiences. Local, site-specific or participatory content can work against the universal face of modern architecture.

Eye-catching media façades may appear as provocative communication tools by the owner or building management, and this could influence their relationship with the locale. For example, the Moodgasometer and O₂ World monuments are perceived as iconic markers of the redevelopment of Berlin, and the impending gentrification of the affected areas. It culminated in a heated debate by local residents.

Artists at the Media Façades Festival in Berlin always reflect on these issues and the role of the media façade as a communications medium with participatory potential. Moodgasometer transformed the structure into an indicator that could reflect residents' moods.

Advertisers BBD2 produced personalized content after it had asked residents to contribute their ideas for their desires and values. Artist Georg Klein's "Sonic Parole – Think different, Be yourself, Join the revolution!" for the O₂ Entertainment Arena was an ironic commentary on radical social and political slogans of the 1960s and 1970s that are now frequently transformed into messages of radical chic in contemporary advertising.

As a forum for user-generated content, urban screens may help to redefine our notions of urban communities, mobilizing citizens to take part in actively shaping the public space and its urban interactions.

Media art should open a field of experimentation through which urban screens gain a growing potential for building community and shared experiences, binding together a diverse urban society and facilitating exchange.

**What do you see as the future of LEDs in this area and its impact on the world?**
-
More competencies in the application of LEDs not only in media façades, but also in the general lighting design of cities is still needed. This should contribute to energy saving and reduction of unnecessary light radiation, while increasing the aesthetics of urban areas.

**NEW VISUAL
CULTURE**
-
**Urban
Media Research**

Collage of Fed Square's large urban screen and The Unique Plaza

**Can you see LEDs altering the way media and advertising markets operate?**
-

New sustainable and humane attitudes and values that direct the application of a product like LEDs will change media and advertising markets — not just the product itself.

**What are some of the things that an investor should know in order to own or operate a media façade installation?**
-

The confinement to a purely visual language is an aspect of working with permanent urban screen infrastructure that must not be underestimated.

In western countries in particular there is little opportunity to work with sound, as it is strictly prohibited. The planning of a media façade is a highly complex project requiring knowledge about the relationship of material, size, resolution, the positioning in the local environment, content and local regulations.

**What is the usual cost of such an installation and how do owners plan their return on investment?**
-

Costs of installations vary extremely, thus it is very hard to generalize. An important condition for positive recognition is the successful aesthetic amalgamation of the screen itself with the architectural building shell — in combination with inspiring content.

The more the light-pixel installation becomes itself an artwork the less it is dependant on constantly changing content and promotion to be acknowledged and appreciated.

As these kind of media façades require more site-specific considerations than a square screen, the possibility for selling it as advertisement space is harder, however high quality site specific content can transform successfully an ordinary façade into an attractive urban highlight catching wide media attention.

**What are some of the best examples you know of internationally?**
-

The artist collective Mader Stublic Wiermann created a very successful animation called "Twist and Turns" for the LED installation at Vienna's Uniqa Tower. It was designed to change completely the image of the building.

The animation was overwhelmingly effective, relying on the skillful application of effects of optical illusions in black and white, which distorted and broke up the façade into a number of weird, three-dimensional objects.

This ordinary high-rise, named after the company, was transformed into a dynamic luminous sculpture and became a new landmark in the city. The Dexia Tower in Brussels as well is an exemplary instance of this kind of corporate effort to create a strong profile for their high-rise.

The special light game "Touch" by Lab[au] used a huge touch screen installation in front of the tower as interface for interactive engagement with the public.

The GreenPix - Zero Energy Media Wall in Beijing is a good example for a connection of a photovoltaic system and light pixels integrated in the glass curtain wall of the Xicui entertainment complex.

The most exciting merger of a TV-format screen and a public urban space has been achieved in Melbourne's Federation

Square with its FedTV. With its agenda geared towards community-building and sustainability, it is a good example of how integrated urban screen projects are utilized to build a sustainable relationship with culturally diverse citizens of a vibrant, modern city.

It represents a unique cultural precinct where the incorporation of various media tools into the design intersects with a careful creation of a public space to achieve engagement with the community and promote exchange.

The main plaza was designed from a conception centered around a prominent 65-square-meter public LED screen, a rare case of early consideration of the marriage of new media and urban design. The project management seeks to primarily make the square with its screen available to local groups for their festive activities.

Another beautiful example for a thoughtful and aesthetic LED installation is part of the façade of the Henry Madden Library at California State University, Fresno. The inspiring visuals show the weaving process of traditional baskets from region's Native American tribes. The images have a calming, meditative impact on the viewer.

The artist Jenny Holzer has worked successfully with the minimal aesthetic integration of LED ticker screens into architectural structures such as at the David Lawrence Convention Center in Pittsburgh or the New National Gallery in Berlin. For the Museum of Contemporary Art San Diego, she created a double-sided red LED installation shooting words from Holzer's writings upward, into the sky.

The most impressive artwork created for an ordinary LED screen is Pippilotti Rist's series of 16, one-minute video segments, *Open My Glade*, originally commissioned by the Public Art Fund in 2000, to air in April 2000 on the NBC Astrovision by Panasonic screen in Times Square, New York.

Media façades can encourage mass social interaction at events like city-center film screenings

It represented one of the most successful treatments worldwide for the format commercial outdoor screens. This work successfully employs the motif of the screen's window-like character to afford fascinating views into an altogether different commercial media universe with its beauty enhanced.

**Do people ever consider a media façade as a source of light pollution or visual bombardment?**
-

So far, media façades play only a minor role in this problem. However there is indeed a growing public intolerance of light constantly emitted from large screens — flickering light is considered more disturbing than "still light." If content lacks popular local appeal tolerance is even lower.

With this experience in mind, the BBC's "Public Space Broadcasting" initiative aimed at the installation of large monitors in central urban locations shifted to include more specifically local content as well as interactive games and artistic films in order to increase popular acceptance. They generate content in close collaboration with local authorities, arts and higher education institutions in each specific location.

The subject of light pollution was also raised at the preparatory stage of the Urban Screens Melbourne Festival. A special "Dark Nights" program for the evening featured video works in darker colors and with reduced, and less hectic light changes. This demonstrated that even with a 20-percent reduction in power, the daylight-enabled screen radiated widely beyond the confines of the square.

**Is there anything you would like to add to the debate?**
-

In general, light and information should be considered as a precious resource. We should aim at a moderate usage of media façades as creative urban communication medium instead of the simple digitalization of advertisement boards.

This might prevent radical actions against the advertisement market as in the case of São Paulo, where all advertisements have been banned from public space.

## NEW VISUAL
## CULTURE

ag4
Lighthouse
Hibino
Join Merit
Urban Media Research

# Imago

Rafel Fors
Worldwide Head of
Architectural Projects
and New Architectural Product Innovator
-

◯ IMAGO
-
Electric Signs

Stunning LED façades greet guests at the W hotel in Barcelona, Spain

NEW VISUAL
CULTURE
-
Imago

IMAGO DESIGNS, DEVELOPS, MANUFACTURES AND SELLS
LARGE LED DISPLAYS THAT INCREASE VISUAL COMMUNICATION
EFFECTIVENESS. WITH ITS HEADQUARTERS IN BARCELONA,
SPAIN, IMAGO BRINGS OVER ONE QUARTER OF A CENTURY OF
EXPERIENCE WITH A PRESENCE IN MORE THAN 40 COUNTRIES.
PRODUCT RELIABILITY AND LONGEVITY IS BACKED BY THE
COMPANY'S PROPRIETARY TECHNOLOGY AND MANUFACTURING
PROCESSES THAT ARE A DIRECT RESPONSE TO REAL CUSTOMER
NEEDS ACROSS IMAGO'S KEY MARKETS.

THE FIRM WAS FOUNDED IN 2006, WHEN QUERCUS EQUITY
ACQUIRED ODECO ELECTRÓNICA WITH THE INTENTION TO
BUILD A GLOBAL LEADER OF VISUAL COMMUNICATION AND LED
ELECTRONIC SIGNAGE.

## NEW VISUAL CULTURE
-
**Imago**

**Imago is separated into Traffic, Sports, OHM and Architecture units. Can you talk about each business?**
-

### TRAFFIC
Odeco's Variable Message Signs (VMS), ADDCO's mobile Dynamic Message Signs and Thomas VT's Fixed Signs offers over 23 years of continuous improvement supporting road management.

Our systems are used by systems integrators, transportation infrastructure developers and concessionaries, and governmental agencies, in more than 3,500 projects installed in over 40 countries.

### SPORTS
We are the inventors of the perimeter system LiveAd, previously known as Speedtime. It enables sports teams, stadium owners, venue operators and sports advertising agencies to deliver profitable rich media to its stadiums and TV audiences through state-of-the-art LED perimeter systems, digital scoreboards and video screens.

LiveSports modular LED systems and displays are easy to install and let you begin broadcasting digital media.

### OHM
For outdoor advertising, Imago OHM, standard or tailor-made digital billboards and modular LED systems enable media agencies to deliver high-impact communication in unique locations at a very competitive price and with reliable equipment.

For indoors, our value-for-money high-resolution LED screens and displays help retailers influence buying behaviour with a point-of-purchase presence and create new environments for differentiation.

### ARCHITECTURE
A history of successful Transvision projects and end-to-end customer support make Imago Architecture a reliable partner to help architects transform buildings into communication media. Our integrated architectural structure LED systems have made legendary symbols in some city skylines such as Arles or Barcelona.

The Nasdaq screen at Times Square, New York City

**What changes have you observed in the field of LED technology during your time in the industry?**

-

Basically, changes in the industry have been linked with improvements to LED technology. This is especially true with SMD LEDs, where there has been a reduction of pixel pitch of up to 3mm in outdoor daylight SMD screens.

Now we're seeing the growth of low consumption and high-efficiency products.

**How do you foresee LED technology's growing influence in the future?**

-

We have to wait and see how OLED technology evolves, and also we have to see improvements in LED efficiency. A massive uptake in domestic usage is also expected, for example backlighting for TVs, and general lighting, where standard bulbs will be replaced with LEDs.

**Do you feel that this uptake is essential given the environmental benefits of LED technology?**

-

For sure. Nowadays it is the most efficient light source that we can use domestically, but we still have to improve, and even more importantly, reduce prices. Consumer LEDs are still too expensive to be a truly mass market product.

**What are your expectations about the future of LED technology?**

-

I'm expecting OLED products to revolutionize the industry once more, but probably in about five years.

The Torre Agbar has become a colorful and striking icon
for the skyline of Barcelona, Spain

**What are your latest, most exciting projects?**

-

We're working on several media façade projects, and we expect that some of them will soon become a reality. Stadiums and emblematic buildings are our goal right now.

We're discussing agreements and partnerships with important firms in this market, but also increasing our presence to the intelligent lighting market, so we'll be able to offer complete solutions.

**What are the major R&D challenges in this type of project?**

-

We have to integrate as much LED technology into the buildings as possible. Lighting and video screens must be part of the building, not just an added part on top of them.

This means developing projects together with architects, glass, metal and mesh providers, so our solutions (we're beyond products) achieve what designers and final customers desire.

**How do you incorporate these low- and high-resolution technologies together in your designs? Do they provide solutions to each other?**

-

It's important to understand client expectations and then find the product that fits the best. Size of the screen or type of content that they want to show normally defines what resolution you are going to use.

Normally you use high-resolution screens for small screens, high-definition content or OHM purpose screens. On the other hand, low-resolution technologies are used when big surfaces have to be covered (for example at the Grande Halle in Arles or the Barcelona's Agbar Tower). Alternatively, low-definition content in fact needs to be displayed — as in the W hotel in Barcelona, where the screen creates a special atmosphere within the lobby.

The impressive Grande Halle in Arles, France

## NEW VISUAL
## CULTURE

# Electric Signs

Alice Arnold
Non-fiction Filmmaker and Educator
-

ELECTRIC SIGNS

Screen Shots, Hong Kong 2007

183

ALICE ARNOLD MAKES DOCUMENTARY FILMS THAT EXPLORE
URBAN EXPERIENCES AND VISUAL CULTURE. SHE ALSO TEACHES
MEDIA STUDIES AND MEDIA PRODUCTION COURSES. MS. ARNOLD
HAS TAUGHT AT PARSONS, CSI/CUNY, HUNTER COLLEGE/CUNY,
POLYTECHNIC/BROOKLYN AND HOLLINS UNIVERSITY.

**Can you define media façade culture?**
-

I would not define media façades as a "culture." The term simply refers to the exterior cladding (the façade) of a building that is equipped with media technology.

There are many different applications of media façades, ranging from video screens to programmable light discs. Media façades are a new type of city surface, formed from the intersection of architecture, signage and screens.

**You are making a film on this subject matter. Can you tell us something about it?**
-

The goal of *Electric Signs* is to create media work that is rooted in social and cultural history and that is relevant to issues affecting people's social conditions.

The project is structured as a documentary essay in the spirit of city symphony films. It is organized into five sequences: New Sign Systems, Mobile Marketplaces, Pale Daylight, Media City, and Urban Lightscapes.

Screens — whether they are on the tops of skyscrapers, in ATMs or on our iPods — are reshaping urban environments and redefining areas of public space by intensifying the commercialization of the public sphere.

*Electric Signs* is a feature documentary that explores this new screen culture as it unfolds in several world cities, though with an emphasis on New York and Hong Kong, both cities that have pushed global trends, from the emergence of electric street signs in the early 1900s to today's new urban lightscapes.

**Who is your major target audience for the film? How do you expect this film will impact its issue?**
-

*Electric Signs* is created for distribution to a television audience in the United States, Europe and Asia. In addition, the film will be submitted to festivals so as to increase its screening and marketing opportunities.

Another key distribution outlet is the educational market, where this program has the potential to spark awareness and discussion in the fields of media studies, visual culture, public policy and urban studies.

**What are some of the popular design trends now?**
-

I think many architects and designers are thinking about data visualization techniques and dynamic walls (or screens) that can be programmed and updated via software.

Media façades, as well as digital billboards, impact public space by increasing the amount of marketing and advertising images in the public sphere.

They are changing the experience of architecture, from something solid to something permeable. They are shifting visual culture and they are changing people's experience of space and time in cities.

LEDs are more sustainable than incandescent lighting but at the same time, they are driving an increased use of lighting and video boards.

On the other hand, the ability to program light (to change color values and color temperatures, and create different patterns) is a very positive development.

Yes, they already have.

– Chanel Shop, Ginza
– Bix for Kunsthaus, Graz
– Uniqa Tower, Vienna
– Galleria West, Seoul
– Star Palace, Taiwan
– Greenpix Media Wall, Beijing

I've read that light from Las Vegas now infiltrates Death Valley and that this affects astronomy in that region. People can no longer easily see the stars and planets.

This is a serious concern and a problem that needs to be addressed. Visual bombardment also occurs because more and more screens are now in the public realm and these screens show a stream of images instead of just one — as does a static billboard.

Screens both frame and mediate the way we access, use and absorb visual culture, communications and information.

As the framing device for digital data and communication flows (from photos to financial information), screens enable new ways to experience and conceptualize space, time and speed.

Digital media concepts and technologies expand our sense of space to include desktop and virtual space, and alter our measurement of time to include real, download and upload time.

Another essential facet about screen culture lies in the dual meaning of the word "screen." In the digital age a screen is a viewing device, but it also means to hide, partition and conceal. So as we are watching are we are also being watched?

Panopticons and closed-circuit TVs are visual-based forms of surveillance, but there are other, softer forms of control that screens help to enable, such as image control and control of people's attention.

Las Vegas at Night
Photo credits: Nasa

# DESIGN
# AND
# INTERACTIVE
# WORLD

The fields of automation and interactive media have experienced an unprecedented leap in the past decade. Now that the developed world is infused with so many connecting technologies, our current culture has become completely reliant on global communication systems, information networks and digital interfaces.

Remote locations and cultural differences are no longer the barriers they once were. Contemporary work habits, with the help of the world wide web and global travel, mean that almost any level of connectivity is possible.

Likewise, interactive designs allow and encourage us to test the unknown and unexpected. Interactivity now gives us the courage and capability to manipulate and experience any kind of environment and social group — real or virtual.

One of the most interesting trends resulting from interactive media takes place in lighting and media design. LED technology's innate environmental and dynamic qualities allow it to be widely applied on new architectural designs, visual arts, industrial products and installations projects.

Through this bleeding-edge development, an interactive understanding of "fourth dimension" or "time-based nature" has entered the workplace, retail sectors, the entertainment and leisure, as well as the domestic arena.

Designers create a context that makes the human and environmental response a constantly active and evolving interface. In this new era, the fourth dimension has been incorporated into a variety of architectures, installations and spatial designs. As a result, there is a greater focus on research and development. Labs, design agencies and institutions are globablly active in this erupting field, while trans-disciplinary collaborations now explore the new social and technological realities.

Whether it is the macro data from the universe or micro data from nanotechnology, our species is developing a new sense of perception of our responsive environment. This new sensual experience and psychological landscape will mark our ulterior lifestyle.

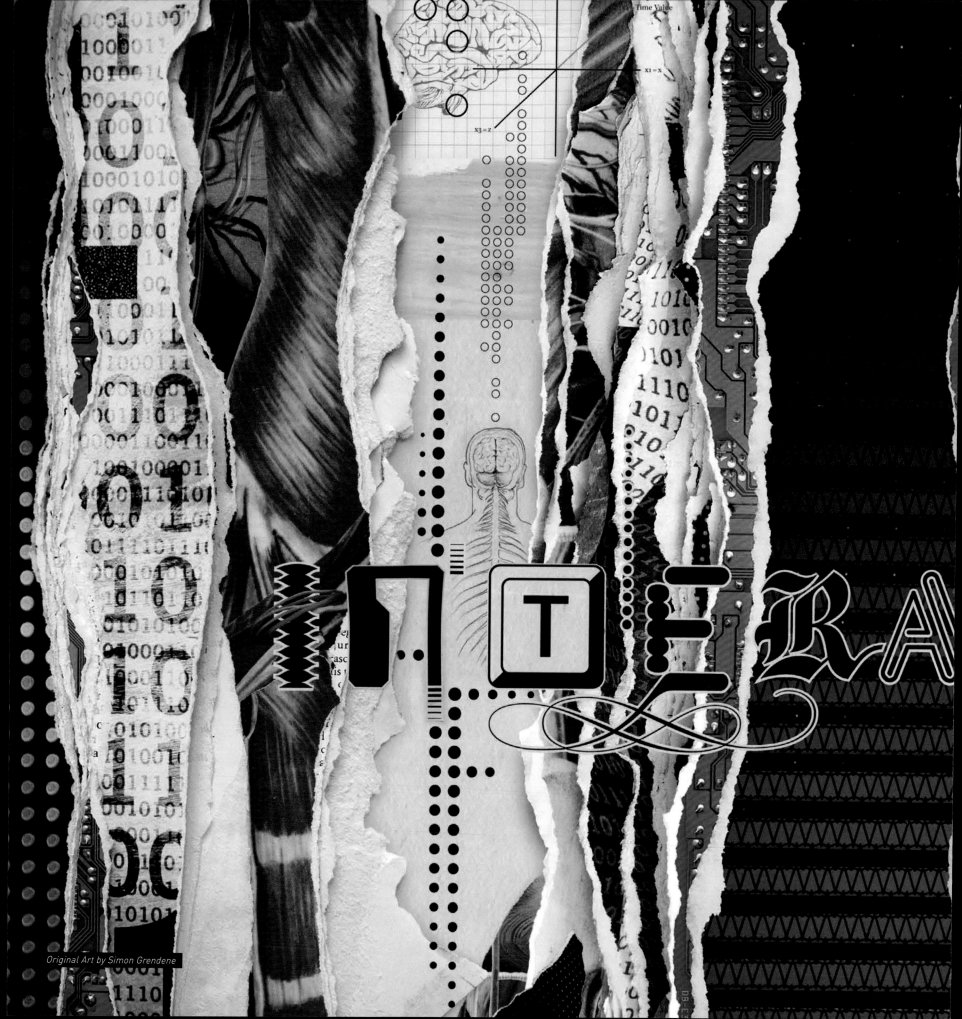

Original Art by Simon Grendene

PLANET LED
-
Chapter 04

DESIGN
AND
INTERACTIVE
WORLD

# United Visual Artists

Matthew Clark
Founding Partner
-

**UnitedVisualArtists**
-

LEDARTIST
Cinimod Studio
Jason Bruges Studio
Electroland
New York University
James Law Cybertecture
Arup Lighting
Licht Kunst Licht
Webb Australia Group

Volume at London's iconic V&A museum
*Photo credits: United Visual Artists*

PLANET LED
-
Chapter 04

DESIGN
AND
INTERACTIVE
WORLD
-
United
Visual Artists

ESTABLISHED IN 2003, UNITED VISUAL ARTISTS (UVA) IS AN ART AND DESIGN PRACTICE BASED IN LONDON. UVA PRODUCES PROJECTS AT THE INTERSECTION OF SCULPTURE, ARCHITECTURE, MOVING IMAGE, LIVE PERFORMANCE AND DIGITAL INSTALLATION.

UVA'S TEAM MEMBERS CONSIST OF MANY DISCIPLINES INCLUDING FINE ART, ARCHITECTURE, COMMUNICATION DESIGN, MOVING IMAGE, COMPUTER SCIENCE AND ENGINEERING. THE CROSS-POLLINATION OF DIVERSE SKILLS INSPIRES NEW FIELDS OF EXPLORATION, WHICH IS CORE TO THE FIRM'S ETHOS.

On tour with Massive Attack. Back in 2003, UVA became the first company to use LED screens as a data display
*Photo credits: United Visual Artists*

Many of UVA's projects take the viewer or audience beyond a passive
experience. Constellation, London, November 2008
*Photo credits: United Visual Artists*

**DESIGN
AND
INTERACTIVE
WORLD**
-
**United
Visual Artists**

Chorus, Leeds, February 2009
*Photo credits: United Visual Artists*

**Your work emphasizes interactivity. Why do you prioritize this?**
-

Yes, we have made a number of responsive works, but the priority isn't for all of our work to be interactive. We always aim to create work that feels alive and which takes the viewer beyond a passive experience. However, this can be achieved in many ways other than the call-and-response approach.

**Why is an interactive experience important? And why have you chosen to involve the spectator in such innovative ways?**
-

This question of participation is wider than what can be termed an "interactive" experience. In some ways everything we involve ourselves in during a normal day can be seen in terms of interaction. When we create a new installation, one of the first elements we consider is who is the space for and what is its identity. The physical form of the installation is a response to its environment. Following on from this we consider how we wish the installation to behave and respond.

Chorus, which is a series of pendulums of light and sound, comes from that process. The context of the space is a newly renovated assembly hall— traditionally a working-class and social space.

In its new role the assembly hall becomes home to Opera North with a radically different social context. The architecture is breathtaking, and it was important that the installation complimented rather than invaded the space. The performance of Chorus is contained in three movements; the intensity of swing from the pendulums dominates the piece.

We felt it unnecessary to introduce any kind of "interactive" technology to the piece. Instead we allowed the audience to choose their level of involvement. Integrating responsive technology into an artwork needs questioning and must have purpose and resonance with the idea and not just the function.

**Your choice of experiments questions our sense of identity. How does the general public respond to this?**
-

The success of an installation can be judged by the way the media responds to it. In this case we don't just mean "column inches" in press, but also social networking media such as Flickr, blogs and so on.

Acknowledging and appreciating how people choose to document their social experiences is important to us. If we have a temporary installation in a public space that thousands of people experience and share, that is a successful transformation of a social space.

On another level, our work reaches out to contemporary society by inviting intimacy with surfaces and technology that in the majority of cases is untouchable.

**Why is LED technology such an imaginative material?**
-

We often use LEDs as they offer a versatile way to work with light, in terms of form, intensity and programmability. LEDs have a very cold and digital aesthetic which gives it an other-world quality. They can be beautiful when used in contrast to more natural surroundings and materials.

However, LED technology also has its limitations when you consider resolution and color depth. It is all too often used in a garish manner without any consideration to the environment it occupies; this particularly applies to modern architectural lighting schemes.

**In what capacity can LEDs reach an audience?**
-

LED functions as an emissive and intense carrier of light, and this adds a visual impact to any show. However, we would say that it is not the LEDs themselves that reach the audience in different ways, but the whole aesthetic and narrative arc of a show.

**How do different genres of music and new locations affect your choice of experiment and mode of communication?**
-

When we create live shows for musicians we see the heart of the show as a collaboration. Each location on a tour has its own requirements, but a tour is not really site-specific, like a public art installation.

Touring shows are usually based on the same footprint and design. Different artists require different treatments. It really depends on what seems to "fit." We take each artist on a case-by-case basis.

Array, YCAM Japan, December 2008
*Photo credits: United Visual Artists*

## DESIGN AND INTERACTIVE WORLD

-

**United Visual Artists**

**How has the world of entertainment contributed to new areas of development within the field of LED?**

-

When we started working in this field, there were very few LED technologies available for concert touring and live performances. On the Massive Attack 100th Window Tour, we became the first people to use a LED screen as a data display using pixel-perfect graphics.

At the time, LED screens were driven with analogue video signals, but now everything is digital. The cost of LED has dropped considerably, and, as it is has a much lower energy usage, it is a sensible move for the industry. There's also been a convergence of the worlds of lighting and video.

**Why do you think it is important for the public to view such large-scale LED art productions? What are you hoping to create for them and the performers?**

-

Public art is important for many reasons, and this is true for all artworks, LED or otherwise. These kinds of LED technology are usually used in commercial applications, like sports stadiums and advertising boards. It's interesting to see the public's reaction when they are able to walk up to, and even touch this technology.

The emissive nature of the LEDs also gives a brilliant, and ethereal illumination, which is at times artificial and otherworldly. Seeing yourself and others bathed in this light gives people pause for thought and allows them to view themselves in a new environment. We are hoping to blur the line between the performer and the stage, bringing the audience into the environment and allow them to play within it.

Kabaret's Prophercy restaurant, London
*Photo credits: United Visual Artists*

**What value does this add to the integral meaning and focus of the work?**

-

Allowing the viewer to participate either passively or actively creates a sense of involvement for both the individual and the group. The focus is at one time on the artwork, and at others on the space it is in, and at other times on those participating with you.

**How do you feel technology can meet and adapt to the wider reaching needs of social responsibility?**

-

We are keen to create more permanent artwork and LEDs lend themselves very well to this aspiration as it is both energy efficient and long lasting, minimizing the need for bulb replacement.

As artists, we have a social responsibility to create objects and environments that are both compelling and memorable, but at the same time, as humans we have a responsibility to the environment.

Back on the road with Massive Attack
*Photo credits: United Visual Artists*

Success of a project can be measured by media and also audience response

Photo credits: United Visual Artists

**DESIGN
AND
INTERACTIVE
WORLD**

United Visual Artists

# LEDARTIST

Angus Yu
Business Director and Head of Business Development, Sales & Marketing
-

**LEDARTIST**™

-

Cinimod Studio
Jason Bruges Studio
Electroland
New York University
James Law Cybertecture
Arup Lighting
Licht Kunst Licht
Webb Australia Group

Dynamic LED Lighting Lantern, Lee Kum Kee Lantern Wonderland 2011
*Photo credits: LEDARTIST*

**DESIGN
AND
INTERACTIVE
WORLD**
-
**LEDARTIST**

LED Facade Festive Lighting, Tsim Sha Tsui East, Hong Kong

LEDARTIST (LEDA) IS A VISIONARY COMPANY THAT PROVIDES LED LIGHTING DESIGN AND CONSULTANCY, ART DIRECTIONS AND INTERACTIVE DESIGN. LEDA IS BASED IN HONG KONG, SHANGHAI AND NEW YORK CITY.

LEDA BELIEVES IN COMMUNICATION THROUGH LIGHTS. THE STUDIO IS COMMITTED TO LEADING THE WAY IN INNOVATIVE LIGHTING AND MEDIA DESIGN. IT SEEKS TO PUSH THE ENVELOPE OF BUILDING A FUTURISTIC, ENVIRONMENTAL, VISUALLY COMPELLING AND COMMUNICATIVE WORLD.

LEDA'S DYNAMIC, MULTI-CULTURAL TEAM CONSISTS OF LIKEMINDED VISUAL AND LIGHTING DESIGNERS, ENGINEERS, PROGRAMMERS AND LED EXPERTS WHO SHARE THE SAME DREAM TO LEDIZE® THE WORLD.

Dynamic LED Lighting Lantern, Lee Kum Kee Lantern Wonderland 2012

## DESIGN
## AND
## INTERACTIVE
## WORLD
-
## LEDARTIST

**What changes have you observed in the field of LED technology during your time in the industry?**
-
The LED industry is similar to the computing industry. New models and major technological improvements appear all the time. Complete dedication to the industry is needed to keep up with the pace in development.

LEDs have been popular in electronics applications — VCRs, mobile phones, monitors and TVs. Also in digital media — outdoor big TV screens, digital banners, dot matrix displays. And signalling devices — traffic lights and road works. But in recent years, growth has been focused on illumination.

Major players in lighting estimate that LED lighting will represent over 50 percent of total spending in the global lighting market by 2015. No lighting technology has grown and penetrated the market this quickly since Edison invented the first light bulb.

There have been a lot of newcomers to the industry lately. But certain key entry barriers, such as high investment costs and drastic technology developments, are pulling.

In the past few years, we've seen a majority of industry investments gradually moving from decorative and color-change lighting to white lighting. Figures show that LEDs for illumination purposes represents only five percent of the whole industry in 2011, but it's going to reach double-digits very soon.

Some manufacturers offer one-stop-shop design, installation, programming and after-sale services, in addition to simply supplying a product.

Lighting designers are using more LED fixtures than ever before. This is mainly due to increased demand driven by energy-saving benefits and environmental consciousness of property developers.

**How have these changes resonated through your company?**
-
The transformation from color-lighting to white-lighting is a tough lesson for many industry players. Unlike the traditional lighting market — where there are clear international standards that guide product development — the white-lighting market now has many rivals on industrial design, research and development. The industry has slowly turned from what was once a blue ocean to a bloody battlefield.

To cope with this rivalry, we chose to remain strong on creativity and work with only the biggest and most reliable manufacturers. LED illumination has caught the "green" wave.

We have learned that LEDs have become an important branding tool for many corporations. Especially when they want to bring attention to their corporate social responsibility characteristics.

**What are your opinions on the popularity of LED as method of lighting?**
-
LEDs are one of the most energy-efficient illumination technologies. And the increased awareness of environmental issues has turned LED into a popular tool of property developers and socially responsible corporations.

Inconsistent adaptations, non-binding industry standards, and high production costs fortify rapid development in replacing traditional lighting methods.

But it will take more time for the industry giants to migrate from their traditional lighting to investment more in LEDs.

HSBC Hong Kong headquarter 10th year
MPF anniversary façade lighting

Shanghai JinQiao Interactive Christmas Tree

**Which major project are you most proud of?**
-
The media façade of the HSBC headquarters building in
Hong Kong.

**What is the philosophy behind LEDARTIST's designs?**
-
Our philosophy is to maintain a high level of creativity and value-
added services in our lighting designs. And, at the same time,
uphold our in-depth knowledge on LED illumination technology
and its development.

We continually challenge ourselves on research and
development to ensure we bring new ideas to our clients.

**What is the future of LED technology?**
-
LEDs will revolutionize the lighting market, especially in the area of illumination. The
potential of LEDs in illumination is enormous and just keeps increasing all the time.

It allows us to demonstrate what happens when creativity merges with LED technology.
What can be achieved are advanced technologies such as interactive solutions that
enlighten the world. We believe that LEDs can help to bring a new definition of
illumination to people and can forge a new kind of relationship between people and light.

Ultimately, LEDs will be both a major illumination technology and an intangible
medium technology that brings people together.

## DESIGN
## AND
## INTERACTIVE
## WORLD
-
## LEDARTIST

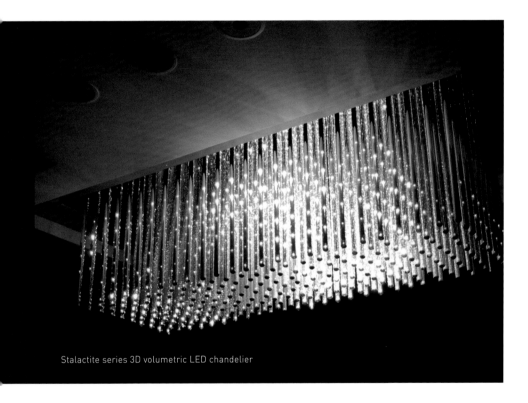

Stalactite series 3D volumetric LED chandelier

**Can you talk about a current project that you are excited about?**
-
Our next exciting project is to create an adaptive lighting solution that focuses on lighting control, rather than traditional lighting fixtures.

We are putting different system hardware and LED lights to different experiments in our Lighting Lab. Hopefully someday, we can offer a truly energy-saving lighting system that is smart and flexible, and can be applied to all situations.

**Do you have a final thought you'd like to share?**
-
We believe that with every new technology that replaces old technology there will be an inevitable sacrifice. It will also take time to implement. But we need to have courage to try new because that is the key to a better life.

We hope that everybody can be more open-minded and introduce LED technology in all kinds of ways. This is the way we contribute to the earth. Be green with a new technology.

Media Facade Lighting of Huizhou Zhong Kai Government Economic Headquarter Building

PLANET LED
-
Chapter 04

**DESIGN
AND
INTERACTIVE
WORLD**

United Visual Artists
LEDARTIST

# Cinimod Studio

Dominic Harris
Founder and Creative Director
-

-

Jason Bruges Studio
Electroland
New York University
James Law Cybertecture
Arup Lighting
Licht Kunst Licht
Webb Australia Group

"Untitled (UFO)" is an art project conceived by established New York artist Peter Coffin. Cinimod Studio was hired to realize the project

*Photo credits: Michal Slaga*

**DESIGN
AND
INTERACTIVE
WORLD**
-
**Cinimod Studio**

DOMINIC HARRIS QUALIFIED AND WORKED AS AN ARCHITECT IN LONDON BEFORE JOINING JASON BRUGES STUDIO. HE THEN FOUNDED CINIMOD STUDIO, DRIVEN BY AN INTEREST IN INTEGRATING TECHNOLOGY AND INTERACTION WITHIN ARCHITECTURE, WHICH NOW FORMS THE BASIS OF THE DESIGN STUDIO. HE HAS A FASCINATION WITH LIGHTING AND ELECTRONICS, WHICH IS EVIDENT IN THE HIGHLY INNOVATIVE LIGHTING SCHEMES THAT HE BRINGS TO EACH OF HIS PROJECTS.

This lighting feature at SNOG in Soho, London, is comprised of 700 glass globes containing LED lights and presents a new level of visual excitement and public engagement
*Photo credits: Cinimod Studio*

"Beacon" is a kinetic light installation with a mind of its own.
An array of emergency beacon lights interacts with visitors, tracking
their movement through the space, creating an immersive and playful experience
*Photo credits: Chris O'Shea*

## DESIGN
## AND
## INTERACTIVE
## WORLD
-

**Cinimod Studio**

### What does Cinimod Studio do?
-

Cinimod Studio is a cross-discipline practice based in London specializing in the fusion of architecture and lighting design. The ongoing work of Cinimod Studio is both visually stunning and technologically advanced.

A dedication to research and development ensures that the studio stays abreast of the latest technologies and fabrication techniques. The studio is currently involved in several projects in both the UK and abroad, and has designed bespoke lighting products that are now in production.

### What is the importance of an interactive experience, and why do you choose to involve the spectator?
-

Lighting, color and form are everything to me. I am obsessed with these qualities in all of our projects. Each project must have a considered approach and sensitive response to the brief.

If we are working with fully color-controllable lighting, then we will take major steps to prevent any appearance of the "default rainbow test pattern" that I despise so much in large scale lighting projects.

Instead we will create bespoke control systems and interfaces to ensure that the lighting control is relevant and, above all, always beautiful.

Much of our work is interactive, which is a whole new art form that combines science and technology with human and environmental interaction. Bringing the spectator into a project in a way that becomes an active part of the artwork will fundamentally change a project.

The interaction leads to new and unexpected behaviours, and for me there is a real passion and reward in seeing "users" of an artwork become entangled and immerged within it.

Cinimod's ongoing R&D programme has generated some fascinating technologies and solutions to unusual design briefs. We now routinely utilize multi-touch tracking surfaces, multiple thermal-camera setups, and bespoke electronics and software solutions.

### Do you have an example of that?
-

Recently, a large scale interactive project that we were involved in was the "Light Symphony" for Subranic that can now be found at the European Shopping Centre in Moscow. While traditional chandeliers are static objects, the Light Symphony is designed to engage with the public and become active and animated elements within the space.

It comprises 240 light tubes suspended in space to create a falling volume of red, gold and white light. The overall height is 15 meters, and the scale of the piece feels both natural and appropriate to the cavernous atrium where it is located.

The real magic comes from when members of the public become "conductors" of the Light Symphony. Standing at a special plinth that is reminiscent of an artist's easel, the user can orchestrate complex color movements throughout the Light Symphony by using his hands and arms across a highly innovative LED touch panel. The response is immediate, and the effect clear, fluid and rewarding.

### Your choice of experiments questions our sense of identity. How do you feel your creations and manipulation of them reach out to society?
-

Much of Cinimod's work can be described as projects that engage and delight the public. We strive to achieve this in all of our work, be it a standalone artwork, a retail store, or a façade of a building. When I first approach a project I look for clues as to what is achievable within the brief, and how far we can push our response to achieve extraordinary results.

Modern society, our target audience, is comprised of technologically savvy consumers who have grown up surrounded by color and light stimulation. In order to be noticed by this audience, I make sure that are work is refined and precise, and that the aesthetics are beautiful and innovative.

The greatest testament to the success of our projects within this contemporary society is seeing our work published by the public across all the social media sites — photos on Flickr, videos on YouTube and commentary on Facebook.

Photo credits: Cinimod Studio

### Do you see LED technology as an imaginative material?
-

Light is one of the most awesome architectural materials. Light forms a central part of my palette of materials. I treat it as a fully integrated element of design rather than as a later-stage bolt-on.

LED technology harnesses an added level of controllability and flexibility to light, and that allows us to use light as an even more imaginative material.

LED technologies have matured significantly in recent years, and now exhibit both proven reliability and longevity. They are also increasingly easier to install and control.

With the current generation of fixtures available from the big suppliers one can now be confident that equipment specified and installed today will not appear primitive or, even worse, obsolete, in the years to come. Both the lighting designer and the end client can be sure that their respective designs and investment of today will still look good for many years to come.

The main island of this kiosk in London is a striking organic form with a continuously undulating surface that is studded with LED "dimples"
*Photo credits: Cinimod Studio*

### What influences your artistic endeavours?
-

My studio and I are connected and involved with a number of regular events and groups of people. We attend and speak at hardware and electronics workshops, we display at and visit gallery openings, and we regularly meet up with our peers for discussions on our industry as a whole.

It is very important to me that I am surrounded by this network of interaction. I find that the feedback from one's peers is often the most constructively critical, and ultimately the most valuable.

### How are your stylistic choices matched by the materials you use?
-

It is my fundamental belief of the studio that we should design the experience first and then use our best technologies and techniques to make it a reality.

We have a workshop with engineers where we continuously experiment with new lighting technologies, electronics hardware, and software development.

While there is a general and continuous Research & Development program that is being pursued, we do try and make the R&D respond to specific projects as much as possible. I have no desire to undertake projects that exist solely to show off technology and I steer clear of any artworks that would be described as "techno-art."

A Cinimod Studio project must always have a more emotional and experiential quality to it. In the studio there is a highly skilled and dedicated team of designers and engineers from a mixture of backgrounds. One of the most important aspects of my studio is the architectural background of many of the team members. We are able to use this to our advantage as we have the experience of interfacing between different professions and suppliers, developing the design in an organized and robust manner, and ultimately delivering projects of impeccable architectural detail.

We work closely with a regular network of consultant structural and electronic engineers. Many of these consultants have worked with us on many projects, and there is a natural and smooth continuous dialogue of ideas between us. Ultimately we assume responsibility for the overall design solution.

The overall UFO structure is seven meters and carries 3,000 bright and individually controllable Color Kinetics LED nodes. An on-board 6kw generator provides the system power, and the UFO can be controlled via SMS messaging
*Photo credits: Peter Turo*

**DESIGN
AND
INTERACTIVE
WORLD**
-
**Cinimod Studio**

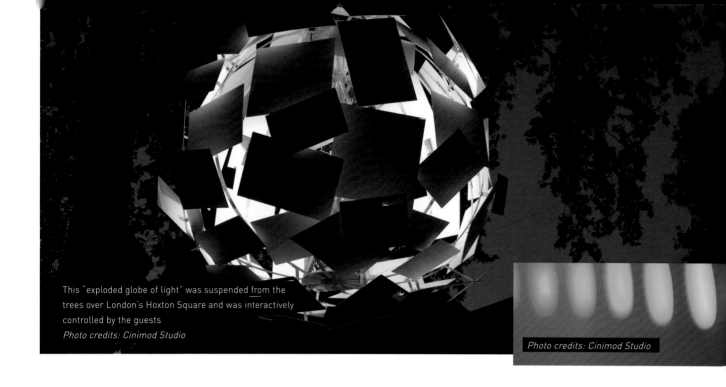

This "exploded globe of light" was suspended from the trees over London's Hoxton Square and was interactively controlled by the guests
*Photo credits: Cinimod Studio*

*Photo credits: Cinimod Studio*

**How do you feel your work has changed traditional perceptions of sculpture?**
-
I strive to create truly unique lighting solutions for our projects. Although they are usually comprised of groundbreaking forms and designs, they ultimately end up looking perfectly natural and suited to the interior. The key is to create a special lighting design that people notice but that does not appear alien.

In London we completed a series of projects called "Butterfly in Flight" for the Itsu sushi restaurant group that show the use of highly integrated lighting solutions which provided a radical improvement to the interior. The brief was to capture the elegance and freshness of their brand while bringing a new excitement and visual prominence to the stores.

Cinimod developed a concept inspired by Itsu's butterfly motif which was brought to life as an animated visible sculpture. The dynamic form is based upon the cinematic motion of a butterfly's wings as it takes flight.

This was modeled as a continuous sequence in 3D software and then sliced at time intervals to determine the evolving angled shapes which comprise the final artwork. The illusion of the butterfly's flight is completed by the bespoke software controlling the color of each wing, allowing for the illuminated and highly visible fluttering of butterflies through the piece.

The "Butterfly in Flight" installation demonstrates the benefit of integrating physical and electrical aspects of lighting at the design stage. The result is a surreal and ephemeral lighting sculpture that provides an adventurous and effective addition to the Itsu shop design, and an intriguing and beautiful new lighting addition to an otherwise dreary high street.

**To what extent can your public projects be integrated into the environment and community?**
-
Often we find ourselves working within the public realm. We are used to working through various consultation processes, and a great deal can be learned through the important of local community consultation.

When working in the public realm it is important that the local community take pride in the work. Making a connection to the history and context of any given site is very important. This possibly stems from my training as an architect where I am always seeking to make connections to the past, present and future.

**What are your hopes for your future work, and how do you feel technology, in particular LED lighting, can meet and adapt to these needs?**
-

The future projects and dreams of Cinimod Studio will invariably continue the pattern of extreme innovation, beauty and technology.

I will continue to guide and encourage my talented team of designers towards exploring new technologies whilst seeking artistic inspiration from the worlds of nature and art. LEDs are clearly going to remain an important part of our material palette, but at the same time we are also working on some cutting-edge projects where there are no LEDs in sight!

Beyond my studio, I believe we will see more avant-garde art that combines multiple disciplines. My personal hope is that there will be less techno-art, and instead artists and lighting designers will collectively focus on beauty and concept rather than the expression of technology.

**How do you foresee LED technology developing?**
-

One area that we have spent considerable time debating is the rapidly increasing use of media façades across buildings. While some LED-lit buildings seem to be left in their rainbow-chase patterns, it is perhaps not surprising that some of the most experimental and innovative building lighting schemes can be found installed at art galleries and cultural institutions.

I think the coming decade will see the demand for much more considered lighting design and media content on such large scale installations; lighting designers in the coming years will have great social responsibility for creating considered and beautiful content for their media façades.

**Given the increase in awareness of social and environmental issues, is this essential or inevitable?**
-

Sustainability is an important issue, and while there have been some less-than-ideal solutions in the past, I do genuinely believe that energy-saving technologies are moving in the correct direction.

In my personal life I have always been very environmentally aware, and this is something I have extended to our studio. As a digital lighting designer I do find a conflict between a desire to use LED fixtures which are energy-efficient, and a desire to use LED fixtures in great quantities.

I suspect that many lighting designers seem to forget that even a scheme based entirely around LED fixtures can still consume vast amounts of energy. While LEDs clearly do consume less energy than their counterparts, we must consider the overall impact of each given scheme.

At Cinimod Studio I encourage a balanced view of the environmental implications of our schemes. I dismiss the idea that using LED fixtures alone is a big enough step. Instead we look at the overall control systems and applications, and develop highly tuned and responsive controllers that tweak our lighting output (and therefore energy consumption) throughout the day.

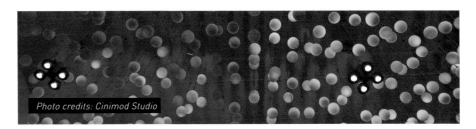

*Photo credits: Cinimod Studio*

**DESIGN
AND
INTERACTIVE
WORLD**

United Visual Artists
LEDARTIST
Cinimod Studio

# Jason Bruges Studio

Jason Bruges
Founder
-

jason bruges studio

-

Electroland
New York University
James Law Cybertecture
Arup Lighting
Licht Kunst Licht
Webb Australia Group

*Mirror Mirror* in London, United Kingdom
Photo credits: Tom Bland, onedotzero.com

PLANET LED
-
Chapter 04

DESIGN
AND
INTERACTIVE
WORLD
-
Jason Bruges Studio

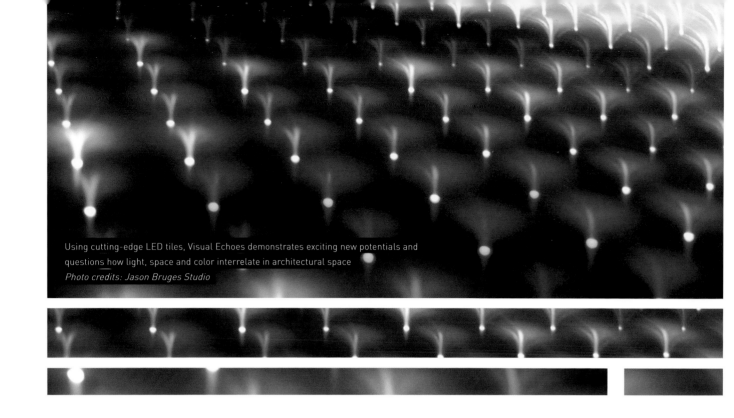

Using cutting-edge LED tiles, Visual Echoes demonstrates exciting new potentials and questions how light, space and color interrelate in architectural space
Photo credits: Jason Bruges Studio

FOUNDED BY JASON BRUGES IN 2001, THE UK-BASED STUDIO CONSISTS OF AN EXPERIENCED TEAM OF ARCHITECTS, LIGHTING DESIGNERS, SPECIALISTS IN INTERACTION AND INDUSTRIAL DESIGN AND PROJECT MANAGERS.

THE STUDIO CREATES INTERACTIVE SPACES AND SURFACES THAT SIT BETWEEN THE WORLDS OF ARCHITECTURE, INTERACTION DESIGN AND SITE-SPECIFIC INSTALLATION ART. ITS PROJECTS RANGE FROM LARGE-SCALE BUILDING FAÇADES AND PUBLIC ART TO INTERACTIVE INTERIOR ENVIRONMENTS AND PRODUCTS.

Memory Wall is integrated into a hotel lobby space and interacts with passersby
Photo credits: Jason Bruges Studio

## DESIGN AND INTERACTIVE WORLD

-

**Jason Bruges Studio**

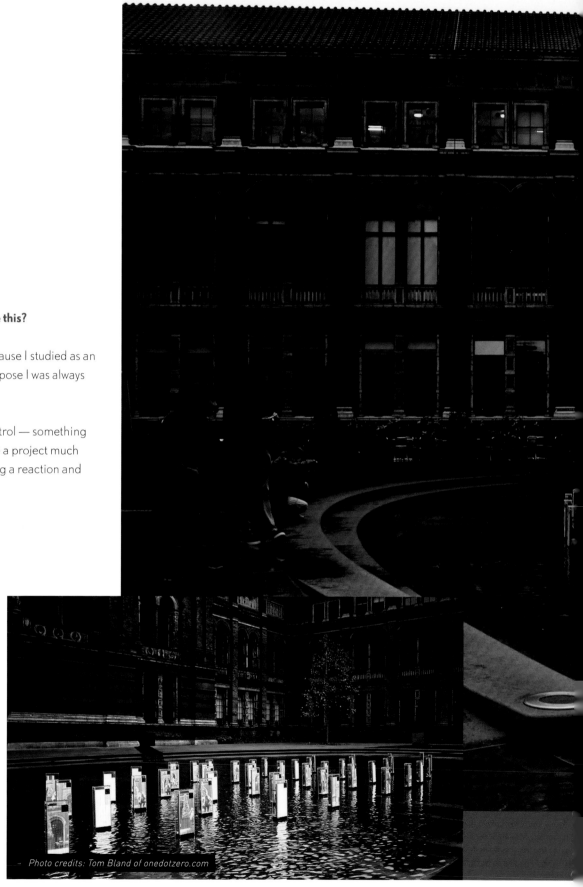

Photo credits: Tom Bland of onedotzero.com

**Your work emphasizes interactivity. Why would you say you prioritize this?**

-

I suppose it evolved out of a general interest in the subject and because I studied as an architect at university. It wasn't really anything intentional but I suppose I was always thinking about it and this led me towards the field.

With interactivity, there is a richness and a texture that you can control — something that is more dynamic [than conventional architecture]. It can make a project much more than simply a static form. For me, what we do is about creating a reaction and an interaction.

**What is the importance of an interactive experience to you, and why have you chosen to involve the spectator in new and innovative ways?**

-

In terms of creating an interactive experience, we try and demonstrate as rich a palette as possible. It is about creating a dynamic space, and if a spatial 3D designer can do that and you add interactivity as well, it becomes a kind of a fourth dimension.

We've found that this really engages people and encourages them to look at the environment around them. But interactivity doesn't always have to be something obvious, it can be something subtle, sub-narrative. If you think about the way people react to fireworks, there is something innate, maybe even primeval, about the way we view nature and space.

Mirror Mirror was commissioned by the V&A museum in London for the Decode exhibition in 2010
Photo credits: Tom Bland, onedotzero.com

**Your choice of experiments questions our sense of identity. How do you feel your media, and your manipulation of them, reach out to contemporary society?**
-

More often than not our projects are in the public realm. "Litmus-Havering Roundabouts Project" on the A13 [four interactive LED sculptures located at major roundabouts in the UK] provoked plenty of discussion and debate. It was a trigger for people to drive past something and question what they had seen.

As a result, people are coming to us and asking us to do projects that can be woven into society, even simple signage projects.

LED lighting is a medium that is instantly gratifying. It can react to vibration or sound and is part of the rich palette that I mentioned. Generally, all the pieces we do are concept driven and are dependent on what the scenario is. But certainly LED projects are great feedback devices.

**Why do you feel LED technology is an imaginative material?**
-

For me, I remember the initial joy as an eight-year-old child when I plugged in and passed a current through my first LED. I remember watching it glow with fascination!

LEDs are "humanly-accessible." They are bright, solid-state and low-energy. The technology is rapidly developing. There are continually more functions and they just get brighter and brighter. It's very exciting to be a part of this development and I suppose that is why LEDs are so imaginative.

**What sort of modern icons or movements inform your artistic endeavours?**
-

I get my inspiration from almost anywhere. But things that I notice in nature — for example, biological signals — definitely influence what I do.

**How is your stylistic lexicon matched by your choice of material?**
-

That's quite a tricky one…The materials that we use are governed by all sorts of things. First of all, there is normally a functional element to a project. For example, if we are doing something in a hotel lobby, we'll generally use materials that are unobtrusive, hidden and quiet. Longevity and wear-and-tear are also issues to be aware of. Sometimes style sits back a little and the priority is that the item is seamless and is able to blend in.

But we're also interested in the intrinsic aspects of a product. Ecology is something that our clients are also thinking about.

Recently we created a camera obscura made with aluminium. It was light and transportable but also had a "space pod" aesthetic. There was a mystery aspect and it gave off a "how do they do that?" feeling.

Sometimes I think that what we do is a little bit like being a magician.

# DESIGN
# AND
# INTERACTIVE
# WORLD
-

## Jason Bruges Studio

**Your sculptures and works are physically ambitious in terms of spatial definition and awareness. What is the role of sculpture as it inhabits our 3D world, and via extension, a public space such as London Bridge?**
-

There are many, many reasons for realizing and commissioning people to build sculptures in public space. There is a matter of civic pride and a way for a local council to show that they are able to spend money, for example. But they are also there to enhance and enrich the surroundings.

London Bridge is generally seen as dirty and an uninspiring part of a walk to work in the morning. For a lot of people, this project [a Bluetooth-enabled project which ran in London in February 2007] made their day. Again, it opened up public debate and people started to ask what was appropriate for public artwork.

**Traditionally sculpture is a form of art that can be easily replicated — how do you feel your work has changed this perception?**
-

I do see different styles and genres that are imitated, but that is always going to be the case. But some can also be pioneering. Passing ideas on to the next generation and influencing them is not necessarily a bad thing. Everybody can learn from everyone else.

For us, though, we're usually site-specific and limited edition. There is rarely a cross-over of agenda.

**You place an emphasis on experimenting with our familiar 3D world, questioning and agitating our expectations of the status quo. What considerations have you explored through method and impact within the creative process of your work?**
-

I like to challenge things and I also like to start projects completely from scratch. I recently started on a project at a school and I know nothing about schools, but I'm not going to start looking at what other people have done in similar environments. I come to a project without preconceptions and I always ask questions driven by ideas…what is interesting and how can we help?

Litmus Lux project. Four landmark sculptures that work like giant litmus papers to respond to a variety of environmental stimuli
*Photo credits: Jason Bruges Studio*

"Wind to Light" was an idea that visualized wind movement across the built form with the use of mini turbines and LEDs and draws attention to the potential of harnessing wind power as a source of energy
*Photo credits: Jason Bruges Studio*

**How do you feel your contribution to public projects shares a community of thought with the goals and ambitions of the public and to what extent can it be integrated into the environment itself?**

-

I am very keen to involve as many people as possible.
I love that there can be a public involvement in what we do.

We have worked in downtrodden neighbourhoods and in some more luxury areas. The latter gives you a better chance of experimenting with technology and spending money, but when we work at the former, it's usually about regeneration and you immediately affect the way a space is conceived. There can be a big contrast from the before and after.

**What are your personal aims in creating these unique interactive experiences?**

-

For me personally, the kinds of projects I have already mentioned explore the opportunities of interactive space. But it's really about building them rather than engaging in an academic debate.

It's about building and making and doing something that is going to work and hopefully last.

**Why do you think it is important for the public to participate in fine art productions such as yours?**

-

Like all things, if people haven't had the opportunity, being involved in a project like one of ours is a great chance to doing something you haven't done before.

Art is still undersubscribed. So, any chance to "get it out there," so much the better!

**What are your hopes and aspirations for the future of your work, and how do you feel technology can meet and adapt to these needs?**

-

I aspire to create world-class environments. I enjoy looking at the impact that these have on people and am really pleased that technology can facilitate that.

With technology, things are easier to control and embed into our environment. Researching and developing ways that we can do this in new spaces is particularly exciting to me.

Generally, LED and other kinds of technology are filtering down into more "standard" architecture and design. However, the more we become accepting of that and the more technology is challenged, the more this process will be tested.

PLANET LED
-
Chapter 04

**DESIGN
AND
INTERACTIVE
WORLD**

United Visual Artists
LEDARTIST
Cinimod Studio
Jason Bruges Studio

# Electroland

Cameron McNall          Damon Seely
Principal               Partner
-

-
New York University
James Law Cybertecture
Arup Lighting
Licht Kunst Licht
Webb Australia Group

"Enteractive at 11th and Flower" comprises 176 LED tiles in the electronic carpet are 16" square, with a layer of glass covering a bright square of red LEDs, for a total of 23,000 LED lights

Target Breezeway, a unique experimental space for environmental interactivity, which is powered by Tyzx 3D vision technology and located on the 69th-floor observation deck of Rockefeller Center in New York City.

ELECTROLAND IS A TEAM THAT CREATES LARGE-SCALE PUBLIC ART PROJECTS AND ELECTRONIC INSTALLATIONS. EACH PROJECT IS SITE-SPECIFIC AND MAY EMPLOY A BROAD RANGE OF MEDIA, INCLUDING LIGHT, SOUND, IMAGES, MOTION, ARCHITECTURE AND INTERACTIVITY.

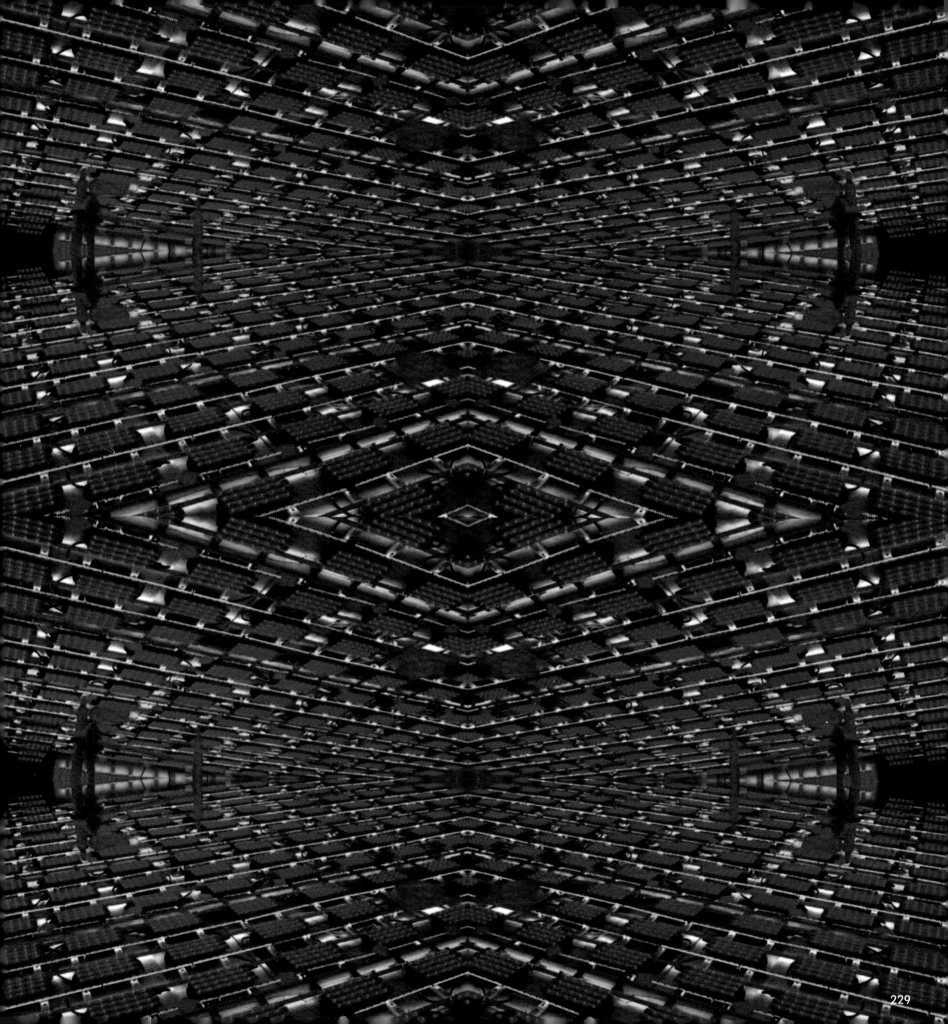

DESIGN
AND
INTERACTIVE
WORLD
-

Electroland

Environmental intelligence and surveillance of human activity are combined with a video-game sensibility. The "Enteractive" building face displays the human interactions occurring below

**Who are the people involved?**
-

Electroland Principal Cameron McNall is an architect and educator with 20 years of experience designing and realizing all scales of projects. His combined experiences in public art and architecture, university research, and cutting-edge technologies make him uniquely qualified to forecast the implications of new technologies and how they may be integrated into environments and information systems.

Partner Damon Seeley has worked on a great variety of technically challenging projects for 10 years with an emphasis on the design of interactive environments and information systems.

**What was behind the installation at the Rockefeller Center?**
-

Target approached us with a "branding opportunity." Rockefeller Center was poised to reopen its top-floor observation decks, and Target was to have a small room that connects the North and South decks on the 59th floor, called the Target Breezeway.

The room is 20 feet by 20 feet, and has almost no walls — two sides are all doors, and a third side is all glass and visually connects with the lower Rainbow Room area. Target wanted to do something fun and thought we might be suited for the task.

**What is its design concept?**
-

We were given an absolutely impossible task. In addition to the lack of walls, the ceiling is only 8 1/2 feet tall, and we only had about four inches of ceiling depth to work with. We could do nothing with the floors.

The space gets bombed with light for several hours, so any light-based solution would have to be very bright to be effective. We had only five months to come up with a concept and get it built in time for the opening.

**How important were LEDs in the project?**
-

LEDs can be compressed into a small or thin package, and you can get a lot of light for relatively little power. We needed something that would be maintenance free for a three-year period. And we needed quick dimming control.

We devised a thin package of white strip LEDs for an overall ambient light and clusters of RGB capable lights, all under translucent glass that met our four-inch requirement. We lined the entire ceiling, one wall, and most of the other pilasters with this LED package. It is a very intense concentration of over 20,000 LEDs.

**Why was LED used as opposed to other lights?**
-

There are many reasons. Probably most important for many of our installations is that the lights are placed in somewhat inaccessible and difficult to reach locations, so they have to last a long time.

Low power and longevity are very important. The small size and weight of LED fixtures make more types of installations feasible. Quick dimming control over smaller areas allows for more varied programming.

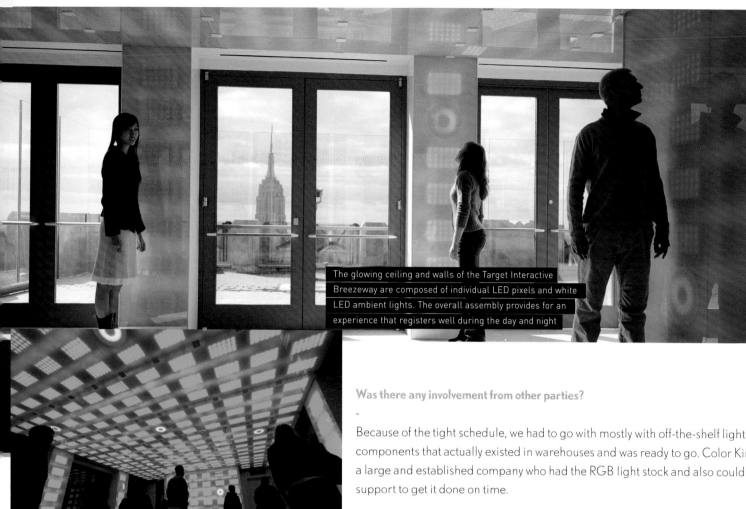

The glowing ceiling and walls of the Target Interactive Breezeway are composed of individual LED pixels and white LED ambient lights. The overall assembly provides for an experience that registers well during the day and night

**Was there any involvement from other parties?**

-

Because of the tight schedule, we had to go with mostly with off-the-shelf light components that actually existed in warehouses and was ready to go. Color Kinetics is a large and established company who had the RGB light stock and also could offer us support to get it done on time.

We found white strip lights also in stock from another vendor. We did have to custom-fabricate the 11 Target logo lights, but this was not too difficult. However, we had to write significant amounts of code to control the lights to our satisfaction.

The people-sensing is done via a four-camera stereo vision tracking system from TYZX, which has its own computer to analyze the video data. We wrote code to translate the location data from the TYZX system to our control computer.

Our control computer sent data to Color Kinetics proprietary data enablers that communicate to the RGB lights. The ambient lights are left on all the time. The Target logo lights were controlled by a special proprietary low-voltage dimmer device we had custom fabricated. Four high-quality speakers are embedded into the ceiling for sound, and receive their signal from the same control computer.

**What was the reaction?**

-

The Breezeway space is not a gallery or museum, so people have no forewarning about what they are walking into. Everyone is also in a state of extreme distraction, and it is a real shock to go from an outdoor observation deck with expansive views and then walk into our crazy space. So we had to devise ways to grab people's attention immediately, and then give them a little more to explore.

This element of interactivity — of interacting with a space — is very difficult and requires fine tuning once the space is complete. It is about theatre and timing more than anything else. Once refined, the visitor response has been terrific.

People understand immediately that they are in some sort of folly, and seem to enjoy the space, whether they just walk through it or remain to dance around and explore it more fully.

## DESIGN AND INTERACTIVE WORLD

-

**Electroland**

**What questions did the project make you consider?**

-

This space is a very good test for some elements of interactive spaces. As our reliance on electronic connections increase it will be a natural development to access this information and capability in a transparent and gadget-free manner.

**How do you make this possible? How do you communicate interactive capability without being intrusive?**

-

The Breezeway space is extreme and is clearly just a folly, however we still had to grapple with these issues with each action we programmed. With each interactive response we had to ask: how loud, how bright, how often, where, in what way?

**What was the most interesting observation about how it was received?**

-

Despite the extremely programmed environment where almost the entire point is the tracking of individuals, it seems that no one is threatened by this. Perhaps it is the humorous play of lights and somewhat humorous sounds, or perhaps it is because through interactivity they feel in control.

**What other creative LED installations have Electroland executed?**

-

We completed Enteractive in Los Angeles in 2006. Movement on an "interactive carpet" causes patterns to simultaneously appear on the carpet and on the building face.

The LEDs on the building are in "U" channels and face out, so although they are very bright they do not bother the building inhabitants. It is video-game interactivity at an urban scale.

**Can you tell us about your next LED projects?**

-

We have another two other LED projects in Los Angeles. For the LA FACE project we have designed a blue array five meters tall by 42 meters long lit by rows of LEDs that will react to traffic with multiple patterns.

We have another project in North Hollywood where 40 alphanumeric characters each two meters tall and stretched over a distance of 73 meters will spell out phrases from films based on a text search a visitor can do with a mobile phone. Each dot is actually a cluster of four RGB-capable lights, individually addressable.

**How do you see the future of LEDs over the world?**

-

Anything that uses low power will be called upon to address power needs. However it must be said that we have never seen an analysis of the lifecycle issues of LEDs, answering these questions: how difficult are they to manufacture; how many resources and how much power is needed for manufacture; recyclability of product; overall lifecycle toxicity.

**DESIGN
AND
INTERACTIVE
WORLD**

United Visual Artists
LEDARTIST
Cinimod Studio
Jason Bruges Studio
Electroland

# New York University

Todd Holoubek
Adjunct Professor,
Interactive Telecommunications Program,
New York University

-

 **NEW YORK UNIVERSITY**

-

James Law Cybertecture
Arup Lighting
Licht Kunst Licht
Webb Australia Group

**NEW YORK UNIVERSITY'S INTERACTIVE TELECOMMUNICATIONS PROGRAM (ITP) WAS FOUNDED IN 1979 AS THE FIRST GRADUATE EDUCATION PROGRAM IN ALTERNATIVE MEDIA. IT HAS GROWN INTO A LIVING COMMUNITY OF TECHNOLOGISTS, THEORISTS, ENGINEERS, DESIGNERS, AND ARTISTS UNIQUELY DEDICATED TO PUSHING THE BOUNDARIES OF INTERACTIVITY IN THE REAL AND DIGITAL WORLDS.**

**A HANDS-ON APPROACH TO EXPERIMENTATION, PRODUCTION AND RISK-TAKING MAKE THIS HI-TECH FUN HOUSE A CREATIVE HOME NOT ONLY TO ITS STUDENTS, BUT ALSO TO AN EXTENDED NETWORK OF THE TECHNOLOGY INDUSTRY'S MOST DARING AND PROLIFIC PRACTITIONERS.**

**TODD HOLOUBEK IS ADJUNCT PROFESSOR OF THE "LIVING ART," "SYSTEMS: HACKING EVERYDAY OBJECTS" AND "PRACTICAL APPLICATIONS OF TECHNOLOGY" COURSES OF ITP AT NYU.**

## DESIGN
## AND
## INTERACTIVE
## WORLD
-

**New York University**

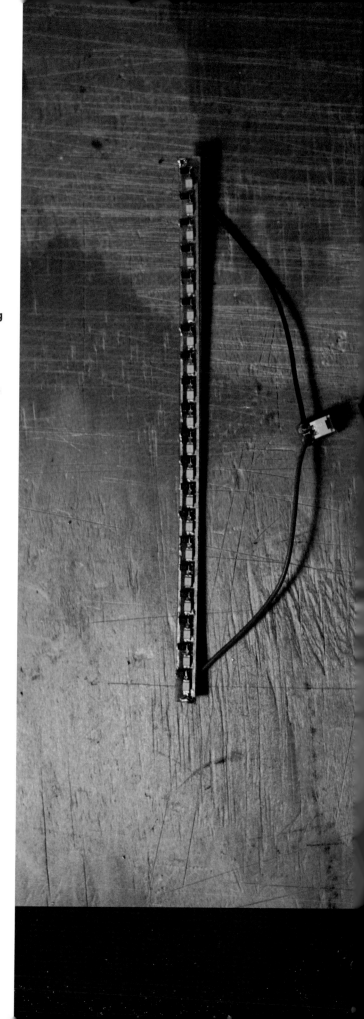

**Why was this program developed?**

-

ITP was created to give people the opportunity to make change using media tools either pre-existing or self made.

**How is this program still changing, and what about it is addressing the interests of students and meeting them with academia?**

-

The program is constantly changing and much of this change comes from the students. If you listen to others and what they are interested in, you realize that you are seeing the world through someone's unique vision.

This is fertile ground for change. It's almost inevitable the more we communicate. These diverse interests are what come through the community and the community itself changes.

**What role do you feel education has in regards to LED technology and programming?**

-

I read in a *New York Times* article that teachers are the people who see their subject in a way that the rest of us haven't yet. LEDs are more than lights. They are a yes or a no, sometimes a maybe. An LED can be stubborn, humbling and unforgiving. The role of education is to provide the opportunity to see not just these things but also, with our own vision, see something that hasn't been seen.

We can discover these gems through programming. We can coax behaviour from an LED with the code. Through the code, through the LED, I can speak to others. Learning the "technologies" (if we can give them a name) are becoming basic survival skills at this point.

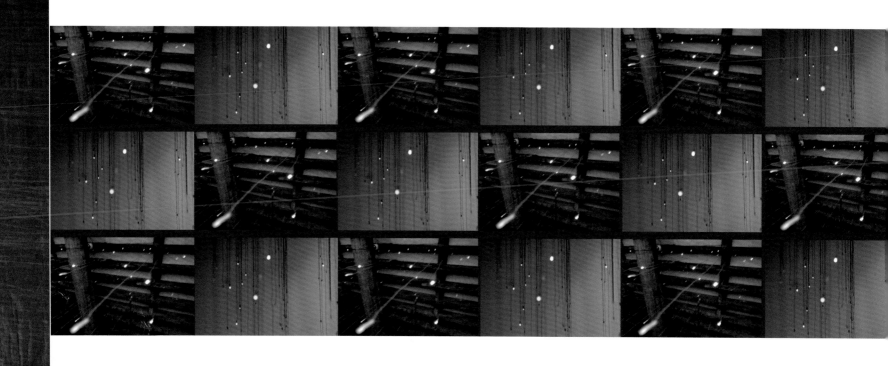

**What measures do you take to ensure that the program is up to date with the latest technologies?**

-

It is important to study one's job. When you are doing this, you are aware of what is up to date. This isn't easy, especially with LEDs. There are branches of LED technology that are a far step from where the LED began. The development of a light-emitting diode is enjoying a hearty momentum. This carries into not just the uses for LEDs but the making of LEDs — OLED, AOLED, or even LEPs themselves.

**How important are LEDs?**

-

The LED is a cheaper, more cost-efficient producer of light. I can't think of many things that have credentials of this caliber. It's this fact alone that allows it to be used where there is little or no electricity.

It saves energy by using less. On batteries alone an LED lamp will fare better than for those before us who had oil lamps when that was the hot technology. When we look at quality of life the LED is a silent warrior helping our environment via energy conservation. One simple example is that Manhattan changed its traffic lights to LED.

**What goals and values do you hope the students take away with them beyond graduation?**

-

That a student walks away with a greater curiosity, a sense of wonderment, and a respect for that which is foreign to them.

**What are the program's chief aims and aspirations?**

-

This is a long list. I would begin though, by saying that the alumni take what they learn while they are at ITP and apply it.

**What do you feel is the projected growth pattern of the demand for learning in such a program?**

-

Exponential.

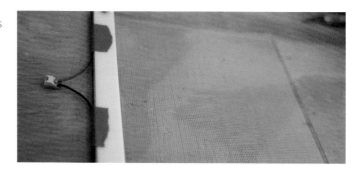

# DESIGN
# AND
# INTERACTIVE
# WORLD
-

**New York University**

PLANET LED
-
Chapter 04

DESIGN
AND
INTERACTIVE
WORLD

United Visual Artists
LEDARTIST
Cinimod Studio
Jason Bruges Studio
Electroland
New York University

# James Law Cybertecture

James Law
Founder
-

James Law
Cybertecture®

-
Arup Lighting
Licht Kunst Licht
Webb Australia Group

Much more than just a pretty face. The illuminating Cybertecture
mirror is web-connected with programmable applications and digital
display for the home, office and public environments

DESIGN
AND
INTERACTIVE
WORLD
-
James Law
Cybertecture

JAMES LAW CYBERTECTURE INTERNATIONAL WAS ESTABLISHED IN 2001 AND HAS FUSED ARCHITECTURE, TECHNOLOGY, AND ENGINEERING, RESULTING IN CYBER-BASED SOLUTIONS.

THE PRACTICE HAS MORE THAN 100 PERSONNEL BASED IN OFFICES IN HONG KONG, THE UAE AND INDIA. ITS CYBER DESIGN DIVISION UNDERTAKES "CYBERTECTURE" BUILDING, INTERIORS, MULTIMEDIA, AND URBAN DESIGN / MASTER PLAN COMMISSIONS WITH SUSTAINABILITY AND THE ENVIRONMENT IN MIND.

ITS SPECIAL PROJECTS DIVISION ALSO DESIGNS, DEVELOPS AND MANUFACTURES CYBERTECTURE TECHNOLOGIES AND PRODUCTS WITH I.T., SOFTWARE AND HARDWARE COMPONENTS.

Infused with visual technology innovations, the core auditorium of Olympic Pavilion X contains an internal 360-degree display screen. Three external visual devices composing hundreds of minuscule LCD monitors are designed to relay and display the live 2012 Olympic games in real-time

PLANET LED
-
Chapter 04

DESIGN
AND
INTERACTIVE
WORLD
-
James Law
Cybertecture

**Define cybertecture...**
-

In essence, cybertecture is about all things that we design — not only buildings. Our philosophy of cybertecture is to "innovate the fabric of mankind" through the things we design, make or build that will create a better world.

Cybertecture introduces a philosophy that a building is not just a building — it's much more than that. It is a device that carries new technologies and possibilities of a better life within the building for the people who will inhabit it.

**Why LED?**
-

LED lighting enables stunning creativity and artistic expression. It becomes a useful tool to redefine and highlight leading structures, spaces and shapes.

Cybertecture always tries to embrace the very latest technologies. LED lighting technology is now blended into buildings more so in the last decade than before, and for good purpose.

Architects and designers require the use of new materials and technology that go beyond the conventional concrete, steel and glass. Moving forward, we are looking at a new form of materials including the delicate yet powerful silicon chips, electrons, interconnected internet, and the intelligence of automatic systems for a stunning and seamless fabric of coming leading buildings.

In our work so far in Asia, we have taken initial steps to educate our clients and partners to this comprehensive and futuristic approach. We are not just making buildings, but "super buildings" that live, breathe and think for and with the people that inhabit it.

If done successfully, LED and other technologies will together help shape and style some of the smartest buildings ever built on the planet empowered with cybertecture.

The Pad Tower in Dubai, UAE, is a 26-floor building containing over 231 "intelligent" apartments

**Future of lighting...**
-

Looking beyond the contemporary use of LED lighting, its effects on mostly building façades and interior spacing will probably be very different to even the modern buildings of the late 20th century. The world has changed so much at the beginning of the 21st century, and the world's resources are decreasing rapidly at this point in time.

We predict that visual and environmental needs would further be addressed in the lighting of new cityscapes, road grids and buildings being built in the near future. LED lighting will eventually meet the concerns as a more environmentally friendly measure. We will be better equipped to support the latest intelligent buildings as well as new kinds of lighting effects that are designed especially for the new generation of business offices, living spaces and leisure areas.

Inspired by the fluid shape of a raindrop splash, Olympic Pavilion X becomes a modern iconic landmark to inject both fun and flair to London's monumental Trafalgar Square

## Ultimate potential...

LED lighting adds to the dimension of architecture with both creative flair and greener energy consumption capacity. It is widely expected to merge into the DNA of architectural themes and culture as modern buildings are incorporated with modern aesthetics.

## LED versatility...

Stretching imagination into reality, our project The Pad is a specific design which is a collection of inspiring LED lighting blended in with a touch of contemporary modernity and forwardly futurism.

In tune with the emerging trends of enhanced personal expression, digital interconnectivity and social involvement, we placed LED lighting inside the building as a visual notification tool corresponding to incoming emails, voice messages and visitors.

To capture the audience's imagination and ignite visual impact, the exterior façade of The Pad is filled with fluid flow of lighting effects to fabricate a style and sense of free expression.

DESIGN
AND
INTERACTIVE
WORLD
-
James Law
Cybertecture

### Challenge?
-

As usual, the prime obstacle is the education and understanding of developers, builders, and people in general to understand this changing trend of LED lighting mechanism.

More and more people are beginning to understand why a new building shouldn't be designed with conventional ways or older techniques in lighting. They are openly welcoming new methods and technologies as a sound investment into the future of the global landscape and lifestyles.

I am optimistic that this generation has more forward-looking people, and that soon, they will see the great upside in LED lighting as an iconic and advanced element of design.

### Saving the world...
-

LED lighting is being driven, at least in part, by the double advantage of increasing standards of living whilst minimizing the use of natural resources.

### Impact...
-

In the world of today and tomorrow, our computational power has increased and so has the manipulation of dramatic lighting effects available. Being "green" is now an important aspect for the architecture industry. LED lighting will probably be dealt with in greater complexity and dexterity by cybertecture, which always strives to use new systems and technologies.

Moving forward, time will tell how the design community and society evolve. Together they continue to reward ideas that are more environmentally friendly, sharpen contemporary interior blueprints and exceed conventional expectations of visual impact.

249

**DESIGN
AND
INTERACTIVE
WORLD**

United Visual Artists
LEDARTIST
Cinimod Studio
Jason Bruges Studio
Electroland
New York University
James Law Cybertecture

# Arup Lighting

Simone Collon
European Leader
-

ARUP
-

Licht Kunst Licht
Webb Australia Group

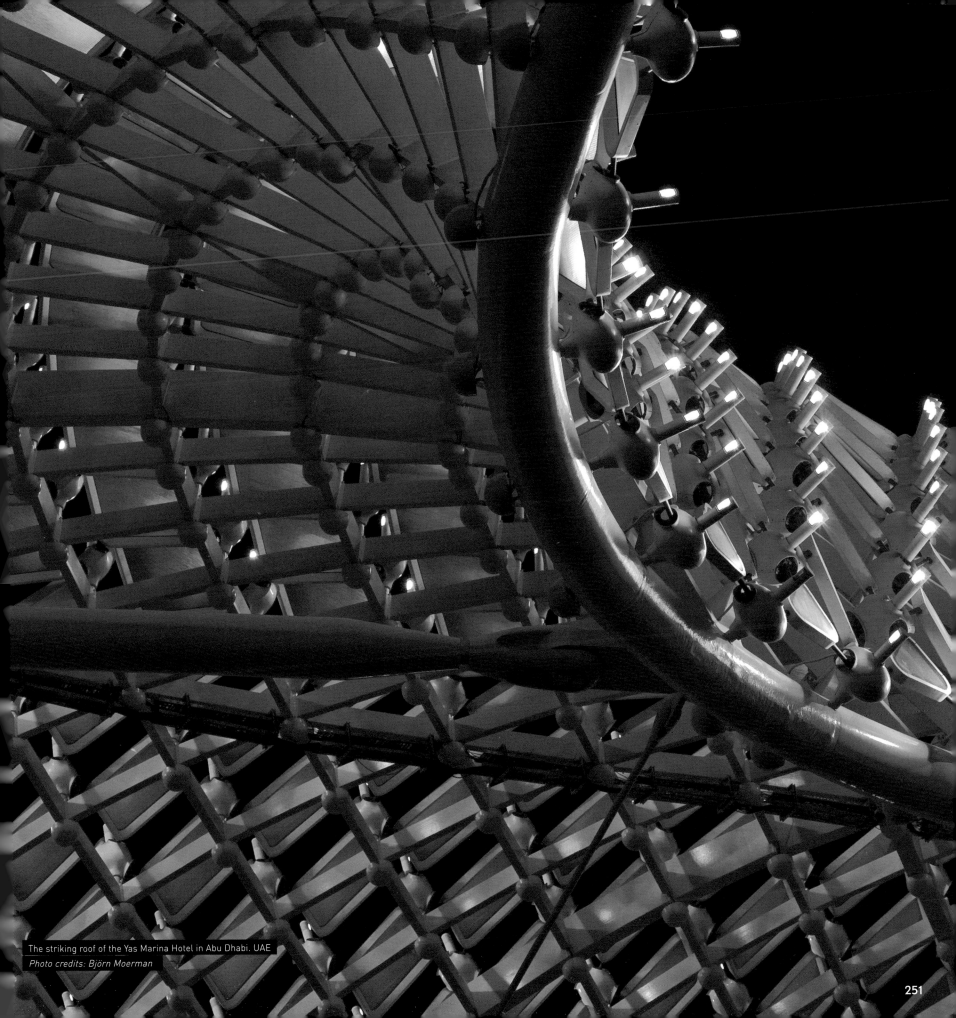

The striking roof of the Yas Marina Hotel in Abu Dhabi. UAE
*Photo credits: Björn Moerman*

251

PLANET LED
-
Chapter 01

DESIGN
AND
INTERACTIVE
WORLD
-
Arup Lighting

ARUP LIGHTING IS THE LIGHTING DESIGN STUDIO OF ARUP, A PROFESSIONAL SERVICES FIRM PROVIDING ENGINEERING, DESIGN, PLANNING, PROJECT MANAGEMENT AND CONSULTING SERVICES FOR ALL ASPECTS OF THE BUILT ENVIRONMENT. ARUP LIGHTING HAS EIGHT GLOBAL ARUP OFFICES AND PROVIDES A COMPREHENSIVE INDEPENDENT ARCHITECTURAL LIGHTING DESIGN SERVICE TO CLIENTS AROUND THE WORLD.

GREAT LIGHTING DESIGN RELIES ON USING NATURAL LIGHT EFFECTIVELY. IN ADDITION TO ELECTRIC LIGHTING DESIGN, ARUP LIGHTING IS A MARKET LEADER IN DAY-LIGHTING.

### What are Arup's specialist areas?

-

We specialize in turning strong, unique visions into detailed technical specifications. Multidisciplinary project teams consisting of lighting designers, architects, product designers, electrical engineers, interaction designers and artists work in close collaboration with architects and clients from various sectors.

"Branding with light" enables the creation of memorable unforgettable luminous spaces. A strong vision and a unique conceptual design approach are crucial to the success of all our projects.

Innovation and unique custom designed solutions are the key factors in our creative design approach. Our intention is to "weave lighting into architecture." The integration of light into architectural materials and façades is one of our key specialist areas.

In our vision, we use the metaphor of architectural spaces dressing up at night. The metamorphosis of a lit space after sunset can be described as a three dimensional space transforming to glow in an unexpected and amazing way. The lit nightscape is inspiring, unforgettable and can touch people's souls. Lighting is the fourth dimension.

## DESIGN
## AND
## INTERACTIVE
## WORLD
-
**Arup Lighting**

**What prompted you to construct the installation at the Galleria Fashion Mall in Seoul?**
-

The lighting design concept was used as a strategic branding tool that transformed a shopping mall into a hip and trendy place with extraordinary spike in turnover.

A media façade is wrapped around the building to form a fluid, dynamic skin. Custom designed in close collaboration with the architects UN Studio, nearly 5,000 glass discs make up an ocean of colors and movement.

The effect of the Galleria lighting design goes much beyond a fancy color projection. People stop in the street, take pictures, interact with the façade, take video — all of them are amazed.

Nothing is left to remind them of the dull, blind, concrete façade that Galleria was until recently. The design's subtle color changes and abstract images perfectly fit the contemporary image of the building.

The luminous cladding system was used in a unique way to present a fluid, changing architectural skin at night.

**What makes the installation's design so special?**
-

LEDs covering façades is nothing new. But LEDs wrapping around the volume, forming a skin to a building, fluid and dynamic is!

It is a sophisticated frosted-glass façade with a mother-of-pearl effect during the day, and transforms into a vibrant and scenic experience at night through the 5,000 glass discs, with their own RGB luminaire.

The control system runs 15,000 DMX channels and is arguably the most elaborate system of its kind.

**Why were LEDs used as opposed to other lights?**
-

LED technology offers dynamic color changes while guaranteeing low energy consumption. This results in amazing effects with low operating costs. The lifetime of the used LED fixtures is estimated at 25 years, which minimizes maintenance efforts.

No other light source can fulfill the requirements to build up luminous façades of that kind. Innovative LED technology has fundamentally changed the possibilities and freedom in lighting design.

**Does the installation contribute to the local community?**
-

The media façade reacts to its environment. After sunset, fluid color movements and intensity of the light increase gradually. At around 8pm, the shopping center reflects Seoul's busiest time of day to its urban environment through strong color movements.

Late at night, the façade dims down and offers subtle dimmed lighting effects that do not disturb people in the surrounding residential areas.

People love that the façade is "alive" and come to watch the fluid artistic patterns at night.

**What are the most interesting aspects of LED technology, during your time working with it?**
-

First of all I find it amazing that electroluminescence was discovered in 1907 by a British experimenter H.J. Round.

Since my first exposure to the industry in 2003 it was amazing to watch such rapid developments in the increase of output and efficiency, as well as color rendition developments — something which I find crucial.

Last but not least, I find it very inspiring to see implementation of LED technology in a big variety of products. Most fascinating are modular LED pixels for outdoor media solutions, dynamic powerful floodlights for outdoor applications and the increasingly good quality of dynamic indoor LED fixtures.

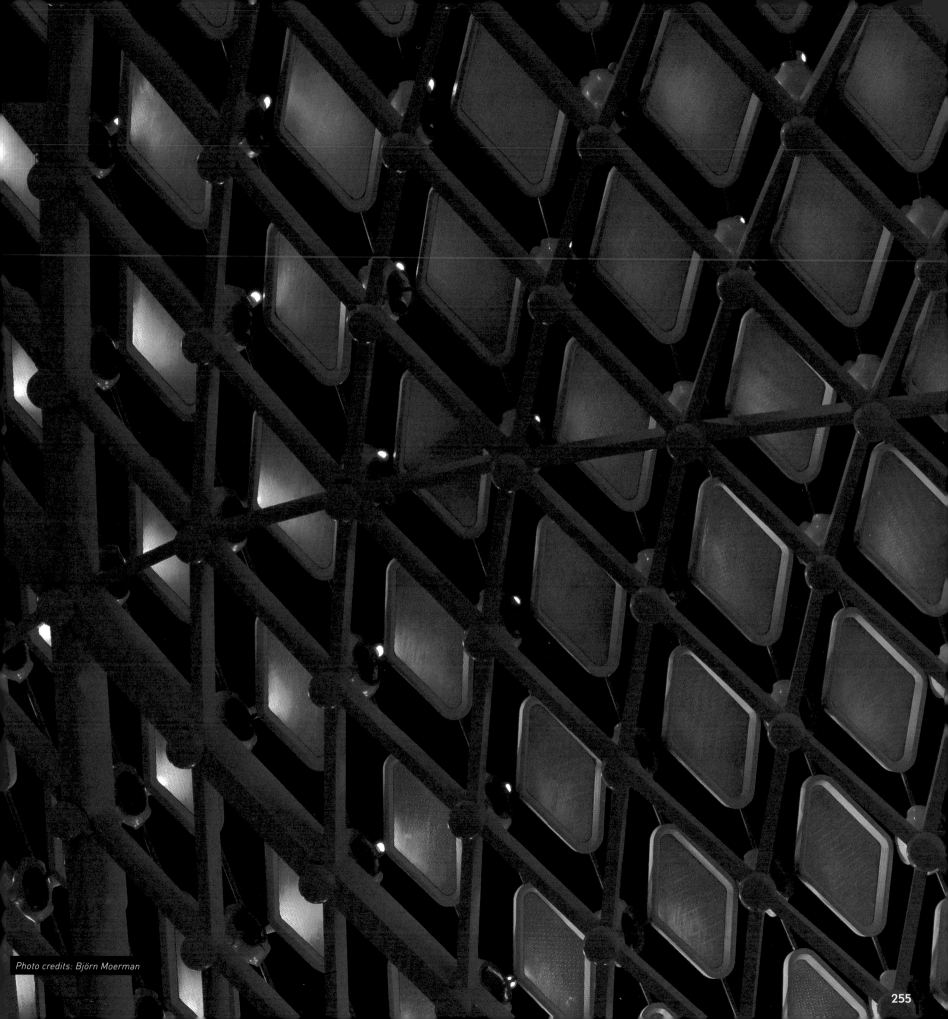

255

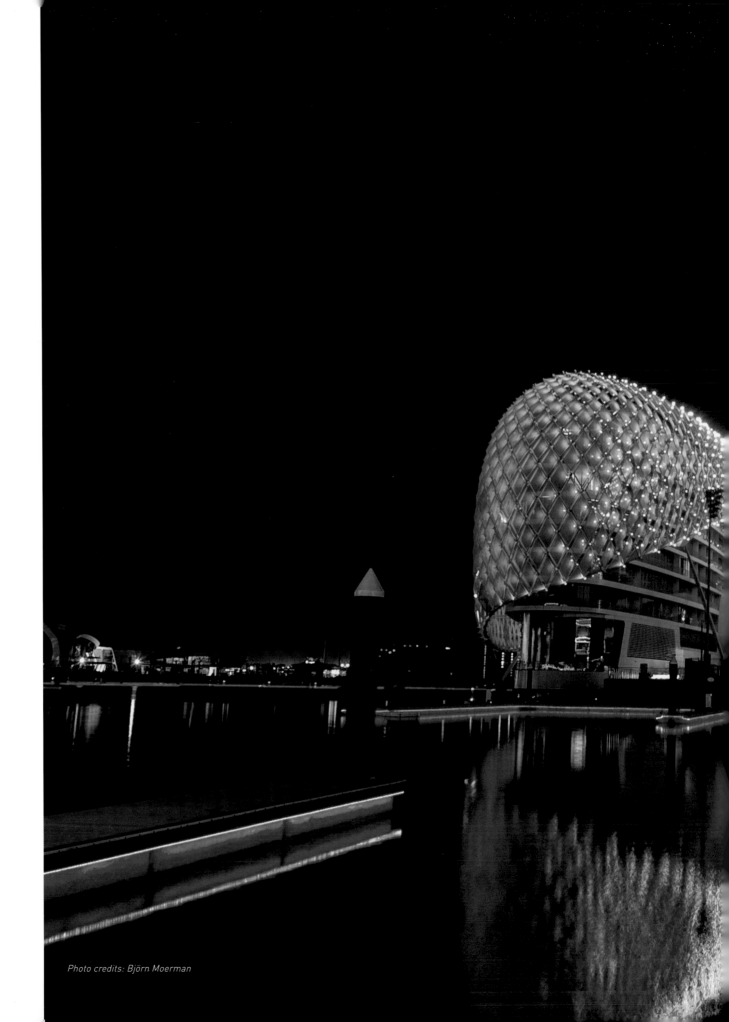

PLANET LED
-
Chapter 04

## DESIGN AND INTERACTIVE WORLD
-
**Arup Lighting**

*Photo credits: Björn Moerman*

## DESIGN AND INTERACTIVE WORLD
-
**Arup Lighting**

### Can you tell us about your next LED project?
-

We are working on a design development phase of a project in the Netherlands using dynamic LEDs in urban chandeliers to illuminate a street. An amazing tensegrity (tensional integrity) structure houses thousands of LED pixels which are able to react to people's movements below. The chandeliers in the nightly streetscape fulfill both functional and atmospheric lighting requirements.

I cannot wait to see how people will react to the gigantic chandelier responding to their individual movements. A cloud of light illuminates the street, enriching the urban streetscape with fluid color movements and changing intensities.

### How do you foresee this kind of technology developing further to influence society?
-

LEDs offer a dynamic character which opens endless new possibilities for innovative applications. I see LED technology as the tool to create "personal light." It becomes extremely easy for a user to change intensities and colors manually, or to regulate the dynamic effects via sensor technology. With great pleasure I call LED technology "the light which is alive."

### Do you feel that LEDs will become an essential part of a more ecologically minded world?
-

LED technology will continue to innovate our lifestyles — of that there is no doubt. Apart from low energy consumption I see a lot of potential with regards to sustainability. This is connected to LEDs' dynamic character and that they can be controlled in an intelligent way.

LED light is able to react fast by means of dimming the intensity of light depending on its need. In a more ecologically minded world, the sustainable approach would be to maximize the light to a certain intensity, but only when it's really required.

As soon as a person comes close to the fixture, the light increases to full intensity, if people leave the illuminated area, the light reacts fast and dims to low intensity or switches off. An unbelievable amount of energy could be saved globally if all lighting installations used this principle.

Photo credits: Björn Moerman

Photo credits: Björn Moerman

Photo credits: Arup

**Do you still consider LEDs to be an exciting new technology for the lighting design industry? If so, why?**
-

I believe that lighting designers, manufacturers and other developers are only starting to discover the endless range of options that LEDs can provide.

The possibilities of using the source are boundless. New innovative creations which exist in the lighting designer's fantasy can be realized and will continue to enrich the visual environment.

**What are your predictions for the future of LED technology and how will that affect your company?**
-

I am expecting that further development of OLEDs will change our design freedom significantly. Imagine luminous ink which can be printed on fabrics, cladding materials or any kind building materials, which is able to provide functional lighting.

I am very much looking forward to these developments as they will foster our design intent of "weaving light into architecture." The light fixture actually becomes a surface — that's the promising future I cannot wait to see.

The importance of hiring a lighting designer for specific and attractive solutions is increasing constantly. I am expecting a growing professional guild of lighting designers who take the serious responsibility of creating a fantastic luminous world.

**DESIGN
AND
INTERACTIVE
WORLD**

United Visual Artists
LEDARTIST
Cinimod Studio
Jason Bruges Studio
Electroland
New York University
James Law Cybertecture
Arup Lighting

# Licht
# Kunst Licht

Andreas Schulz
Chairman
-

Webb Australia Group

Uniqa Tower, an illuminating part of Vienna's skyline

Photo credits: Werner Huthmacher

PLANET LED
-
Chapter 04

DESIGN
AND
INTERACTIVE
WORLD
-
Licht
Kunst Licht

PROFESSOR ANDREAS SCHULZ OF LICHT KUNST LICHT (LKL) HEADS A TEAM OF 25 DESIGNERS, ARCHITECTS AND ENGINEERS, WORKING IN THE WIDE-RANGING FIELD OF LIGHTING DESIGN WITH PROJECTS THAT INCLUDE ANYTHING FROM MUSEUMS TO MEDIA FAÇADES. HAVING STUDIED ELECTRICAL ENGINEERING, HE DOES HAVE A TECHNICAL BACKGROUND BUT HAS ALWAYS BEEN PASSIONATE ABOUT ARCHITECTURE AND DESIGN.

DURING THE LAST 15 YEARS, PROFESSOR SCHULZ AND HIS TEAM HAVE CONTRIBUTED TO THE WORLD'S MOST EXCITING AND AMBITIOUS ARCHITECTURAL MISSIONS.

LKL APPROACHES ALL ITS PROJECTS WITH PASSION AND COMMITMENT. FOR LKL, SIZE OR APPARENT SIGNIFICANCE OF A PROJECT DOES NOT CONSTITUTE A DIFFERENCE.

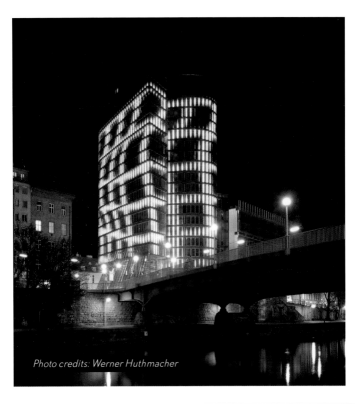

Photo credits: Werner Huthmacher

**What is the main focus for your company?**
-

Our main objective is to create an atmosphere within a space by means of light. Mainly working artificial lighting projects, we also develop sophisticated day-lighting concepts; a good handling of daylight especially for museum projects is of great importance.

Most essential though is the right handling of light as a medium — the fixture or light-producing element lies second within our approach.

Prominently located in the 1st District, the Uniqa Tower stands at 20 floors and has been fitted with 45,000 Barco LED blocks covering a staggering 7,000 square meters. The LED blocks, attached to profiles in between the window panes, bring the building to life and make it one of the most striking towers in Austria

Photo credits: Werner Huthmacher

**What prompted the idea to construct the installation at the Uniqa Tower in Vienna?**
-

We entered a competition dealing with the façade structure and the performance of the façade of the Uniqa Tower. We won the competition hoping to implement a large-scale display utilizing the entire surface of the tower covering 360 degrees and the full height of the building.

We had the courage to achieve this although the necessary elements were not yet available at the time. Our original idea was to split a large LED screen into stripes and to arrange them at the façade in order to create a complete overall image.

We accommodated these particular components in a custom-designed profile — with the advantage of being extremely powerful and low-maintenance, the building of the Uniqa Tower could be viewed as an expanded LED screen.

We also strived to create a system that would be easy to maintain by the facility management. The outside surface of the interior façade turned out to be the perfect location to house the LED fixtures.

DESIGN
AND
INTERACTIVE
WORLD
-
Licht
Kunst Licht

Photo credits: Lukas Roth

**What is the design concept behind the installation?**
-

We wanted to offer a performance surface for media artists, and all possibilities for future performances were to be established. We made a lot of mock-ups to find the perfect vertical distance of the linear profiles and the spacing of the pixels with the goal to achieve a good resolution of the image. At the end, costs were subject of argument, however.

**Was there any external participation?**
-

No, the project was completely carried out in our office — going from the idea to the technical planning and the logistical transfer (during the installation work the building was already occupied). For the production of the contents displayed in first performance we worked together with the artistic group Mader Stublic Wiermann.

**Why was LED used as opposed to other kinds of lights?**
-

We needed a fast-switching light source with high intensity and color miscibility allowing for an individual control of pixels within the matrix. The only light source satisfying these criteria was LED.

**What is the installation's contribution to the general community?**
-

Well there is a nice story to this answer. During the competition process, we needed to get to our first appointment in Vienna. We tried travelling from the airport to the Uniqa Tower by taxi. However, the taxi driver did not know the address since the building was still relatively unknown in Vienna.

A few months later, at one of our last appointments after the completion of the installation, another taxi driver asked us if we wanted him to drive past the tower which, he claimed, was the most exciting place in Vienna.

The building gained such a degree of popularity within just a couple of months and evoked many positive reactions. Even the investor himself was surprised about the results of the installation. Vienna is a very art-minded town, therefore the whole art community is pleased about this symbolic icon that had demonstrated it had arrived in the 21st century.

**What do you see is the future of LED technology?**

I am certain that we are facing a massive change within the lighting field. Ten years from now, we will see the spread of LED lighting that will make our current light sources look ancient. LED lighting will shed new light on our world. It will become our light for the future.

*Licht Kunst Licht's most recent exclusively LED lighting scheme is a beautiful component of the Telekom Bridge in Bonn, Germany*
*Photo credits: Lukas Roth*

PLANET LED
-
Chapter 04

DESIGN
AND
INTERACTIVE
WORLD
-
Licht
Kunst Licht

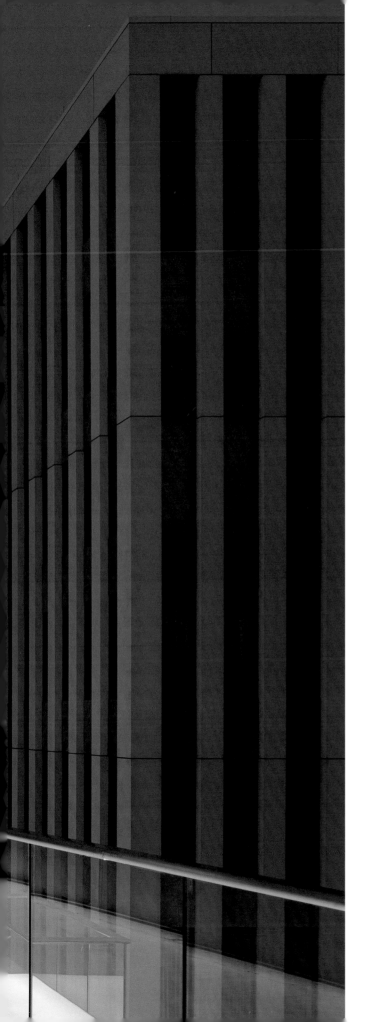

**Will environmental aspects help this development?**
-

LED light sources will be much more efficient in the future than any other light sources we are using right now. If the lighting industry clarifies the status question so that LEDs are not necessarily connected to lamp-housing, the LED will be reasonably considered ecological. But today, the LED is still not considered part of the environmental balance.

**Are you still excited by LEDs?**
-

Yes, they are very exciting. But for the lighting industry, they still represent a risk. For 100 years we have had manufacturers for light sources and we have had manufacturers for fixtures. In the future we will just have one line — manufacturers of the LED light source are the manufacturers of a fixture as well. That is why we will experience a considerable shift in the markets.

Also, we require much more know-how regarding the handling of LEDs because they are more technically demanding in comparison to prefabricated old lamp types.

The parameters of LED can be read on data sheets. But even so, the technology is new and there are a lot of unknown problems which big industry might be afraid of.

But all in all, we are facing a positive development because a lot of innovative solutions lie ahead. Think of perfect control, fast activation, dimming and compact dimensions of a light source…here there are a lot of new possibilities available to designers and the industry as a whole.

**DESIGN
AND
INTERACTIVE
WORLD**

# Webb Australia Group

Garry Lowe,
Director
-

WEBB
AUSTRALIA
-

Along the side of the Craigieburn Hume Highway.
A Webb project in Melbourne, Australia

PLANET LED
-
Chapter 04

DESIGN
AND
INTERACTIVE
WORLD
-
Webb
Australia
Group

ELECTRICAL ENGINEERING AND SPECIALIST LIGHTING CONSULTANCY, WEBB AUSTRALIA GROUP, WAS ESTABLISHED IN 1973 BY FOUNDERS WITH A PASSION FOR LIGHTING DESIGN.

WEBB SUCCESSFULLY PROMOTED LIGHTING AS AN IMPORTANT COMPLEMENT TO ARCHITECTURAL DESIGN IN AUSTRALIA. WHILST THE COMPANY HAS EXPANDED INTO OTHER SPECIALIST AREAS, LIGHTING REMAINS A KEY FOCUS OF EXPERTISE WITHIN THE BUSINESS.

**What are your main priorities when taking on a new project?**
-

Our main objectives are to provide our clients with the best solutions that meet their project needs with respect to design and budget, in whatever discipline of service we are offering.

As lighting designers, we aim to promote lighting as an integral part of design solutions that should be taken into consideration from the outset of project, and not an "afterthought."

In design, our objectives are to provide solutions that not only excite and complement the built form of the project, but are economically and environmentally sustainable.

**What was the challenge for the lighting design for the Olympics in Australia?**
-

Our involvement with the Sydney Olympics in 2000 included many lighting elements including sports lighting for various venues, feature lighting of many public icons such as the Harbour Bridge and the public domain lighting at the new Olympic Games precinct at Homebush Bay.

Each element presented its own challenges, but having to complete the work within an unmoveable deadline was an overriding issue.

Perhaps the most challenging element of lighting was the public domain at the Olympic Precinct, which included many layers and areas of lighting to create the overall solution. This included lighting of plazas, streets, water features, buildings, signage, transportation areas, parklands, temporary facilities and other public amenities.

Two lighting schemes were required, one for operations during the Games and one for everyday use upon completion of the Games. The complexity of developing and completing the design in time was the first challenge.

This was further complicated by the need to ensure that lights could be supplied and installed on time. This required restrictions on the selection criteria of light fitting and development of procurement strategies to source and purchase the lights whilst concurrently trying to develop and finalize the design.

**What was the overall design concept for this project?**
-

The Sydney Olympics included many lighting design elements and therefore many different concepts. One of the key design elements for the public domain at Homebush Bay Olympic Precinct included the lighting of Olympic Plaza, which spans approximately 700m x 100m.

The concepts included design of multifunctional towers that were 35 meters high and incorporated purpose built lighting 4.5-square-meter reflectors and solar collection.

The design presented many challenges and results were aesthetically dramatic. The solar installation resulted in an energy-neutral lighting installation.

**Why did you not consider LEDs in this project?**
-

Quite simply, LEDs were not a mainstream lighting product available at that time.

Until recently, most of our use of LEDs on large scale projects was primarily for "decorative" purposes, utilizing LED source as a feature enhancement of the architectural form. The designs relied on the brightness and visibility of the LED source, rather than the ability of the LED to illuminate.

Such a project was the Craigieburn Hume Highway Bypass Project in Melbourne. This highway project included landscaping elements to reduce noise from the highway to adjacent residential area. The system was designed as a dynamic installation and is responsive to the traffic density and time.

**With incandescent lighting being phased out in Australia, will LED take over and compete with compact fluorescents?**

There is no doubt that LEDs will take over some technologies. Only time will tell which lamps will be phased out and totally replaced by LEDs.

# DESIGN
# AND
# INTERACTIVE
# WORLD
-
**Webb**
**Australia**
**Group**

Like Beijing for the 2008 Games, the Sydney Olympics in 2000 brought lighting projects onto the world stage. During those eight years, LEDs became a mainstream option unlike for Sydney's Olympic Plaza (pictured) which used more traditional lighting sources

## DESIGN AND INTERACTIVE WORLD
-
**Webb
Australia
Group**

The Sydney Harbour Bridge with the iconic Olympic rings

**What changes have you observed in the field of LED technology during your time in the industry?**
-

The changes in LED technology have been particularly significant over the last five to six years. Perhaps the most significant observations have been the development of white light LEDs, particularly in development of various color temperatures and the increase in their efficacy.

**What is your next LED project? Can you tell us something about it?**
-

There are now several LED street lights on the market, each with its own design idiosyncrasies and strategies for addressing performance, distribution and lamp failures.

One current LED project that we are undertaking involves the review of various LED products for street lighting application. Working with the City of Melbourne, we are assessing each product presented to us and where appropriate, installing a sample of the product in an LED trial area. The products will be assessed over a period of time.

In the next phase of the project we will be expanding this trial and converting a precinct within the city to LED street lighting. This is currently in the planning phase and selection of a preferred LED product is yet to be finalized.

**How do you foresee LED technology developing in the future?**
-

Improvements in efficacy must get to a point where increases are more "incremental" rather than with "quantum leaps," as they seem to be at the moment. Greater focus on heat dissipation techniques should become more prevalent in design of LED light fittings to optimize the efficacy and life of the LEDs.

**Do you feel that this is an essential route on a social and ecological level?**

-

Any route that promotes technological advances to provide better lighting quality, lower energy consumption and provide improved sustainability, is essential to our society.

Whether the technology is LED or fluorescent or metal halide or any other lamp is not the important issue. What is important is that all technologies take the path of improvement to achieve better performances that ultimately provide benefits to the environment.

LEDs are probably the most obvious technology to exploit at the moment as it is with this technology where the greatest gains in performance are being achieved.

**Do you think LEDs are still seen as a new exciting technology for the lighting design industry and if so, why?**

Yes, LEDs are still very much at the forefront of topical discussion and design innovation in the industry. The ever-increasing application platforms for the LEDs seem to constantly move to new levels at a rapid rate. Like digital technology, there seems to be something new to look at and play with every day.

It will be interesting and exciting to see just how far boundaries can be pushed as LEDs develop in the next five years.

**What are your thoughts on the future for LED technology?**

Well-engineered and more flexible LED light fittings for application in large scale public domain lighting is where I have aspirations for the development of LED technology.

Use of LEDs in urban scale functional lighting will be a natural progression for product development. LED products that are currently available can very restrictive and inflexible in their design use.

Reliability, robustness and heat dissipation are key areas where the technology has long term impacts on what we deliver as part of our design solutions. Better engineered products, leading to greater reliability will be a driving objective in our future direction and use of LEDs.

There is no doubt that LED technology will play a greater role in our design solutions and this inherently leads to the technology becoming an extension to our company as an important design tool.

**Are LEDs ever misunderstood?**

-

Anyone who has worked closely with LEDs over recent years would appreciate how LEDs can be misused and misrepresented in what they capable of achieving.

I cannot count the number of times clients have wanted to use LEDs because they "hardly use any energy" and "they last forever." Many project managers, architects and end user clients are often only told part of the story. I have seen examples of installation where the client has been told that a new LED installation will save them 70 percent in energy. What they have not been told is that their illumination levels probably decreased by 90 percent.

LEDs will continue to improve in all respects and great claims will truly become more real. Education and appropriate application, however, will always remain the keys to good designs and client satisfaction.

Beijing & Tianjin at night
Photo credits: Nasa

# ENVIRONMENTAL
# AND
# HUMAN FACTORS

Peter Boyce
Queensland University of Technology
LED City
ECOLS
PLDA
Diamond Therapy
PlantLab
Talika
Philips

All living things react to electromagnetic (EM) energy. It stands to reason, then, that we are all sensitive to the effects of lighting. Both lighting and color can affect our growth, moods and our physical being.

Using different parts of the EM spectrum to influence our physical reality is becoming more and more important. Science tells us that animal and plant cells contain light and emit radiation; LED is therefore a new way of interacting and communicating with other living beings.

Every day we are exposed to a wide range of visible and invisible sections of the EM spectrum. Traditional artificial lighting is known to give off harmful infrared and ultra-violet frequencies. LED, in contrast, has no such adverse effects as it has no IR, UV (unless specified) and a very narrow-range spectrum.

Advancements in LED technology mean that we can manipulate a particular visible spectrum to increase the welfare for all of us. These benefits extend far beyond human exposure to light and into the world we live in.

In the past few decades, LEDs have emerged as a genuine competitor to traditional light sources like incandescent, fluorescent and halogen. Energy consumption and savings are now inextricably linked to the development of LEDs. The advancement of its efficacy (lumen per watt) will significantly increase the potential for fiscal savings and lower the world's reliance on non-renewable energy sources.

In 2002, a global survey showed that there were 1.6 billion people living without electricity, primarily burning wood and kerosene for their lighting. At the time, this represented about 17 percent of global lighting costs while generating only 0.1
percent of the world's total light output. How can this situation change?

Solid State Lighting (SSL) is the most viable alternative to artificial lighting. Indoor white-light LED applications have recently become available due to the advancement of high-brightness technology. This area of lighting offers the greatest potential for energy saving.

It has been estimated that 131 TWh per year of electricity could be spared — the equivalent of more than 20 large, 1,000MW power plants or the annual electricity consumption of 11 million typical US households.

Progress so far has been slow and internationally there have been less than three percent of traditional light sources converted to LED fixtures. But this also means that the potential for energy-saving is enormous.

In 2009, China officially overtook the United States as the largest energy consumer. Even though the country devours an astonishing 26,250TWh, China's energy usage per capita is four times less than America. Nevertheless, Beijing is looking to reverse this trend.

Since 2008, China has been promoting its "Ten Thousand LED lights in Ten Cities" policy. The country is in the process of replacing its 35 million street lights with LEDs.

It goes without saying that reducing energy costs is not just about the money. LED implementation would also mean the reduction of millions of metric tonnes of carbon dioxide emissions. Companies and governments could also reduce environmental tax levies. Every country and energy association will soon have to change its energy conservation standards and energy legislation to encourage a greener world.

There are many countries already phasing out traditional lighting due to low efficiency rates. The policies targeted to minimize carbon footprint have encouraged various energy-efficient technologies. LED technology has already proved that it can be a serious part of a solution.

Australia, Japan, Canada and parts of the US have begun this mind shift. Governments and LED manufacturers have joined hands to start initiatives like LED City. They have established energy-efficient labels like the UL and Energy Star, in addition, setting standards for LED products worldwide.

These projects have spread internationally in order to gauge the pros and cons of applying LED lighting in major infrastructure applications.

Barriers still exist, however. Initial investments in LEDs can be high, but LED believers feel that with further education about return on investment and greater emphasis on the positive environmental impact, decision-makers will be swayed.

Commercial financing strategies like the Energy Management Contract (EMC) and governmental support through sustainable technology subsidies are lucrative and meaningful catalysts for the industry. But for LEDs' ultimate success, everyone from large corporations to individuals will have to play their part. As market demand grows, economies of scale will encourage lower production costs. That will be the tipping point.

With a change in mindset and a change in a lighting source, we can save anywhere between 20-80 percent of the world's energy costs without any substantial change in lifestyle. It should be the easiest conversion we can make for the planet, but will we?

## ENVIRONMENTAL AND HUMAN FACTORS

# Peter Boyce

Queensland University of Technology
LED City
ECOLS
PLDA
Diamond Therapy
PlantLab
Talika
Philips

PETER R. BOYCE, PH.D., FIES, FSLL, IS A PROFESSOR EMERITUS AT THE
SCHOOL OF ARCHITECTURE AT RENSSELAER POLYTECHNIC INSTITUTE IN
TROY, NEW YORK.

WHILE A RESEARCH OFFICER AT THE ELECTRICITY COUNCIL RESEARCH
CENTER IN THE UNITED KINGDOM, HE CONDUCTED RESEARCH ON
VISUAL FATIGUE, THE INFLUENCE OF AGE ON VISUAL PERFORMANCE,
VISUAL PROBLEMS ASSOCIATED WITH VISUAL DISPLAY UNITS, HUE
DISCRIMINATION, SAFE LIGHTING FOR EMERGENCY CONDITIONS AND
SECURITY LIGHTING.

HE WAS ALSO HEAD OF HUMAN FACTORS AT THE LIGHTING RESEARCH
CENTER AT THE RENSSELAER POLYTECHNIC INSTITUTE. PROFESSOR BOYCE
CONDUCTED RESEARCH ON VISUAL PERFORMANCE, VISUAL COMFORT,
CIRCADIAN EFFECTS, EMERGENCY LIGHTING, PERCEPTIONS OF SAFETY
AND LIGHTING FOR DRIVING. HE DIRECTED LIGHTING EVALUATIONS AND
PRODUCT TESTING.

HE IS RETIRED AND IS PRESENTLY WORKING AS TECHNICAL EDITOR FOR
THE LIGHTING RESEARCH AND TECHNOLOGY.

The relative efficiency of electromagnetic
radiation of different wavelengths in
stimulating the human circadian system,
using melatonin suppression as a marker

REFERENCE:
Brainard, Hanifin, Greeson, et al, Journal
of Neuroscience, 2001; 21: 6405-6412,
and Thapan, Arendt and Skene, Journal of
Physiology, 2001; 535: 261-267)

Courtesy of "Human Factors in Lighting,
Publishers: Taylor and Francis"

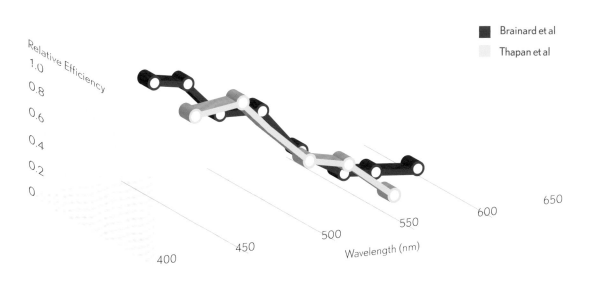

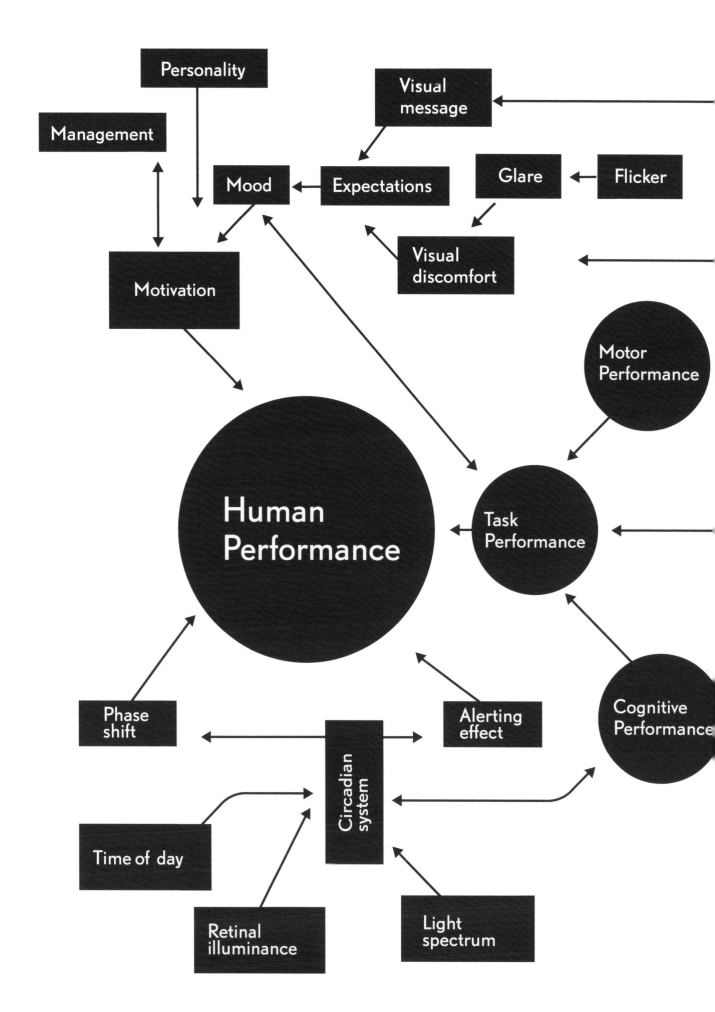

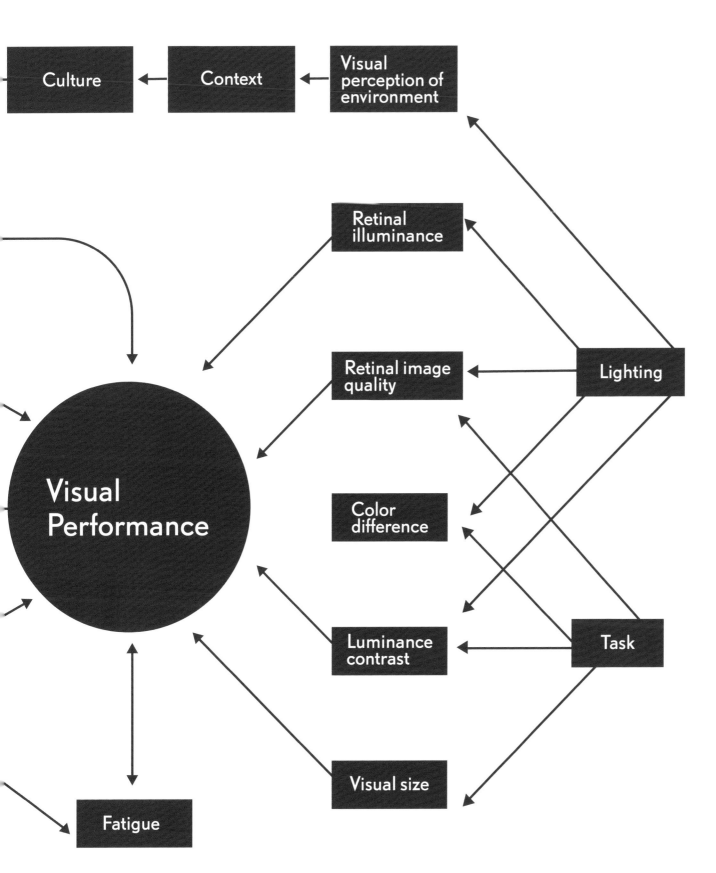

A conceptual framework setting out the three main routes whereby lighting conditions can influence human performance. The arrows in the diagram indicate the direction of effect

*Courtesy of "Human Factors in Lighting, Publishers: Taylor and Francis"*

ENVIRONMENTAL
AND
HUMAN FACTORS

Peter Boyce

Visual discomfort due to lighting glare in a parking area

*Photo credits: Peter Boyce*

## In what ways can lighting affect the human condition?

-

Human factors in lighting are the study of the effects of lighting conditions on human performance, perception, behavior and health.

## What is lighting and visual discomfort?

-

Lighting conditions can cause visual discomfort. For example, lighting can cause glare or flicker. Therefore, if you are designing a lighting installation, one of the consequences you usually wish to avoid is visual discomfort. It is worth pointing out that visual comfort is essentially the absence of visual discomfort, nothing else.

## Does the visual system respond more sensitively to LED compared to traditional lighting technologies?

-

No. The visual system responds to whatever patterns of visible radiation it receives, regardless of its origin. Given the same lighting stimulus, you will get the same response from the visual system.

## How can LED complement the circadian system? And how important is it?

-

LEDs can be used to stimulate the circadian system very efficiently because there are LEDs which emit radiation near to the peak sensitivity of the circadian system, i.e., about 465nm. Other light sources could do this but not so efficiently.

## Can LED improve health in general?

-

No. There is nothing magical about LEDs in regard to health. More generally, however, the effect of light exposure on human health can be positive or negative depending on the amount, type and timing of exposure. We need to know a lot more about this impact before advocating lighting as an aid to health for the general population. There is no doubt that light exposure can help alleviate the effects of some forms of ill health but these are specific cases which have been carefully explored.

## What changes have you observed in the field of LED technology during your time observing the industry?

-

During the past two decades, LEDs have steadily developed into plausible light sources. In that time they have become the standard light source for signs and signals and other applications where lighting is something to "be seen" rather than to "see by." Today, they are moving into the field of general illumination, at least for forms of local lighting—task-lights and reading lights, for example. Over the next few years I expect to see them become more widely used for general lighting.

## How do you foresee LED technology affecting our daily lives?

-

The most obvious area is domestic lighting. There are moves in various parts of the world to eliminate the incandescent lamp. At the moment, the obvious replacement is the compact fluorescent but this is meeting resistance because the compact fluorescent has modest color properties, takes several minutes to reach full light output and cannot easily be dimmed. Within a few years, there should be an LED-based substitute for the incandescent lamp that has good color properties, gives full light out immediately and can easily be dimmed.

## Do you feel that this is essential on a more socially related and ecological level?

-

If you believe in global warming and hence in the need to reduce carbon emissions, then reducing electricity consumption is a good idea, especially electricity consumption derived from fossil fuels. Replacing the incandescent lamp with something with a much higher luminous efficacy without increasing the amount of light is one quick and simple way to do this. One ecological question that the use of LEDs does raise is what happens at the end of life? How easily are they to dispose of without pollution and at reasonable cost?

## Are LEDs still seen as an exciting new technology for the lighting design industry and why?

-

Yes. However, as lighting designers gain experience with the use of LEDs they are revealing areas that need attention, such as the consistency of color appearance. The biggest limitation on the use of LEDs by the lighting designers is still cost.

## Will there be a dramatic change in laws and codes if LED begins to dominate in the lighting market?

-

I hope not. Laws and codes should be technology independent. Laws and codes concerned with reducing energy use should set limits on power density and hours of use, not specify a particular technology.

## What other developments or issues should the lighting industry be addressing?

-

Treat the claims of LED enthusiasts with skepticism. Many of the luminous efficacies claimed for LEDs refer to the LED alone and ignore the power demand of the driver that is needed to make the LED operate. Similarly, we should be asking what is meant by lifespan. Is it the end of a unit's life when it fails completely, or when there is a specified decline in light output? Ask under what conditions these values were acquired, particularly with regard to ambient temperature and current through the LED. Consider the possibility that the life of the LED system may be set by the life of the driver not the LED itself. We should be asking whether if at the end of life, a user has to throw away the whole luminaire or are there parts that can be replaced. *Caveat emptor* ("buyer beware").

## ENVIRONMENTAL
## AND
## HUMAN FACTORS

Peter Boyce

# Queensland University of Technology

Ian Cowling
Associate Professor
-

**QUT** Queensland University
of Technology

-
LED City
ECOLS
PLDA
Diamond Therapy
PlantLab
Talika
Philips

IAN COWLING IS AN ASSOCIATE PROFESSOR IN THE SCHOOL OF PHYSICAL AND CHEMICAL SCIENCES AT QUEENSLAND UNIVERSITY OF TECHNOLOGY IN BRISBANE, AUSTRALIA.

HE IS THE DIRECTOR OF THE QUT PHOTOMETRIC LABORATORY, AN ACCREDITED LABORATORY USED FOR BOTH LIGHTING EDUCATION AND COMMERCIAL CALIBRATION AND TESTING FOR THE AUSTRALIAN LIGHTING INDUSTRY. PROFESSOR COWLING IS ALSO COURSE COORDINATOR OF THE MASTER OF LIGHTING PROGRAM.

# ENVIRONMENTAL AND HUMAN FACTORS
-
## Queensland University of Technology

**Why was this program developed?**
-

The lighting program was developed initially to provide a university-based post-graduate qualification program in lighting for southeast Queenslanders.

However it was also apparent that there were many students outside the capital cities in Australia who were interested in doing the course, so an external program was also introduced. Finally the off-shore program at City University was also set up to meet an obvious need for such a course in Hong Kong.

**How does this program evolve to address the changing interests of students?**
-

The Master of Lighting course has more than 12 lecturers involved in its delivery. All these people are considered experts in their particular area of lighting, and they are encouraged to continuously update their material in keeping with advances in technology and practices in the lighting industry.

Staff members teaching in developing areas are obliged to update their lectures and material in keeping with developments in new technologies.

We are also looking at new units to cover areas of lighting considered not adequately covered in the current program.

**What role do you feel education has in regards to LED technology and programing?**
-

The lighting education program does not attempt to try to be part of the rapid technological development of LEDs themselves, but rather to keep students up to date with the growing range of products and applications available using LED products as they evolve, as well as make them aware of the issues involved in the different types of lighting technologies.

**What are the changes that you've noticed in the LED segment in terms of social responsibility and the ability to solve wider reaching social issues?**
-

The rapid technological development of LEDs, both as an individual light source and in LED-based luminaires, is very strongly driven by perceived energy savings in a world that is now acutely aware of energy generation and carbon-related issues.

Other factors, such as their size, expected long lifetime, price and color versatility have also opened up a wide range of applications that provide exciting and very pleasant colorful lighting experiences. This however can have a negative effect, in that there is evidence that situations are being over-lit, because it is such an exciting and easily applied light source.

So while LED sources will continue to become more energy efficient individually, the additional lighting we are installing for effect may well mean that we are still using as much energy overall as we did with less efficient traditional light sources.

# ENVIRONMENTAL
# AND
# HUMAN FACTORS
-

**Queensland University
of Technology**

**How are the credentials of those participating in your program recognized by the international community?**
-

The QUT Master of Lighting qualification is growing in acceptance in both Australia and Hong Kong. With a new course such as this, it does take a few years after the first class graduates for people in the lighting industry to appreciate the value of the course and start to recognize graduates of the course as having something to offer. I believe this is now starting to happen.

**What goals and values do you hope students take away with them beyond certification and graduation?**
-

I hope that students have an all-round understanding of lighting from both scientific and artistic viewpoints, and can apply the general principles of lighting in whatever area they work in. I also hope that they continue to grow their lighting knowledge and practice as this exciting area continues to advance.

**Is demand for programs such as yours increasing?**

-

Growing enrollments in both Australia and Hong Kong are proof that the demand for credentialed lighting education is growing. The increasing interest in the course from countries all over southeastern Asia and beyond also shows a growing concern about the energy issues of lighting worldwide.

What is of great interest to us at QUT, arising out of the lighting programs, is the wide range of backgrounds and interests that people who enter the course have. While we are aware that lighting is associated with a number of jobs and professions with a wide range of applications, one does not necessarily expect that they will all be a source of students in a post-graduate lighting course.

Also of interest is that approximately 40 percent of students entering the course do not have an undergraduate degree. Most of these do have a diploma or certificate.

Finally there is a noticeable difference in attitude between students enrolling in the QUT program and the City University of Hong Kong program. While QUT students generally tend to enroll firstly in the Graduate Certificate, then upon completion of this, the Graduate Diploma, then the Masters, students in Hong Kong will, if allowed, enroll directly into the Masters program.

# ENVIRONMENTAL
# AND
# HUMAN FACTORS

Peter Boyce
Queensland University of Technology

# LED City

Chuck Swoboda
Chief Executive Officer, Cree
-

-
ECOLS
PLDA
Diamond Therapy
PlantLab
Talika
Philips

PLANET LED
-
Chapter 05

ENVIRONMENTAL
AND
HUMAN FACTORS
-
LED City

THE LED CITY PROJECT AIMS TO IMPROVE THE QUALITY OF OUR LIVES.
IT IS AN EXPANDING COMMUNITY OF GOVERNMENT AND INDUSTRY
PARTIES WORKING TO EVALUATE, DEPLOY AND PROMOTE LED LIGHTING
TECHNOLOGY ACROSS THE FULL RANGE OF MUNICIPAL INFRASTRUCTURE
TO SAVE ENERGY, PROTECT THE ENVIRONMENT, REDUCE MAINTENANCE
COSTS AND PROVIDE BETTER LIGHT QUALITY FOR IMPROVED VISIBILITY
AND SAFETY.

The LED City project was conceived to improve life in every area of life, including government. Here's a chamber room in Indian Wells, California, United States

**What is LED City?**

-

LED City is a promotional program geared to accelerate the adoption of LED lighting in the municipal market. We promote real LED lighting installations in participating cities to show that LED lighting is beneficial from both a lifetime cost basis and quality of light basis today.

**What is the ultimate goal of this project?**

-

Accelerating the adoption of LED lighting. We are showing that LED lighting is beneficial today. Through real installation business case studies we are proving that cities do not have to wait any longer to gain concrete energy and maintenance cost savings from LED lighting in certain applications.

**Do you promote LED to the mass market?**

-

Our marketing plan does include efforts to reach the mass market to generate awareness. However, most efforts are geared toward reaching organizations that track the energy and maintenance associated with overall cost of lighting ownership.

These organizations are less sensitive to a higher initial purchase price because they track energy and maintenance cost savings over the life time of the light.

**How do you foresee LED technology influencing people's lives?**

-

LEDs have the potential to replace the light bulb, helping to significantly reduce the cost of lighting, both in energy use and maintenance.

**What's next for LED City?**

-

To continue to add new participating cities throughout the world.

**What is the ultimate potential of LED technology?**

-

On average, reducing energy use by 60 percent over traditional light sources and significantly reducing the cost of maintenance for lighting.

**How can someone be a part of what LED City does?**

-

Visit www.ledcity.org.

ENVIRONMENTAL
AND
HUMAN FACTORS
-
LED City

The "LED City" initiative is designed to create a "living laboratory" to deliver the economic, environmental and usage benefits of LED lighting to the residents of Raleigh, North Carolina, United States

# ENVIRONMENTAL
# AND
# HUMAN FACTORS

Peter Boyce
Queensland University of Technology
LED City

# ECOLS

Phoebe Yuen
Co-founder
-

ecols

-
PLDA
Diamond Therapy
PlantLab
Talika
Philips

ENVIRONMENTAL
AND
HUMAN FACTORS
-
ECOLS

ECOLS STANDS FOR "ECO-LIFESTYLE." FOUNDED IN 2008, ECOLS PROVIDES A PLATFORM FOR HUMANKIND TO EXCHANGE ECO THOUGHTS AND IDEAS THROUGH ART, DESIGNS AND COMMUNICATIONS.

ECOLS' MISSION IS TO EDUCATE AND NURTURE THE MARKET ABOUT AN ECO LIFESTYLE AND IGNITE PEOPLE'S ECO ATTITUDE.

Inside Ecols' retail space in Hong Kong

PLANET LED
-
Chapter 05

ENVIRONMENTAL
AND
HUMAN FACTORS
-
ECOLS

ECOLS' Hong Kong outlet selling items for an "eco lifestyle"

### How did the company start?
-

Ronald Lo and I started ECOLS in 2008. Initially we planned on creating a green lighting platform for consumers and industry alike. However, as we further developed the ideas of eco platform, we realised being "eco" is not just about particular habits, but a lifestyle that people embrace.

For example, we educate our customers on how to distinguish between different "green" merchandise. By establishing a retail outlet in the NoHo area of Hong Kong, ECOLS was then able to interact with the public through its products, exhibitions and collaborations with eco artists, designers and social enterprises.

### What are your opinions on the popularity of LED as a medium and method of lighting?
-

As a retail and commercial platform, we have the chance to interact with the market on different levels with retailers and consumers.

I think LEDs are already popular with lighting professionals and are part of an architectural trend. Retailers are also looking to adopt this green technology.

We receive more and more inquiries, especially from retailers about installing LEDs in their shops. On the other hand, consumers increasingly have LED gadgets or LED decorative items at home without even knowing much about this new technology. However, they are also beginning to consider LEDs for more general lighting purposes and consumers are learning more about their environmental and financial benefits.

**What changes have you observed in the field of LED technology during your time in the industry?**
-

After early adoption, LED lighting users are becoming smarter and smarter. They are learning not to rely too much on the price point as the most important sourcing criterion. They are also more aware about performance and understand that low-quality LED products can be a real nightmare.

While the market is evolving, the significant improvement of LED CRI (Color Rendering Index), heat sink management and brightness lower the barriers for adoption in general lighting situations and strengthen the green arguments.

**What criteria do you take into account when buying LEDs?**
-

Efficiency, CRI, lighting effects, lifetime, safety and price.

**How are the needs and priorities of the world changing, and how are LEDs a part of that?**
-

The world needs to deal with the issues of global warming. As all of us know, $CO_2$ emissions are the major cause and anything that can help reduce these emissions significantly alleviates this worldwide problem.

With LEDs consuming considerably less energy than traditional lighting, they also emit confined wavelength without UV and boast a 50,000-100,000 hour laboratory lifetime. This explains why LED is a green choice.

About 10-15 years ago, LEDs were considered only for speciality lighting markets such as the automotive industry. But now, as people see how green LEDs are and how they can help reduce $CO_2$ emissions, more and more LED lighting products have been developed.

General lighting applications are now available on a larger domestic and commercial scale, which has led to a lower price point, better brightness and a relatively good CRI.

# ENVIRONMENTAL
# AND
# HUMAN FACTORS
-
## ECOLS

**How do you foresee the impact of LED technology?**
-
This technology has already been with us since the 1970s when it was only good enough to be a simple indicator light on a computer keyboard or a car's dashboard.

When the technology evolved, they were used in more functional ways such as a car's tail light or roadside traffic light, and also as decorative lighting on a building's façade. Those in the industry now know that LEDs are starting to appear in our homes as more general lighting and this development will only increase.

They will play a key role in fighting the problem of global warming and our growing energy issues. Eventually, every home will adopt LEDs when the price gets down to a point similar to that of compact fluorescent light bulbs.

**What obstacles still exist?**
-
Price and lack of LED knowledge.

**What are your aims and aspirations for the future of LED technology and, via extension, your company?**
-
We believe that more people will embrace an eco lifestyle by taking up eco habits and accepting eco merchandise. That includes using green building materials and LED lighting.

ECOLS will continue to educate the general public about greener choices in lighting, influence as many individuals and businesses to convert into more efficient lighting solutions.

At the moment, LEDs are our most eco choice in lighting technologies, but there is still room for improvement. We will also work with our LED supplier to co-create the most efficient lighting solutions to try and minimize $CO_2$ emissions.

**Are there any other messages that you would like to convey?**
-
Green choices make our world better.

# ENVIRONMENTAL
# AND
# HUMAN FACTORS

Peter Boyce
Queensland University of Technology
LED City
ECOLS

# PLDA

Kevan Shaw
Director of Sustainability
-

PLDA

-

Diamond Therapy
PlantLab
Talika
Philips

Al Tijaria Tower in Kuwait uses color-changing LEDs to create different characters for the tower to reflect different events and seasons

PLANET LED
-
Chapter 05

ENVIRONMENTAL
AND
HUMAN FACTORS
-
PLDA

THE PROFESSIONAL LIGHTING DESIGNERS' ASSOCIATION (PLDA) IS A VOLUNTARY FEDERATION OF LIGHTING DESIGNERS AND LIGHTING CONSULTANTS WHO ARE ACTIVE ON AN INTERNATIONAL SCALE, THEIR PURPOSE BEING TO INCREASE THE REPUTATION OF THE PROFESSION AND TO ESTABLISH THE PROFESSION AS SUCH IN ITS OWN RIGHT.

PLDA MEMBERSHIP IS CENTERED AROUND THE PROFESSIONAL ARCHITECTURAL LIGHTING DESIGNER. THESE MEMBERS POSSESS THE KNOWLEDGE AND EXPERTISE TO CARRY OUT ALL THE WORK REQUIRED TO DESIGN LIGHT FOR INTERIOR AND EXTERIOR ARCHITECTURAL PROJECTS. THEIR GOAL IS TO ESTABLISH AN EFFICIENT, ENJOYABLE, HEALTHY, SAFE, SUSTAINABLE AND WELL ACCEPTED ENVIRONMENT THROUGH LIGHTING DESIGN FOR THE PEOPLE WHO LIVE, WORK AND RELAX IN IT.

KEVAN SHAW IS AN ARCHITECTURAL LIGHTING DESIGNER WHO HAS RUN HIS OWN COMPANY, KSLD, IN EDINBURGH FOR 21 YEARS. HE IS CURRENTLY PLDA'S DIRECTOR OF SUSTAINABILITY.

Aspire Tower uses complex control to create a skin whose color and pattern are changeable according to the events taking place in the adjacent stadium and sports center. This complexity relies on the color and controllability to make it work

313

## ENVIRONMENTAL
## AND
## HUMAN FACTORS
-
## PLDA

**What is the mission of the PLDA?**
-

PLDA is a membership-driven organization whose main aim is to promote the lighting design profession and achieve professional recognition around the world.

**What is the Light Focus conference?**
-

Light Focus is a conference program organized by the PLDA and is held in conjunction with other international events such as Light+Building in Frankfurt, Euro Luce and Light Middle East.

PLDA organizes speakers usually in response to a call for papers. These are moderated by PLDA professional members to ensure a high-quality program.

**What changes have you seen in the lighting design industry in the past few years?**
-

As a profession we are seeing strong moves in Europe and the United States to achieve professional recognition, largely in response to the recognition that, as a group, we hold specific knowledge and expertise.

Lighting design is becoming increasingly important to ensure effective sustainable lighting in response to the requirements to the reduction of energy usage. The advent of new lighting technologies has also required more expert knowledge to use these effectively.

**What are the keys factors in a successful lighting design?**
-

Firstly, a clear understanding of the requirements for lighting and a good understanding of the appropriate lighting design approaches to achieve good lighting. Also, designers require a large degree of creativity to provide outstanding solutions.

**What is your opinion on the popularity of LED as a method of lighting? Do you see our creative lighting landscape changing as a result?**
-

LED technology is being heavily oversold as the solution to all lighting problems. It is not. No one lighting technology will be the best for every situation.

However, LEDs have provided an energy-efficient way to create color and dynamics. And, to this end, it is by far the best solution currently available. For white light applications it is beginning to provide some solutions, but these are normally as replacements for existing fittings and lamps.

Until people start creating lighting forms around the specific characteristics of LEDs we will not see the best possible use of this technology.

**How do you see LED technology's influence developing?**
-

There is a big risk that poor LED products currently on the market will create a general perception that LEDs will not be a quality light source.

The overselling and ridiculous claims for efficiency and lifespan are already beginning to cause a backlash because early products are proving less efficient and less reliable than promised. At some point the technology will mature but this is a long time away.

## ENVIRONMENTAL
## AND
## HUMAN FACTORS
-
## PLDA

**For environmental reasons, are LEDs essential?**

-

No. The right light source for the right task is the best solution — socially and ecologically.

**You also run KSLD lighting design agency. Can you tell us about this company?**

-

We are 21 years old and have worked on more than 550 projects, from small parish churches in Scotland to massive towers in the Middle East. We are a broad-based practice with projects throughout the world. Currently we have six designers, though this number varies according to the workload.

**What are the biggest challenges facing lighting designers?**

-

Lighting design has the same challenges everywhere whether it is in developed markets such as the UK or emerging markets such as Turkey. We are all struggling for recognition and for projects. We all have to teach our clients a lot about what we do.

We all suffer the same problems with contractors changing their minds or altering specifications and making errors in installation. We need to act together through organizations like PLDA to achieve the professional recognition we need.

The Public, an arts center in the UK. Here the color of light and color of forms combine to create a spectacular interior responding to a variety of activity

ENVIRONMENTAL
AND
HUMAN FACTORS

Peter Boyce
Queensland University of Technology
LED City
ECOLS
PLDA

# Diamond Therapy

Magnolia Polley
Healing Artist
-

-

PlantLab
Talika
Philips

ENVIRONMENTAL
AND
HUMAN FACTORS
-
Diamond Therapy

MAGNOLIA POLLEY IS A HEALING ARTIST. THE THERAPIES THAT SHE HAS USED FOR 15 YEARS INCORPORATE A FULL RANGE OF ALTERNATIVE ARTS SUCH AS AYURVEDIC AND CHINESE MEDICINE, SHAMANISTIC AND ALTERNATIVE PRACTICES FROM VARYING CULTURES, MASSAGE AND BODYWORK, AND A BROAD RANGE OF ENERGY WORK THERAPIES. SHE HAS TRADITIONAL AND NON-TRADITIONAL TRAINING AND SHE DRAWS HER STUDIES FROM ANTHROPOLOGICAL SCIENCE, AS WELL THE REALM OF METAPHYSICS.

ENERGY WORK IS PERFORMED USING HEALING TOOLS SUCH AS AROMATHERAPY, LED COLOR THERAPY, GEM STONES, SOUND/VIBRATION THERAPIES, AND LIGHT THERAPY, TO CREATE AN ATMOSPHERE OF ENERGY THAT ENCOURAGES THE BODY TO COME INTO BALANCE OR HEAL.

Magnolia performs up to 10 hours of treatments a day on celebrities, journalists, writers and producers. The diamonds here are worth USD$18 million and are flawless, which makes them more effective and exceptionally brilliant under a controlled LED ultraviolet light. The diamonds include 14 loose two- to four-carat immaculate diamonds and two 12-carat canary diamonds faceted into pendulums

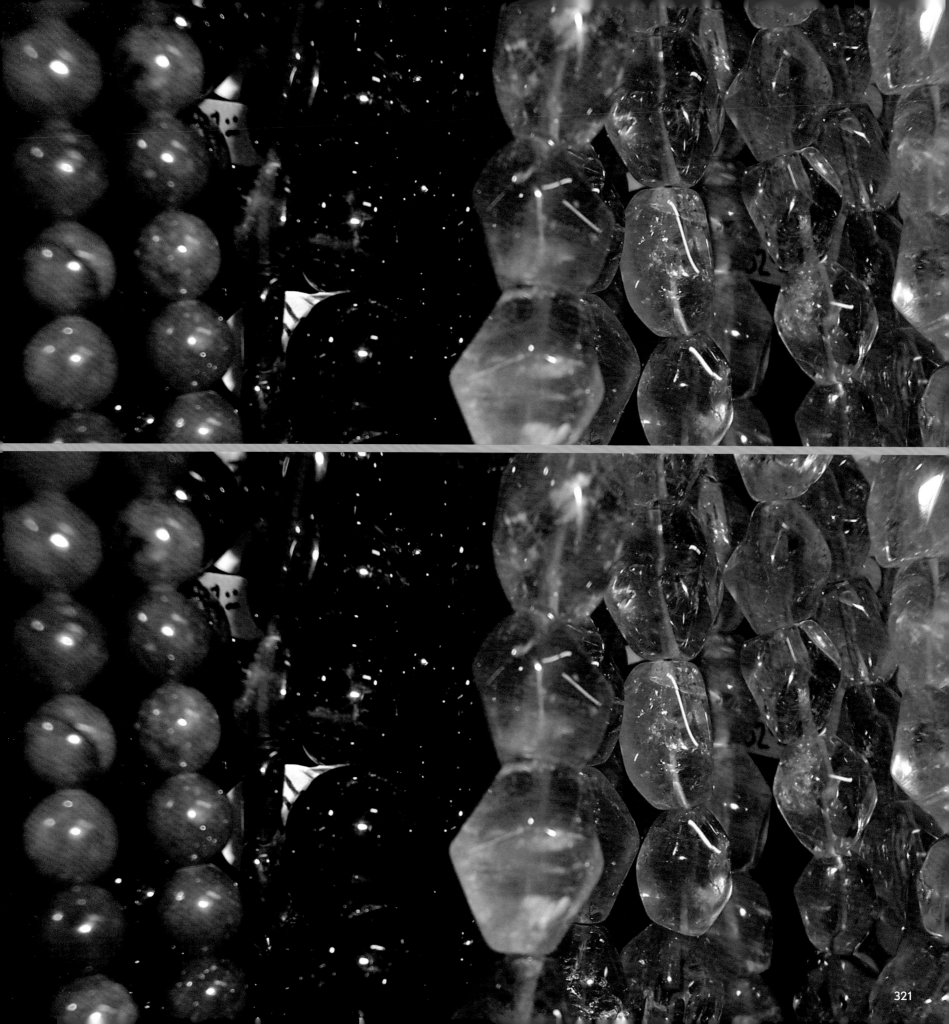

ENVIRONMENTAL
AND
HUMAN FACTORS
-
Diamond Therapy

**How does lighting affect a human's wellbeing?**
-

My work revolves around the theory that if the body receives
the right amount of light from each facet of the color spectrum,
optimum balance can be achieved.

The human eye connects to the optic chiasm, or nerve, which
has an entrainment path or a direct feed to the hypothalamus,
pituitary and pineal glands found within brain. The optic nerve is
present in the eye even if a person experiences blindness.

A human's survival is completely dependent upon sunlight
for the nervous system to use it as an energy source for
communication. Without it, the human body would eventually fall
into dysfunction and disease.

Our hereditary skin coloration is an example of how our bodies
are able to adapt to its environment to be able to obtain optimal
sunlight. The skin is the body's largest organ and is also designed
to absorb additional sunlight.

**What particular spectrum is good for the body?**
-

Each spectrum of color is essential to the body's performance and survival. Chinese medicine and the Indian philosophy of the chakra system both work to
stimulate the meridians and naturally occurring minor and major nerve plexus sites within the body.

A nerve plexus is a bundle of nerves that holds an electrical rhythm that is particular to the functioning system to which it feeds. Major nerve plexus sites
recognized by Western medicine are found at the spinal column and happen to coincide with the chakra system and the colors associated with the chakras.

For example, the third chakra vibrates to the color yellow and is believed to control the function of our kidneys, liver, pancreas, and other major internal organs.
The theory is, if our body receives enough light within the yellow color spectrum, the nerve plexus or chakra has the energy to supply our internal organs.

The catch is, however, that all of the chakras or plexus sites are dependent upon the others' function. If one color spectrum is missing, eventually, the others
will begin to fall out of rhythm and dysfunction will occur.

USD$6 million worth of colored diamonds in Magnolia's hand.
She uses these with UV LED light for chakra balancing and healing

**Is there a spiritual connection between the body and light?**

Light is a form of energy released by an atom. It is my belief that the spirit or spiritual energy is actually found within the light produced by the atoms and cells found within our bodies.

The aura, the body's own electromagnetic field, is the spiritual register to how physically well-balanced our bodies are, how much light we are receiving, and where a dysfunction may be occurring with the plexus or chakra system.

A circadian rhythm is the rhythmic vibration or bio-rhythm that is held by every cell in the human body and can be fine tuned at the plexus/chakra sites that work together to create your whole body's internal clock. Each nerve plexus sight or chakra, meaning "wheel," holds a particular vibration which has a translating color and musical tone.

Color is magnetized and made into a tool for healing, by UV light. The main nerve plexus site is found at the sixth chakra, often referred to as third eye and happens to be an inch above the center of your eyes. This nerve plexus site is called the suprachiasmatic nuclei.

The suprachiasmatic nuclei holds the main circadian rhythm/bio-rhythm, or internal clock. A healing artist properly trained to work with the aura and chakra systems is able use light, color, aroma, and sound/vibration therapies to alter and regulate a dysfunctional or out-of-balance system within the body.

**How does LED fit into all of this?**

All light has an effect on the bodies function and well being, especially sunlight. I use an LED light pen with colored quartz crystal disc lenses at established chakra sites, especially the sixth chakra, and acupressure sites to create the atmosphere of energy (gauged by the scale of hertz) needed by the body to come into balance and health.

The LED light pen simulates UV light and offers each cell just the right amount of energy to stimulate the circulatory, nervous, glandular and lymphatic systems, opening the meridian lines gently and non-evasively. Therefore, light controls our bio-rhythms or circadian rhythms, which are the connection between the physical and spiritual bodies.

**What is your opinion of LED light?**

LEDs make it possible for me to perform my UV light and color therapies anywhere. LEDs are portable, widely manufactured, and best of all small and very bright. If I couldn't use LED light, I would have to perform all of my therapies outside on a sunny day and with large glass color shields to stimulate and balance the body's bio-rhythms through the chakra system.

Of course, in China's history, these natural UV light facilities paired with large color shields were called color halls. It is widely documented that color halls had been created and used to heal the sick. Color halls were also found in both India and Egypt.

I believe that LED companies and those who work with LED have the ability and an opportunity to affect large groups of people in a very positive way, through the combined use of LEDs and color for healing.

## ENVIRONMENTAL
## AND
## HUMAN FACTORS

-

**Diamond Therapy**

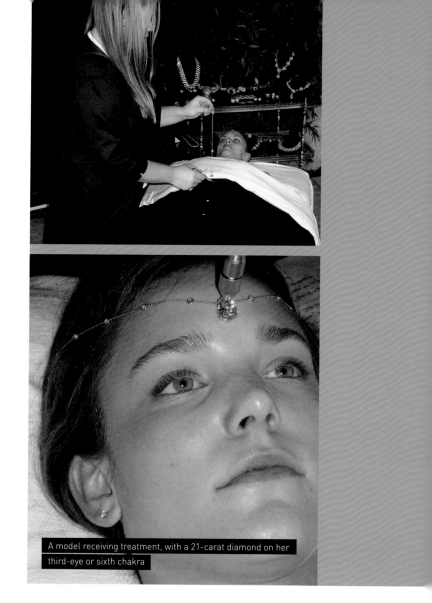

A model receiving treatment, with a 21-carat diamond on her third-eye or sixth chakra

**Are LEDs a major part of your therapies?**

-

I use a technique called chromotherapy or photobiomodulation to perform healing therapies on humans and animals. This is the combination of using combined light and color therapies at specified acupressure/chakra sites to encourage the body to come into balance.

It is essential for me to use a handheld LED UV light pen to perform diamond therapy or other gemstone therapies. It is this UV light that magnetizes a diamond making it a tool for healing.

I look forward to collaborating on a project with LED artists to recreate modern-day color halls.

**What kind of impact have LEDs had on the world?**

-

In the last decade, a wide range of healing tools that utilize LEDs has been created and widely distributed through out the spa and dermatology industries.

Infrared light is commonly used for accelerated cellular renewal to help lighten scaring and skin discolorations by increasing DNA and RNA activity. Infrared can be applied directly to the site of an injury or wound and have a positive effect within just one application as long as the site is exposed to just the right amount of light.

Ultraviolet light is being used as anti-bacterial tool, as well. But LEDs are preferred because their wavelengths are the most penetrating and have very little heat so the application of this form of light is tolerated well by the body and allows the light to affect a deeper level of cells beneath the skin.

LEDs and sunlight have a very similar depth of penetration, between a half to one inch beneath the skin. So, the use of LEDs and the recognition of infrared light as a non-invasive way to heal wounds and various forms of skin damage have revolutionized the availability of these tools to practitioners and to the public.

**Why are diamonds your choice of therapy application tool?**

-

Diamonds are an amazing tool for the amplification and application of light and color therapies. A diamond's immaculately clean carbon structure becomes easily magnetized as soon as UV light is applied to it making the stone a piezoelectric material, able to hold its own vibration or rhythm. This makes the diamond into a superior amplification tool for healing.

I carefully place diamonds that are both clear and of color on the chakra sites to amplify the colored UV light produced by my light pen to amplify it. Amplification occurs as the light enters the diamond, interacts with its facets, breaks the light into spectrums and creates an atmosphere of appropriate healing energy for the body to use for its bio-rhythmic regulation.

This is a naturally occurring healing phenomenon that can be harnessed and used by a healing artist who is practiced and studied in these techniques.

A close-up of the refraction in an immaculate diamond with LED ultraviolet light

Peter Boyce
Queensland University of Technology
LED City
ECOLS
PLDA

# PlantLab

Gertjan Meeuws
Managing Partner
-

-
Talika
Philips

Dutch agricultural company PlantLab wants to change almost
everything you know about growing plants

ENVIRONMENTAL
AND
HUMAN FACTORS
-
**PlantLab**

PLANTLAB BELIEVES THAT HUMANITY CANNOT CONTINUE WITH THE EMPHASIS ON TRADITIONAL METHODS OF GROWING CROPS. THE SCARCITY OF WATER WILL HAVE A LARGE SAY IN THIS. PLANTLAB PROVIDES RESEARCHERS AROUND THE WORLD WITH THE LATEST FACILITIES. BY DEVELOPING SPECIALIZED PLANT PRODUCTION UNITS AND THROUGH GAINING SPECIALIST KNOWLEDGE, THEY PRODUCE HIGH-QUALITY FOOD FOR THE SHORT TERM AS WELL AS PLAN FOR FUTURE DEMAND.

IN ITS GREENHOUSES, PLANTLAB USES LED LIGHTING THAT PROVIDES EXACTLY THE COLORS THAT THE PLANT NEEDS FOR PHOTOSYNTHESIS. PLANTS MAINLY NEED BLUE AND RED LIGHT FOR PHOTOSYNTHESIS AND FAR-RED, A COLOR NOT VISIBLE TO THE HUMAN EYE BUT VISIBLE TO THE PLANT.

PLANTLAB CONSIDERS THAT A SIGNIFICANT PART OF THE FOOD PRODUCTION CAN MOVE RIGHT INTO THE CENTER OF CITIES, IN A BASEMENT OF A GREENGROCER OR IN A MULTI-STORY, MULTI-LAYER VERTICAL NURSERY.

Imagine our farms of the future—all inside, dedicated and
efficient labs, closer to consumers

# ENVIRONMENTAL
# AND
# HUMAN FACTORS
-
## PlantLab

Inside a PlantLab facility

### How and why was this method discovered?
-
Using a unique combination of technology, growing ideas and mathematical models, PlantLab has created a revolution in growing. Four engineers developed the Plant Production Unit in a PlantLab R&D laboratory in Hertogenbosch in the Netherlands. This patented system can be used anywhere from the North Pole to the equator, on a small or a large scale, and adjusted to local demands.

All the requirements "from seed to harvest" are captured in a growing recipe. In these plant paradises, no pesticides are needed and the savings on the water use are over 90 percent compared to traditional systems. PlantLab's ultimate goal is to get the most out of plants in order to contribute to a world where everybody can have fresh food — at any time and any place.

### What is the significance of LED lighting on your system?
-
To create a Plant Paradise, you need light that has exactly the right wavelengths and colors, and that doesn't produce heat. LED technology fits this description perfectly.

### Can LEDs improve the health and production capabilities of plants compared to exposure to other light sources?
-
Yes, but not LEDs by themselves. It's the combination of LEDs and climate control. A Plant Paradise strikes the balance of air temperature, soil temperature, airflow, humidity, carbon dioxide, light intensity and light ratios.

**How important is this discovery in terms of global food production?**

-

Although the system does save energy, it is its water-saving ability that makes it really valuable. Water shortages are the biggest threat to our planet, especially as we grow from seven to nine billion people by 2030.

We need more efficient ways to produce our food and preserve our valuable resources. That means using as little water as possible, without pesticides. It also means having local sources of food that are close to the consumer, appropriate to the size of the market. Our Plant Production Units do so and produce great tasting, high-nutrient value products.

**What changes in LED technology have you witnessed?**

-

When we started preparing Pilot Plant in 2005, the LEDs we used were generating 10 percent light and 90 percent heat. The ratio for the next generation of lights was 16:84. And now, today, there are LEDs available that produce the wavelengths that we need with 27 percent light. These early prototypes are very promising.

**And what about changes in the LED industry?**

-

Producers of LED systems are wrestling with two key issues: high prices and low volume. Basically, they can't yet get a return on their R&D investment quickly enough.

We would encourage them to decrease prices to try and boost sales and make LEDs more affordable for a larger market.

**Do you feel that the ultimate success of LEDs is essential from an environmental viewpoint and vital to achieving social harmony?**

-

When LEDs become affordable for a larger audience and applied in our plant production units, they can really make a big difference in the Western world and especially Third World countries. Again, bear in mind the availability of water and food will be key in the coming decades.

# ENVIRONMENTAL AND HUMAN FACTORS
–
**PlantLab**

Growing tomatoes in a "Plant Paradise"

ENVIRONMENTAL
AND
HUMAN FACTORS

Peter Boyce
Queensland University of Technology
LED City
ECOLS
PLDA
Diamond Therapy
PlantLab

# Talika

Alexis de Brosses,
President
-

TALIKA PARIS

-

Philips

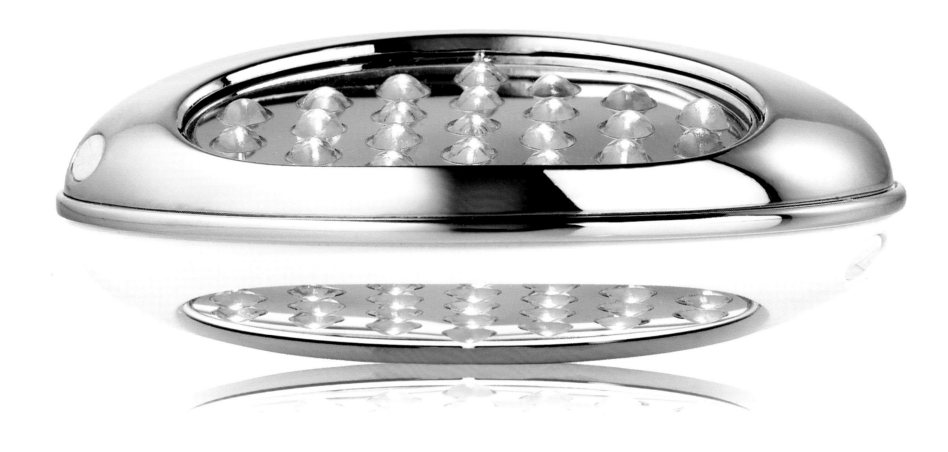

TALIKA Light DUO® collagen booster & skin lightener

ENVIRONMENTAL
AND
HUMAN FACTORS
-
**Talika**

**SINCE ITS CREATION, TALIKA'S LABORATORIES IN FRANCE HAVE BEEN DEVELOPING ORIGINAL AND EFFECTIVE PRODUCTS DIRECTLY TARGETING WOMEN'S NEEDS. MORE THAN 60 YEARS AFTER ITS ESTABLISHMENT, THE BRAND USES BREAKTHROUGH TECHNOLOGIES, INCLUDING LIGHT.**

**TALIKA RESEARCHES, DISCOVERS AND TRANSMITS INNOVATIVE TECHNOLOGIES COMING FROM VARIOUS FIELDS—INCLUDING TRADITIONAL MEDICINES—AND EVEN NASA.**

**What is so revolutionary about your skin rejuvenation research?**
-
Our research has led us to the most efficient, natural and safe solution — light. It is revolutionary because the concept of using natural light to improve beauty is revolutionary in itself. It is based on a new vision for the millennium using quantum theory. Today, this revolution is available to everyone.

But the real revolution is that our product Light Duo is by far more efficient than any other cream or treatment on the market. It is the safest, the purest and the simplest solution ever created to reverse the signs of aging. Today, more and more people are looking for bio products that are pure and natural treatments.

Skin rejuvenation is very important but it's not our only priority. We are inspired by all desires, and all the aesthetic aspirations that men and women have at every stage of their lives.

**Can you tell us more about Light Duo?**

-

Light Duo is a device that offers a complete solution to efficiently treat the signs of aging, especially wrinkles and dark spots. It really is a "time machine" that everybody dreams about.

To develop this revolutionary device, Talika has been inspired by 40 years of NASA research on the benefits of natural light on living organisms. Talika has selected the perfect wavelengths for two products:

• To prevent and treat wrinkles: 590-nanometre wavelength
 (seen as orange light by our naked eye).
• To visibly reduce dark spots and brighten the skin: 525-nanometre wavelength
 (seen as green light by our naked eye).

**So what do these items actually do?**

-

The 590nm-wavelength (orange light) directly acts at the heart of the fibroblasts. These are cells which produce collagen and elastin. Boosting their effectiveness, and therefore improving collagen and elastin synthesis, helps improve skin quality, reduce wrinkles and improve firmness.

Clinical tests have shown that after only 28 days (45 seconds daily use per treated area), this kind of treatment can:

• Reduce skin wrinkles by 32 percent, and;
• Increase skin firmness by 33 percent.

The 525nm wavelength (green light) acts on skin areas that have high melanogenesis activity. The light regulates production of melanin to reduce over-pigmentation (dark spots) and visibly brighten the complexion.

Clinical tests have shown that after 60 days (two minutes of daily use per treated area), this kind of treatment can:

• Reduce dark spots and pigmentation by 46 percent.

**Why did you choose LEDs to power these devices?**

-

Light is the most natural resource in the universe. That's why we really wanted to develop cosmetic products using it and, by doing so, offer the most natural skin treatment.

LEDs enable us to offer selected wavelengths that are very concentrated and very precise. They are consistent and safe, and optimize light's benefits on the skin. LEDs are also very resistant and will last for years.

**What kind of impact do you think LEDs have had?**

-

LEDs have already left a deep mark on our world and in particular in the design field. In fact, designers are now creating objects that are built around LEDs themselves. LEDs are now seen as not just a light source but also as an integral part of the design field. In fact, designers are now creating objects that are built around LEDs themselves—they've already left a deep mark on our world.

As far as the medical field is concerned, LED research will continue and will offer even more new solutions for areas like anaesthesia.

I would also expect to see more ecological and biodegradable LEDs in the future.

**What other lighting projects is Talika working on?**

-

The benefits offered by light are unlimited. So I'm confident that as LEDs are the safest way to transmit light, the future of LEDs is linked to our R&D.

Our challenge is to identify and develop the perfect wavelength to answer problems that we want to solve.

We are currently working on new lighting applications to fulfill needs that have not yet found efficient solutions with existing cosmetic treatments like stretch marks and cellulite.

**What fascinates you about the effects of light on our bodies?**

-

Something that still fascinates me is that light can heal and that it can reverse the damage caused over time.

It was only after we conducted clinical tests on 30 volunteers that we realized the strong regeneration of skin cells that light offers. We discovered that the ATP (molecules that store and distribute energy in the body) was multiplied by 12 after only a few seconds of exposure.

Another amazing result of these tests was the discovery that this therapy was universal. The treatment worked efficiently on 100 percent of the volunteers tested — something which is rarely the case for traditional beauty products.

# ENVIRONMENTAL
# AND
# HUMAN FACTORS

# Philips

Nick Kelso
Senior Communications Manager
Philips Lighting Africa
-

**PHILIPS**
-

LEDs can power all kinds of light on or off the grid

339

## ENVIRONMENTAL
## AND
## HUMAN FACTORS
-
**Philips**

Philips has been testing solar lighting solutions in Ghana as part
of the Sustainable Energy Solutions for Africa project

Kyomugisha Mackline's family enjoying dinner

RwakityokoriGÇÖs grandchildren converge at his home

PHILIPS LIGHTING'S MISSION IS TO SIMPLY ENHANCE LIFE WITH LIGHT. THEREFORE, THE COMPANY IS COMMITTED TO DEVELOPING SUSTAINABLE, AFFORDABLE LIGHTING SOLUTIONS FOR PEOPLE WHO DO NOT HAVE RELIABLE ACCESS TO THE ELECTRICITY GRID IN VARIOUS PARTS OF THE WORLD AND BRINGING THESE TO MARKET.

THE "SUSTAINABLE ENERGY SOLUTIONS FOR AFRICA" (SESA) PROJECT IS A FIRST AND MAJOR STEP IN ITS GLOBAL OFF-GRID LIGHTING PROGRAM.

NICK KELSO IS THE SENIOR COMMUNICATIONS MANAGER FOR PHILIPS LIGHTING AFRICA. IN THOSE REGIONS, IN PARTICULAR AFRICA, THE DUTCH MULTINATIONAL SEEKS TO PROVIDE SUSTAINABLE LIGHTING SOLUTIONS.

# ENVIRONMENTAL
# AND
# HUMAN FACTORS

-

**Philips**

Philips launches the world's first solar-powered LED football
lighting solution in Nairobi, Kenya, in November 2009

# ENVIRONMENTAL AND HUMAN FACTORS
-
**Philips**

### What is Philips' company philosophy?
-
Philips is a health and wellbeing company committed to improving the quality of people's lives. Our vision is that in a world where complexity increasingly touches every aspect of our daily lives, we will lead in bringing sense and simplicity to people.

### Can you explain the goal behind the Simplicity Campaign?
-
In the past few years we have held a series of events where we provide evidence and examples of what we mean by delivering on our brand promise of "sense and simplicity."

This brand promise encapsulates our commitment to deliver solutions that are advanced, easy to use, and designed around the needs of all our users.

### What are your opinions on the popularity of LEDs?
-
LEDs are the future of lighting. LEDs offer greater flexibility, controllability, and lifetime and energy efficiency than conventional lighting.

### Do you see them changing the creative lighting landscape?
-
LEDs are already allowing us to do things we could never do before with conventional lighting. The design possibilities, including the use of color and controls, are only limited by our imagination.

### What do you feel is their ultimate potential?
-
LEDs will transform the world in terms of what we can do with light. They will also play a major role in reducing global energy consumption by lighting, which now stands at about 19 percent.

This means they will be a very important tool in the fight against global warming. Low-voltage LEDs are also ideal for solar lighting solutions.

### What obstacles do you think still exist out there?
-
There are no key obstacles which cannot be overcome. It is just a matter of time.

### Can you tell us more about the SESA project in Africa?
-
In 2008, Philips signed a deal with the Dutch government to jointly develop solar-powered lighting solutions for Africa's sub-Saharan region. This is called the SESA (Sustainable Energy Solutions for Africa) project and its aim is to provide 10 million people with access to new lighting by 2015 across 10 sub-Saharan countries.

This is not charity but involves setting up and supporting new businesses and distribution models and hence creating sustainable employment. Philips' role is to develop a new generation of solar-powered LED lighting solutions which will be sold via these new business models.

Today some 500 million Africans and 1.6 billion people elsewhere on the planet do not have access to electricity. In sub-Saharan Africa it goes dark around 6:30pm all year round.

For these people, nightfall means either darkness or the flickering light of a candle or kerosene lamp. There are many health and safety risks for these options, as well as expensive oil-driven fuel prices. Low-light output also makes reading nearly impossible. As a result, life in many parts of Africa — and India — practically comes to a halt at sundown, including for those children busy with their homework.

Solar-powered LED lighting solutions can make a true difference here and Philips has been involved in a pilot SESA project in Ghana where we have been working with local NGOs.

**Why are you involved on such a large scale in these kinds of projects?**
-
As a responsible company we should play an active role in society. However, we would stress that the SESA project is not charity. It offers what we call a triple win.

Consumers benefit from better, safer, cheaper sustainable lighting solutions, local economies benefit from employment creation and potentially increased productivity, whilst businesses benefit from sales.

**Are there other LED projects that Philips is working on?**
-
Philips is currently involved in many high-profile LED lighting projects all around the world including the Bosporus Bridge, The Cairo Tower, Buckingham Palace in London and the LG towers in Beijing.

**What is the future of LED technology at your company?**
-
We will continue to develop meaningful LED lighting solutions that solve real issues in people's lives.

**Is there an initiative that you are particularly proud of?**
-
Philips has just announced its creation of the world's first solar-powered LED football floodlighting system. This has been tested and launched in Africa and will allow communities to come together after dark.

There are also many other applications for this technology such as security and street lighting. More information can be found on our website at www.philips.com/offgridlighting.

Brazil at Night
*Photo credits: Nasa*

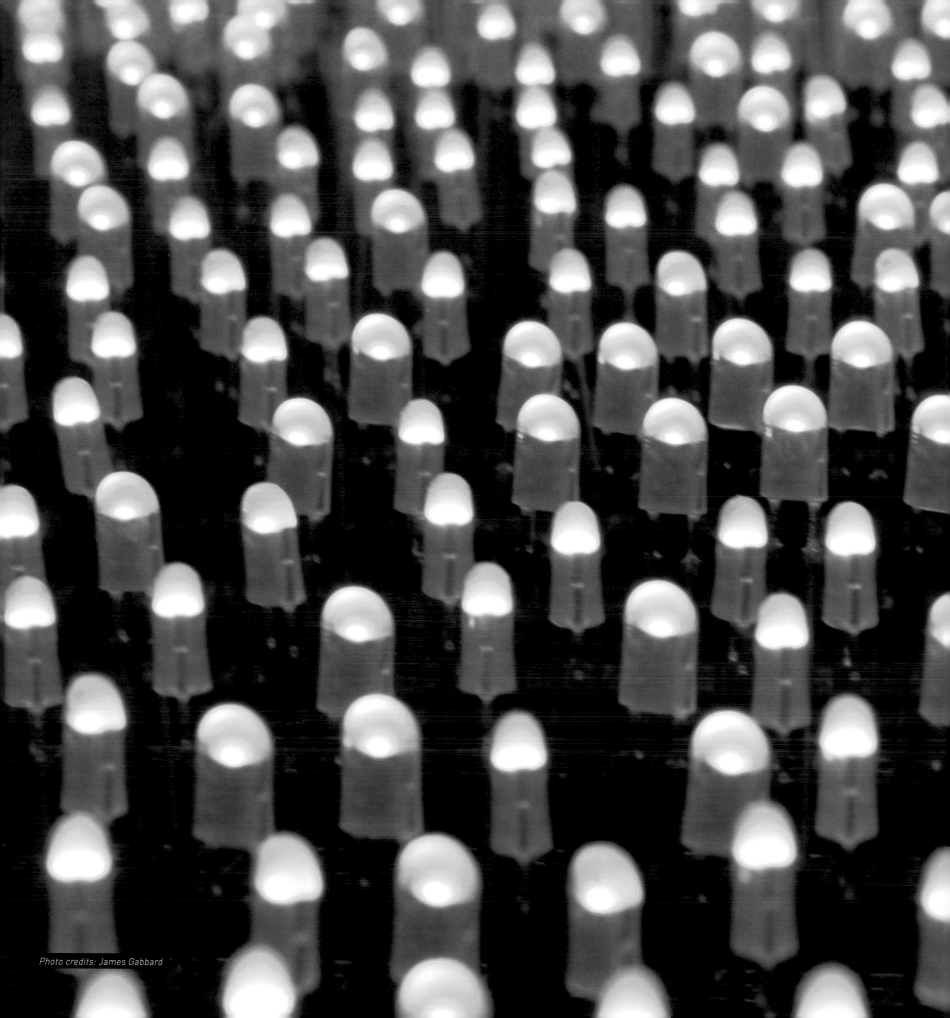

Photo credits: James Gabbard

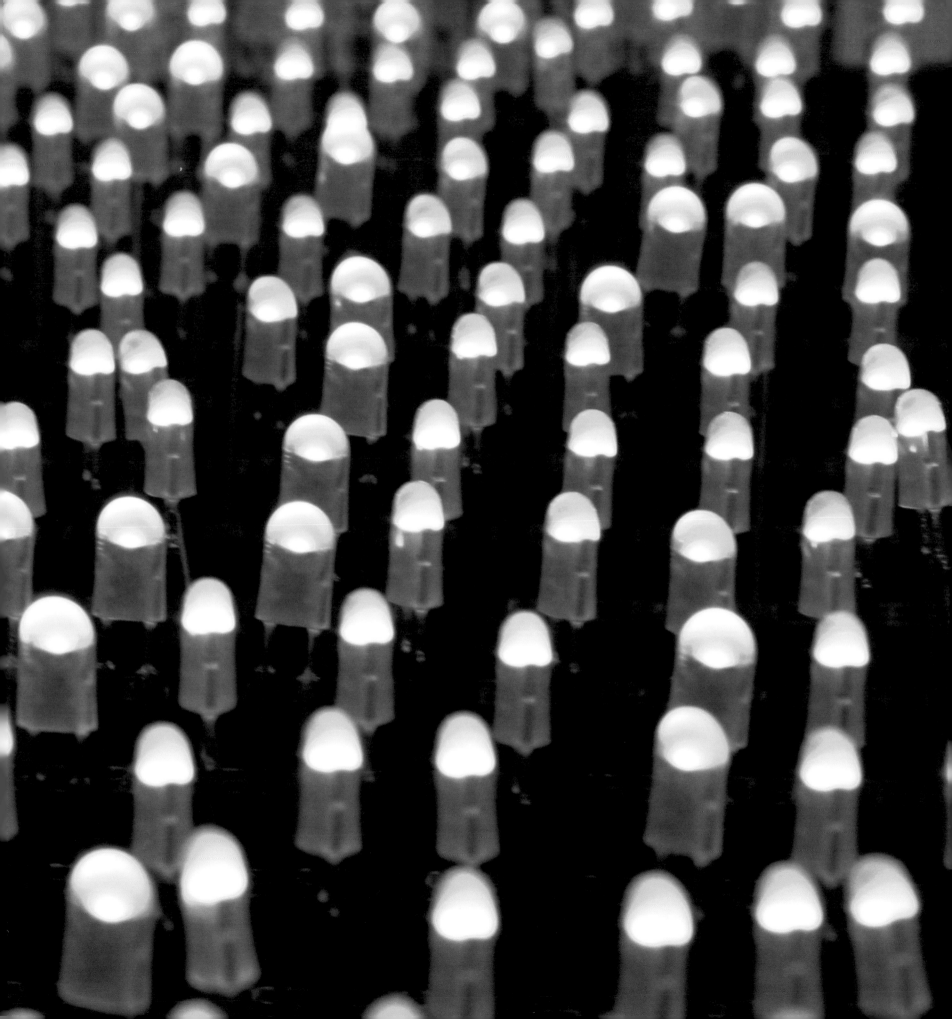

# ART

By using low and high technology, artists and designers can create projects that are both inspiring and fulfilling.

For centuries, we have been fascinated by the interplay between light and darkness. We've experimented with sculptures, architecture, stained glass, zoetropes and painting, and our curiosity still hasn't ended. Many visual art-forms like film, photography, computer and new media have also used light in one way or another. And as technology advanced to artificial lighting, light became critical for artistic expression.

Great designers absorb scientific developments and apply them to our everyday life. For many lighting designers and luminous artists around the world, the introduction of LED lighting provides a fresh palette for their work.

There are several innate capabilities of LED that allow a creator to have more options, control and flexibility during the design process.

- The impressive palette of LED display technologies enable 4.4 trillion colors, which can be manipulated using digital programing system interfaces.

- Its powerful brightness qualities allow it to be the only efficient digital visual medium visible under bright sunlight, making it ideal for outdoor installations.

- The modular capability of LED lights allows the display surface to be assembled in any size, resolution and configuration, enabling a versatile, digital platform that can be created in previously impossible architectural situations.

- An LED unit is very compact and can fit into almost any space and orientation. Its compact and solid state aspects allow the light to be implemented in any environment as well as industrial design.

- LEDs dissipate very little heat so they can be installed with other sensitive materials.

- LEDs have no ultraviolet or infrared, unless specified.

- The response time is much quicker than traditional lighting technology.

- The digital nature of this semi-conductor technology allows designers to control this advanced technology with endless possibilities. The sky is the limit.

We can now program and create appearance and behavior to almost any state imaginable. With the advancement of computer, interactive and robotic technologies, luminous objects have an essentially limitless well of ideas for research and development. With LED technology, artists and designers are now ready to accommodate almost any kind of spatial, technological, structural and architectural demand.

However challenges still exist, although they are not scientific, technological or even functional. The true challenge to achieving good design and artwork will always be of a creative and aesthetic nature. Originality and great conceptual designs are still key to building any true luminous invention.

Artists and designers are only now scratching the surface of this "blue ocean" technology, knowing that one day soon a new lighting paradigm will be on the horizon. We are still only seeing just the tip of this technological iceberg — how exciting is that?

**ART**

# Erwin Redl

*Photo credits: Max Spitzenberger*

-

Leo Villareal
Ingo Maurer
Teddy Lo
Swarovski
Anakin Koenig
Martin Richman
Louis M. Brill
Burning Man

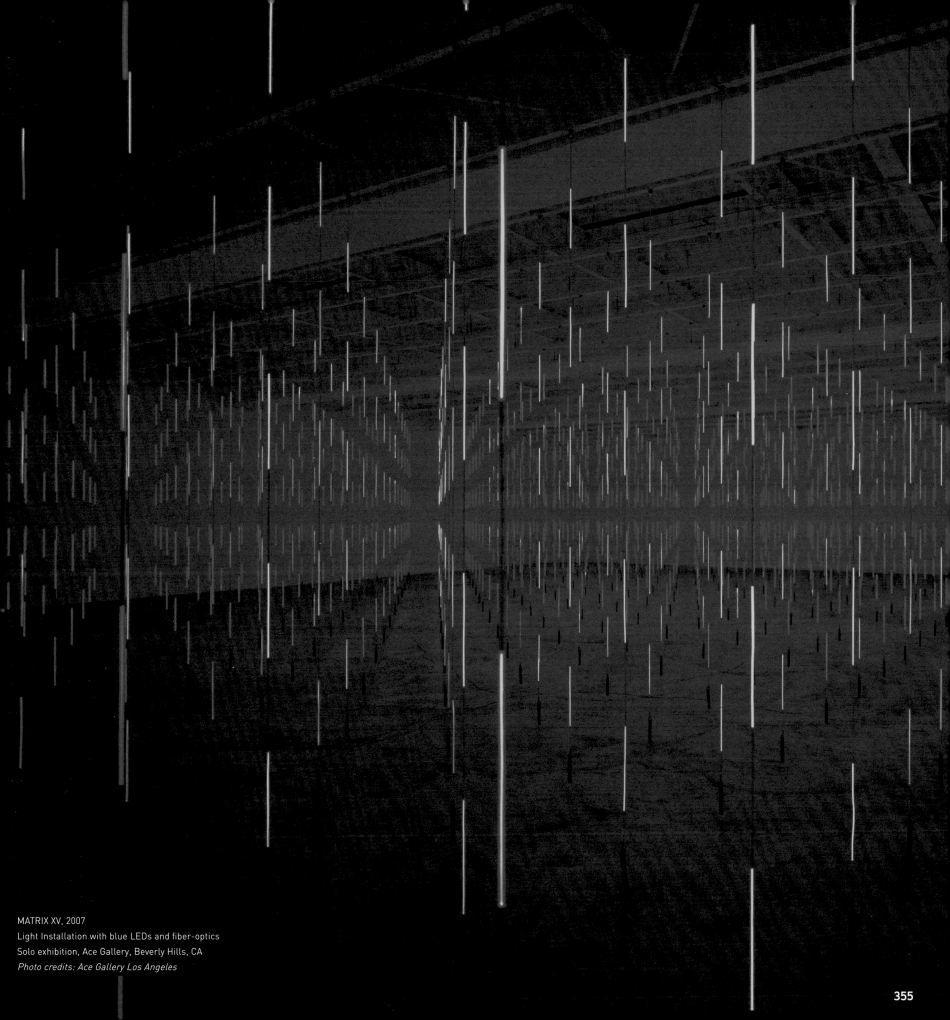

MATRIX XV, 2007
Light Installation with blue LEDs and fiber-optics
Solo exhibition, Ace Gallery, Beverly Hills, CA
*Photo credits: Ace Gallery Los Angeles*

ART
-
Erwin Redl

THE WORK OF ERWIN REDL IS INFLUENCED BY HIS CONCEPT OF "THE DIGITAL EXPERIENCE." HIS VARIOUS ARTISTIC MEDIA ENGAGES IN BINARY LOGIC WITH ITS NARROW SET OF SELF-IMPOSED RULES IN ALGORITHMS. HIS LARGE-SCALE LED INSTALLATIONS ARE THE RESULTS OF TRANSLATING VIRTUAL REALITY AND 3D MODELS INTO ARCHITECTURAL ENVIRONMENTS.

DUE TO ITS ARCHITECTURAL DIMENSION NATURE, VIEWERS SIMPLY BEING "PRESENT" WILL REVEAL ITS VISUAL CHARACTERISTIC IN CONJUNCTION WITH THEIR PHYSICAL MOTION AND THE PASSAGE OF TIME.

"MATRIX XVII" - a permanent light installation with white and blue LEDs at Centennial Towers in South San Francisco, United States
*Photo credits: Erwin Redl*

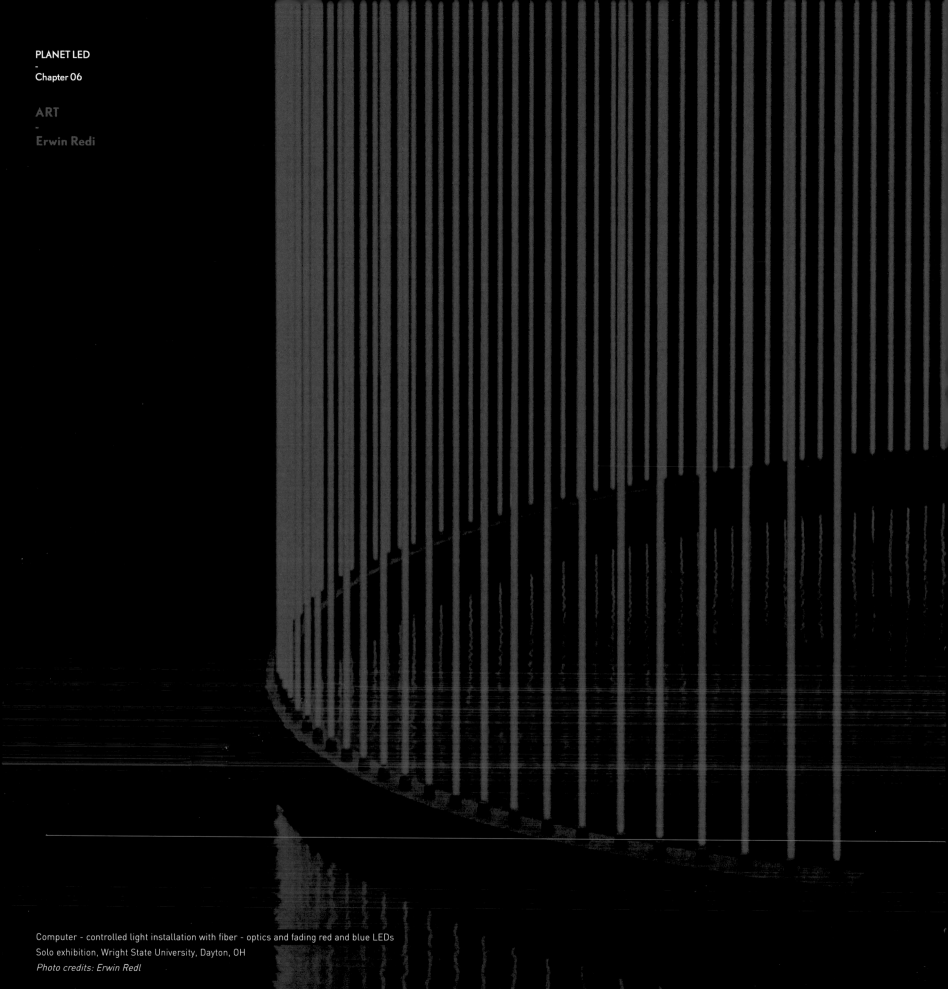

Computer - controlled light installation with fiber - optics and fading red and blue LEDs
Solo exhibition, Wright State University, Dayton, OH
*Photo credits: Erwin Redl*

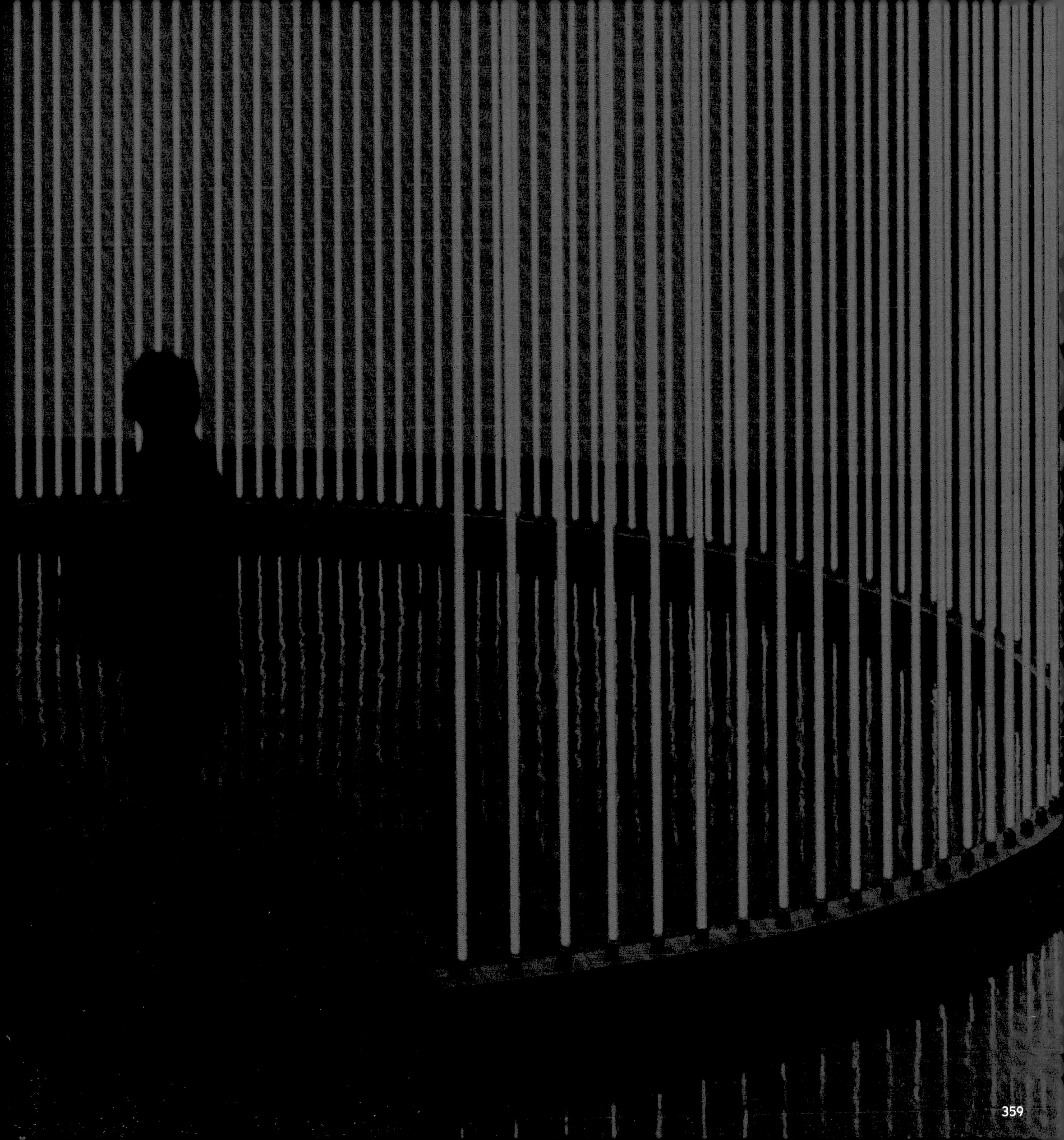

## ART
-
### Erwin Redl

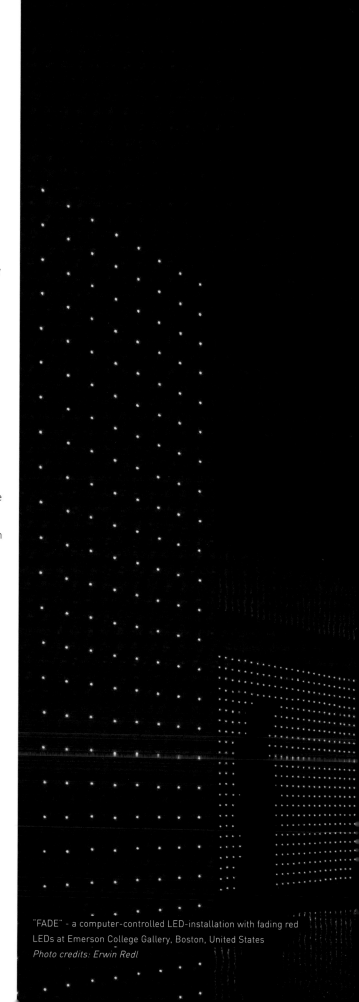

**How do you respond to the label "mental abstraction artist?" What message do you hope to send out to aspiring artists?**
-

I have to admit that I've never heard this term to classify art or my work.

Having said that, I think it actually describes my art quite well because I start with pretty abstract ideas. Not abstract in the sense of "concept art," but abstract in a sense of structural or proportional ideas that I express in a very sensual way.

It is important to note that abstraction in general has always been considered something cold or purely intellectual. I consider abstraction as something that is quite different, something extremely sensual or, if you prefer a more corporeal notion, goose bump-worthy.

**Your choice of experiments questions our understanding of architectural installations. How do you feel your art reaches out to society?**
-

Our perception of space has changed radically over the last decade, mostly through the introduction of virtual spaces into our visual culture. My work is exactly situated at the specific point where the experience of virtual spaces is brought back into the perception of real, architectural space. Parts of my artist's statement, which you can read above, reflect on this explicit condition.

**What modern icons or movements inform your art?**
-

I am extremely influenced by abstract painters like Barnett Newman and Agnes Martin, conceptual artists like Sol LeWitt; minimalists such as Donald Judd, Carl Andre and Fred Sandback; and of course icons of light art, especially James Turrell and Robert Irwin.

At the same time, contemporary music plays a big role in my life — above all the European modernists: Gyorgy Ligeti, Luigi Nono and Pierre Boulez, and the American minimalists Steve Reich and LaMonte Young. The German band Kraftwerk and the Japanese sound artist Ryoji Ikeda are equally important to me.

Of course there are also extremely relevant influences from architects like Tadao Anda and Zaha Hadid.

"FADE" - a computer-controlled LED-installation with fading red LEDs at Emerson College Gallery, Boston, United States
*Photo credits: Erwin Redl*

I'd like use a quote from *Chamber Music* magazine by Frank J Oteri entitled: "Again and Again and Again." It reviews Robert Fink's book *Repeating Ourselves: American Minimal Music as Cultural Practice*. The quote is quite long but in order to emphasize the last sentence I've capitalized it:

> Fink's premise is that both minimalism and disco use repetition
> to reject the teleological trajectory — the feeling that the music
> is going somewhere — that was at the heart of tonal music not
> only in the western classical tradition but in pop and rock. But
> unlike the anti-teleology of avant-garde music — which to the
> uninitiated often sounds like it's going nowhere — MINIMALISM,
> LIKE DISCO IS IN A PERPETUAL STATE OF CLIMAX.

### How does your choice of material match your stylistic lexicon?
-

My choice of material — LEDs — was made from a structural and conceptual point of view. They symbolize the pixel of the computer screen and are the only (almost) economically feasible single wavelength light source.

Because of this limitation and a further restriction to exclusively employ LED grid structures, I opened up stylistic possibilities that would not have otherwise been available.

Within those restricted parameters another aesthetic world unfolds, almost limitless not unlike the restricted parameters of sophisticated games like chess.

### What is the role of an installation such as Matrix X?
-

There are certainly different shades of "installation-dom" in my oeuvre. Some pieces are more "flat" such as MATRIX I, some physically inhabit a three-dimensional environment in a very radical (and democratic?) way such as MATRIX II and MATRIX XV.

The flat, wall-based work is seen in a more painterly fashion, almost purely visual with the audience fixed to a certain viewpoint and squinting their way through perception. Even in these works the regularity of the grid and the intensity of the lights often cause whiteout phenomena.

For works like MATRIX II and MATRIX XV I employ the term "fully immersive." Those room-filling pieces are of a different nature. Seeing them is only a small part of the experience since a single viewpoint within those spaces can not give you the adequate view of the piece. Only corporeal motion and the subsequent discovery of all aspects of the space (visual, corporeal, acoustic, social and so on) slowly reveal the nature of the piece.

Those aspects are highly subjective, based on private, individual memories of the viewer, yet they are experienced in a communal setting which leads to often very surprising interactions between strangers during exhibitions.

The term installation applies to all my work. Simply by the radiating, active nature of light art it inhabits space radically different from traditional sculpture.

An interesting aspect in that regard is Dan Flavin. His early work is purely sculptural but once the entirely new possibilities of light as a medium became clear a radical shift to a new perception of space was obvious. That is when his work suddenly turned from sculpture to installation

### What does the title of this work represent to you?
-

My titles are simple descriptions of the physical appearance of the work. They have no deeper meaning (nor does my work).

I emphasize the most important feature of the work. For example, the MATRIX series employs exclusively unadorned grids, the FADE series uses slow brightness or color fades, and the FLOW series displays a flowing movement, the SPEED SHIFT series juxtaposes movements of different speed.

**ART**
-
**Erwin Redl**

Computer-controlled Light Installation with fading red LEDs
Solo exhibition, Ace Gallery, Beverly Hills, CA
*Photo credits: Ace Gallery Los Angeles*

**What considerations do you explore within the creative process of your work?**
-
My drawings are simple structures manifested on paper.

A single abstract idea is painstakingly executed almost without leaving any room for individualistic expression of the artist beyond the initial concept. Yet the artistic act of creating the drawings myself is important — despite the fact that their minimal aesthetic would lend itself to print making.

Submitting my artistic expression to a strict geometric vocabulary becomes a major emotional force behind these works. The reduction of the field of operation to very precise and smooth pencil and ink work becomes the springboard to an increase in the depth of perception.

To verbally describe the drawings can be very simple. For example, a certain amount of lines, circles or other basic shapes, but it barely touches the visual and corporeal impact of seeing the work. By consciously keeping the narrative, verbally descriptive approach extremely understated, the experience of the work is re-situated on a non-narrative abstract level.

The conceptual methodology of my drawings constitutes a clear link to my large-scale installations. The work on paper offers a laboratory for structural experiments without the obstacles of large-scale production logistics.

**Other than drawings, what else is involved?**

-

I use programs like Maya, 3D Studio Max and MicroStation (something like AutoCAD on steroids). It is the interface and the final result that interests me — the final result being limited to wire frames.

I am definitely not interested in highly rendered environments or 3D architectural simulations but the abstract language of (mostly) simple line-based renderings of early computer games, videos or movies: Tron or the music, video and performance work of Kraftwerk.

The influence of "code" is both literal and metaphorical. For example, some installations like MATRIX XVI are literally created on a spreadsheet using a simple controlled random function.

The same is true for SPEED SHIFT which also incorporates sound (it uses a more complex iterative computer algorithm changing the speed of the movement slowly over time). Other pieces employ code more in a metaphorical or aesthetic manner without actually using computer programing, at least not beyond simple utilization of CAD programs and spreadsheets in the production process.

Most installations of mine are conceived as modular systems (I call them "Lego blocks") which have a certain flexibility both in scale as well as aesthetic possibilities.

MATRIX I is simply defined as a square grid of green LEDs. Once this basic module is established, extremely different versions start to flourish. If you look at MATRIX I's images on my website (www.paramedia.net) you see astonishingly different possibilities.

This second step, applying the module to a given space, is an extremely intuitive process. It almost always requires my corporeal presence in that particular environment. I have to experience its unique atmosphere myself in order to make a valid artistic statement with my work.

**In your artist's statement you refer to "second skin." Can you explain this term?**

-

Our "first skin" is our human skin and clothing, and that defines our corporeality as an individual. Architecture, or space in general, is our "second skin" and defines our corporeality in a social context, as communal beings.

My work acts as an extreme form of second skin by radically changing the environment and providing a very strong context that almost forces the viewer to transcendent his or her individual self. People act extremely different in my installations.

They are outside their usual social context. It certainly has to do with my abstract aesthetic, which a lot of viewers relate to computer or video games. The audience acts like being "only" in a virtual world thus loosing their "normal" social inhibitions. This is especially obvious in fully immersive installations like MATRIX II or MATRIX XV.

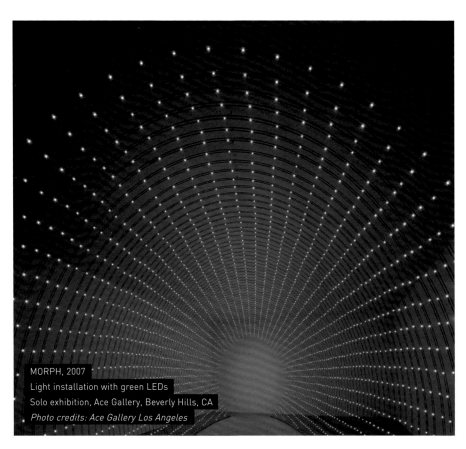

MORPH, 2007
Light installation with green LEDs
Solo exhibition, Ace Gallery, Beverly Hills, CA
*Photo credits: Ace Gallery Los Angeles*

**ART**

Erwin Redl
# Leo Villareal
-

## LEO VILLAREAL
-

Ingo Maurer
Teddy Lo
Swarovski
Anakin Koenig
Martin Richman
Louis M. Brill
Burning Man

ART
-
Leo Villareal

**LEO VILLAREAL IS AN AMERICAN ARTIST LIVING AND WORKING IN NEW YORK CITY. HIS WORK COMBINES LED LIGHTS AND ENCODED COMPUTER PROGRAMING TO CREATE ILLUMINATED MEDIA DISPLAYS. HE IS KNOWN FOR HIS SCULPTURES AND ARCHITECTURAL WORKS. HIS STUDIES AND EXPLORATION IN SELF-GENERATING PATTERNS THROUGH THE "GAME OF LIFE" THEORY IS ENGAGING AND FASCINATING.**

**Why does LED lighting appeal to you?**
-

I studied installation sculpture at college and then became interested in technology in the early 1990s. I began working with light in 1997, initially with strobe lights and then light bulbs. I was attracted to LEDs because of the very wide range of colors that mixing red, green and blue provide. I was also interested in the durability of the LED and its ability to be sequenced.

LEDs have allowed me to make artworks that are fundamentally digital but do not have to be presented on screens or as projection. I can make my own displays in any size, which have a potent presence and that viewers can interact with in the same way they experience painting and sculpture.

With LEDs, my work can come out of the dark rooms it was generally sequestered in and be displayed along side more traditional forms.

**How much of your artistic meaning is derived from technology?**
-

I use technological tools and processes to create my work and I could not do what I do without computers and code. When someone looks at my work, I want them to have an experience. It's not about technology but about responding to sequenced light. All wires, computers and other equipment are hidden and what is presented is the visual manifestation of the programing .

My work is abstract and I do not use words or images. Viewers are presented with information that they absorb and from which they make meaning.

I am interested in pattern recognition and the brain's hard-coded ability to match what we see with what we know. Often the information being transmitted is ambiguous and there is no right answer to what it is.

There is a magic to this process of discovery with open-ended work that is hard to pin down. Because of this elusive quality, I am sure interpretations of the work will continue to evolve over time.

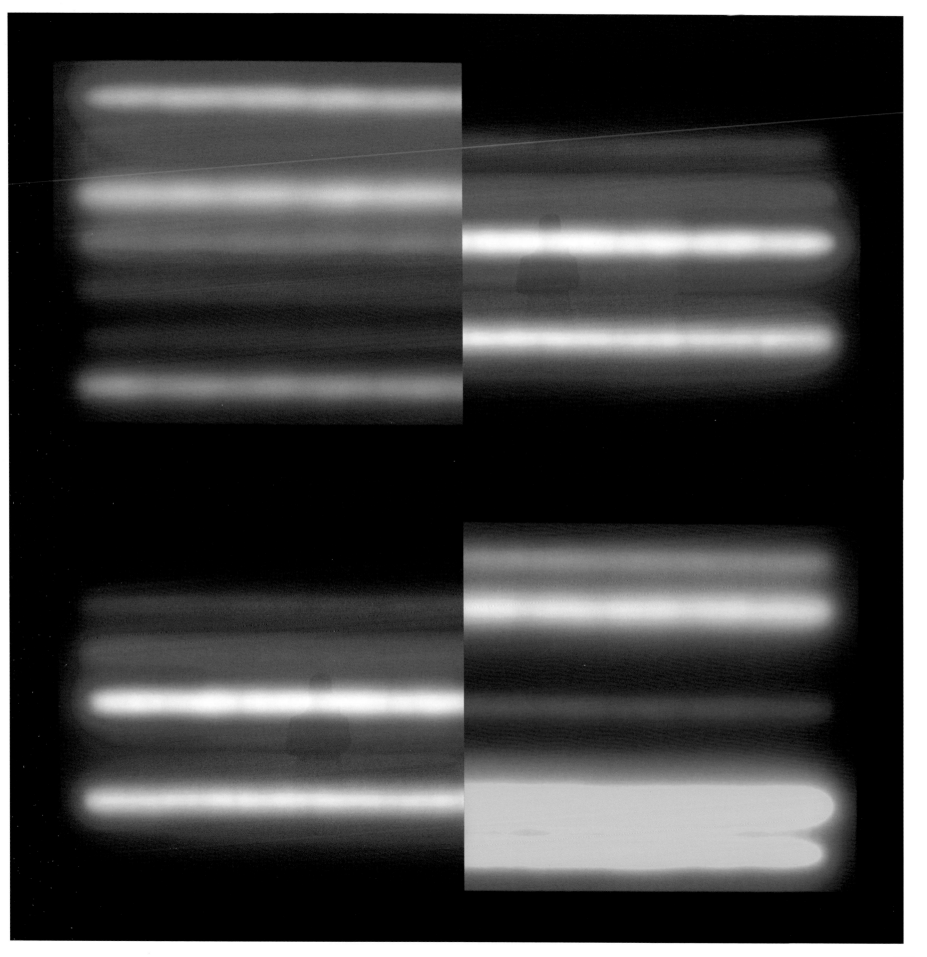

367

## ART
-
**Leo Villareal**

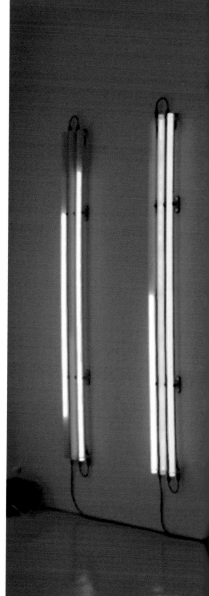

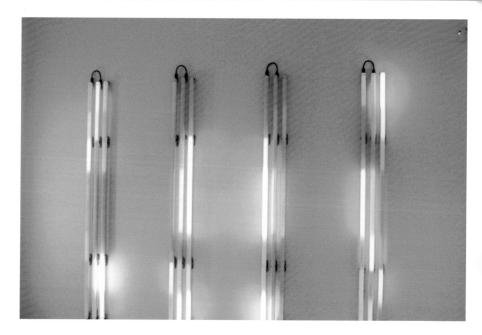

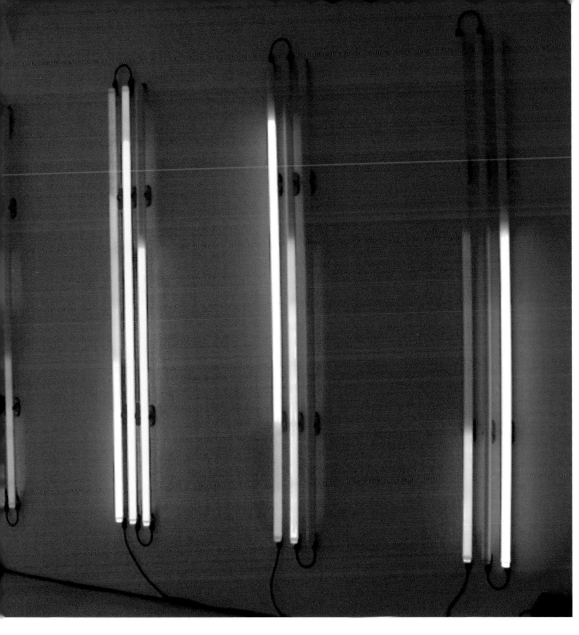

**You have previously expressed an affinity with the laws of physics. What is the influence of natural order in your work?**

-

Recently, I have begun to integrate Newton's Laws into the code that I use to make my work. A pixel may have a certain weight and travel at a specific velocity. When it encounters another element, there is a reaction.

Gravity, air resistance and viscosity are parameters that give a richness to the patterning. Again, we discover something we know from our everyday world and can see even in a 20-by-20 pixel display.

**Do you feel the synthetic nature of technology creates something organic in your art?**

-

Studying the underlying structures in natural systems like cloud formations, water currents and star clusters have inspired my patterning. I have managed to synthesize these elements and evoke them in my work. The very low resolution I work at requires a different approach; simply down-sampling a video does not work. Each pixel matters and must be used efficiently.

**What types of underlying rules do you take into consideration?**

Mathematician John Conway's *Game of Life* has been a great inspiration to me. His cellular automata program exhibits very complex patterns derived from simple rules.

Sometimes the patterns look like something found in nature like an ant colony. Certain forms can even replicate themselves sharing properties of advanced biological systems. Other times the patterns form structures that function as the logic gates of a simple computer. Conway's rules thus become a common denominator between the organic and the synthetic.

**Logistically, what are the differences between working on site specific and *objets d'art*?**

-

I make things that span a wide range of scale. From something that fits in the palm of your hand to arrays of lights that cover entire buildings. Certainly as the work increases in scale, it requires a much larger team and budget to implement.

The complexity can be daunting but the finished products make it well worth it. Regardless of scale, each piece has its own "personality" and set of attributes for viewers to discover.

## ART
-
**Leo Villareal**

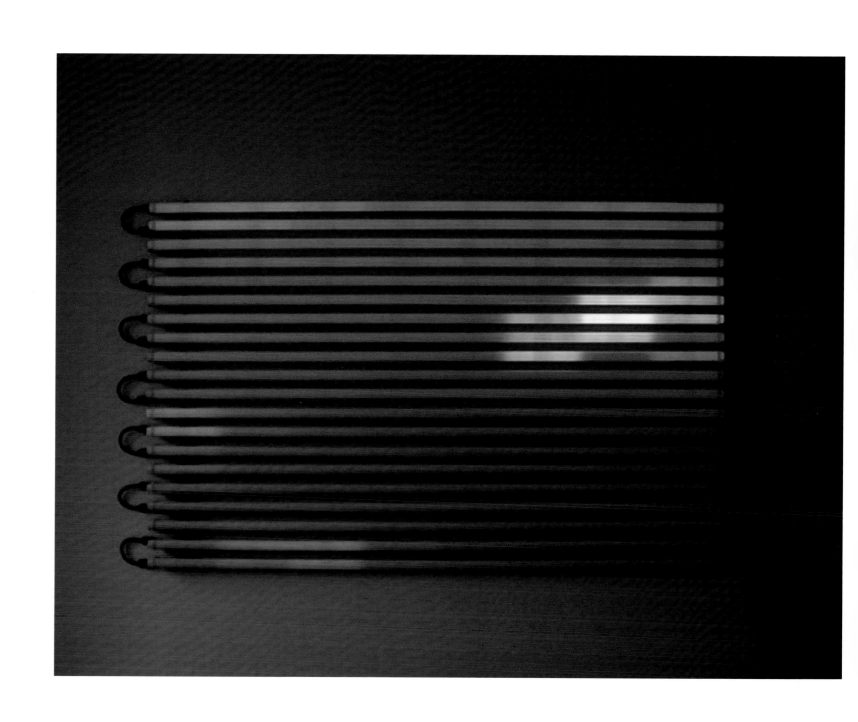

**Do you feel you contribute to the visual landscape of the world and its public arena?**
-

My site-specific works are responsive to their context. I always start with what exists and how people use a space. I ask questions like, "what was the intention of the architect?" and "what systems are at work?" and "how can I best integrate an artwork?"

My desire is to add another layer that activates and energizes. The goal is for the finished product to "work" and not be overwhelmed by any one part.

It is almost like creating a complex musical instrument that when played well, adds to the overall composition, each part augmenting the other.

**ART**

Erwin Redl
Leo Villareal

# Ingo Maurer

*Photo credits: Fico, Paris*

*INGO MAURER*
-

Teddy Lo
Swarovski
Anakin Koenig
Martin Richman
Louis M. Brill
Burning Man

ART
-
Ingo Maurer

**INGO MAURER IS A RENOWNED GERMAN INDUSTRIAL AND LIGHT FIXTURE DESIGNER. HIS COMPANY INGO MAURER GMBH SPECIALIZES IN THE DESIGN OF INTRIGUING LAMPS, LIGHT OBJECTS AND LIGHT INSTALLATIONS FOR PUBLIC AND PRIVATE SPACES.**

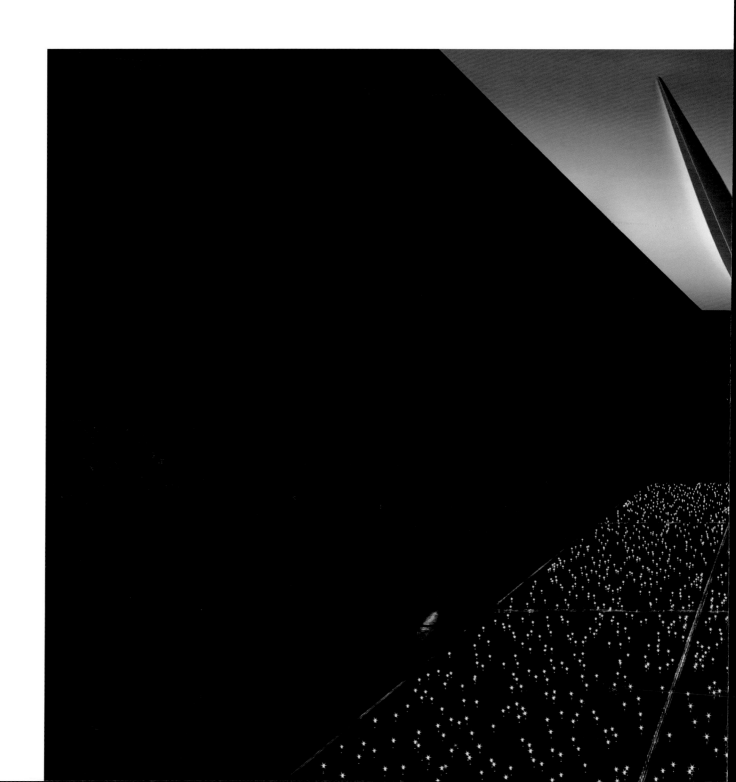

## ART
-
**Ingo Maurer**

**How do you feel the needs and notions of aesthetics have evolved?**
-

Developments and changes in technology always offer new chances that can lead to different aesthetics, which is good in contrast to the established.

**Many of your projects combine high and low technology. Are you addressing particular needs in our contemporary society?**
-

On one hand, it is a natural outcome of the process, on the other hand, low technology has a strong appeal to me.

But I don't want to disclose what's missing in the modern world, it's just that we use it, because we cannot find matchable so-called high-tech solutions for certain demands.

It's the ideas in addition to the technology that make us cutting-edge.

The LED wallpaper
consists of a plastic film
with conductive circuits
and is equipped
with monochrome LEDs
in white, red and blue.
The film is applied like an
conventional wallpaper.
The conductive material
is printed on the film
in three separately-
controllable circuits

ART
-
Ingo Maurer

**What influences your design process?**

-

Influences come through an open perception. The design process itself happens often while making tests with models and materials.

There's so much more about light than what we think it is, so it's a necessity to work on the real configuration, then you'll see.

**There is a growing market for design fixtures in the home. What principles relate to your work in terms of form and function?**

-

I think the coverage and diversity of our collection shows our approach, notably in form and function. There's nothing we're not interested in, and our success seems to prove that we're right.

**LED is a rapidly growing sector of technology — what appeals to you about it as a medium?**

-

Size, efficiency, versatility are welcome attributes, but it is also its different light generation and quality that open a lot of doors for ideas.

**What do you think the future of LED design?**

-

LEDs, as we know them now, are just the beginning of many interesting light components that will lead to exciting products.

Not long ago, for example, we launched the world's first OLED table lamp. And we have many more things in the pipeline...

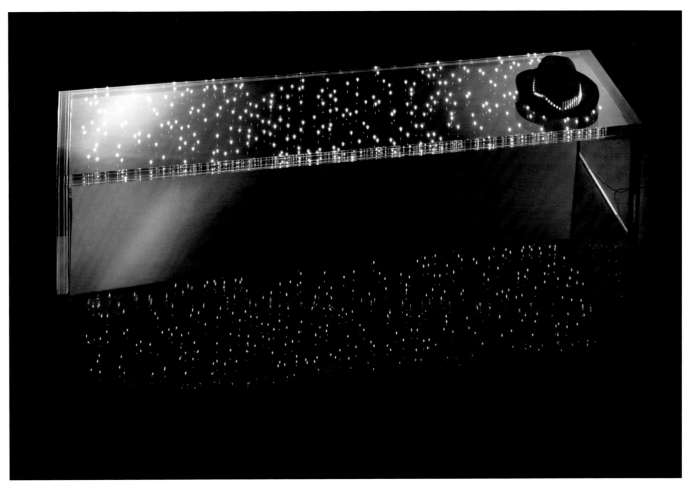

Erwin Redl
Leo Villareal
Ingo Maurer

# Teddy Lo

-
Swarovski
Anakin Koenig
Martin Richman
Louis M. Brill
Burning Man

**ART**
-
**Teddy Lo**

Phaeodaria

**ART**
-
**Teddy Lo**

TEDDY LO IS AN LED ARTIST BASED IN HONG KONG AND NEW YORK. HE'S KNOWN FOR HIS LUMINOUS WORK IN THE "TECH-ART" SCENE AND INTERNATIONAL ART CIRCUITS. HIS BACKGROUND IN ART DIRECTION IN ADVERTISING AND LIGHTING EVOLVES HIS WORKS AROUND CONCEPTUAL, VISUALLY DYNAMIC AND INTRICATE FORMS. HIS WORK INVOLVES LED INSTALLATIONS, PERFORMANCE ARTS, SCULPTURES AND INTERACTIVE ARTS WITH THE INTERPLAY WITH LOW-TECH AND ADVANCED LUMINOUS, COMMUNICATION AND INDUSTRIAL MANUFACTURING TECHNOLOGIES.

Untitled

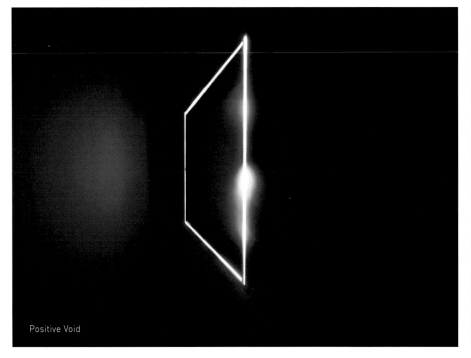

Positive Void

### When did you first come into contact with LEDs?
-

At a young age because my father was in the technological manufacturing business and I remember seeing small samples at home. But I didn't start working with them until art school when I was looking for a medium for my contemporary fine arts project.

Through my research, and as I found out more and more about this technology, I discovered that LEDs are very environmentally friendly and versatile. An LED's physical form is very compact compared to other lighting technologies and the color palette — thanks to computer programing — stretches into millions, trillions. So that's why I love to work with it.

### What differentiates your work from that of other light artists?
-

I guess my background in advertising as a creative art director and master in lighting degree makes me different from everybody else. I always try to mix the conceptual and technical genres and always push the boundaries. I try never to replicate what others have done unless I know how to bring it to a new level of creation.

With my training and with the support that I have built for myself — either working with performance artists, engineers or programers — my concept and execution are unique from other artists working with the same media. I do a lot of research so I do get much of my inspiration from my peers — the kind of work that you can see throughout this book.

**ART**
-
**Teddy Lo**

**Does an LED medium allow artists to be more creative?**
-

One of the advantages of LEDs and one of the reasons that I choose to work with them is because they use a semi-conductor technology. That versatility means that an LED can be integrated into many different electronic components and applications.

The advancement of different programing and system controls gives me greater flexibility to create different forms with different performance and behavior. The solid state and physical size of LEDs also provide me with versatile options to build either massive geometric shapes or small linear intricate sculptural forms. This technology is truly a godsend.

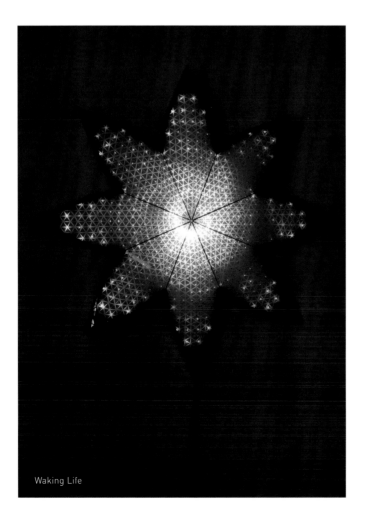

Waking Life

**Which of your projects are you most proud of?**
-

One of the best examples of my work is a project is one I called "Bacillus." It's named after what is supposedly the oldest form of bacteria which scientists found in an ancient dried salt bed.

I've always liked producing sculptures and during the first few years I worked with LEDs I tried to create one. But most of the LEDs that you can buy off the shelf are flat-surfaced and geometric. So after a year or two I kind of felt bored and wanted to push the idea further and make it more interesting by making an LED project "organic."

When I thought about the concept "organic," I thought about nature. And what is "nature?" I thought perhaps plants or trees or flowers but after I explored further I realized that nature was bacteria and after some more research I found out about Bacillus. From that platform I found an image and then with some creativity I drew out the form in a 3D program. I then blew the image up and tried to tackle the problem of actually how to build it.

One of the toughest challenges was how to implement a grid form of LED display on to an organic surface. I realized that in nature, everything that is organic, is composed of triangular forms. With triangles you can lay out the surface of any shape and any form. From that I started designing what I think was the first flexible printed circuit board with LEDs and video circuitry.

It took me three or four months to complete the process, with the help of an iron welder in Brooklyn. When the prototype was finished I realized what I'd accomplished. It was one of the first organic sculptures ever created with full-on video technology. It was big challenge for me.

From the standpoint of both electrical technicality and also structural and modular integration, it's a good example of how I solved the many creative problems.

It took me about two years in research and exploration to produce the second prototype, which was much more challenging because this version had to sustain outdoor environments, be water- and vandal-proof. I was very excited to go through this next stage in the creative process.

Gon Kirin @ Burningman Festival 2012
*Photo credits: Cliff Baise*

389

## ART

**Teddy Lo**

**What is the future of LED? How will the technology develop in the next 10 years?**

I always compare the speed of LED development to Moore's Law. There are many similarities between the development of the silicon chip and LED brightness in relation to cost and efficacy.

I think that with the current trend and the speed of how the industry is currently expanding, in the next decade, a larger percentage of the population will use LEDs for environmental reasons. And if you look long-term, LEDs are much more economical and can save users a lot of energy costs.

LEDs are slowly being adopted by offices and the next step will be the integration of LED lighting systems in the home. As I already mentioned, because it's a semi-conductor technology, many of the systems will be interactive and automatic.

What I would like to see is continued increases in LED efficacy, the efficiency of light bulbs. I think we are already getting really close to surpassing the efficacy of other lighting technologies. As it continues to evolve, we are reaching a stage where we haven't ever seen a light source that's as powerful. An LED can be so small and be powered with such a small amount of energy and yet be so bright.

I foresee that lighting fixtures everywhere will be very different in 10 years time. Many things that you wouldn't expect will be a light source and even a media outlet.

**How are LED advances affecting your work?**

A lot of the work I am currently involved in tries to project information. The information can be something visual through an LED panel or an LED-fixture installation — but I try to do that artistically or, as I call it, more "art directed."

That means that my work is either juxtaposed with a spatial background or seamlessly immersed into a physical reality, without being intrusive.

Right now, if you go out on the street and you see a big LED sign, many people may consider it "in your face." But in the future, when technology advances, maybe the same information could be projected more subtly — on to a handrail or on the pavement, even embedded within a window. Information can and should be embedded gracefully into an environment.

**You describe yourself an "artist." How does that fit in with your business?**

I'm kind of like a hybrid, because my training is in advertising. I try to create a message or imagery using an art director's process. For me, when I create a media message I consider it art, although I know many people would see it as a commercial product.

Anything that you put your heart and mind into it, and when someone comes up with a creation that touches your heart, that can be "art." It is just the same with a lighting installation.

When someone designs lighting for a commercial building or interactive LED installations, do you think of it as an art form? Many people would say no. But what about the lighting at a building like La Louvre in Paris and Millennium Park in Chicago? I think that's definitely artistic.

**Does that mean that art and function are merging?**

-

I think that has always been the case, especially for lighting design. But when you walk into a space, I think that less than one percent of people would even think twice and try and experience the lighting and say: "Ah, the designer did a great job integrating daylight with artificial lighting."

In the future, if the execution of LED media within an environment is done skillfully and with an interesting concept, then lighting will be considered more and more as art.

**So is LED changing that?**

-

Yes. When you work with LEDs, suddenly you have a brand new color palette and brushes which gives you greater amounts of freedom and almost any space can be like a playground for a lighting designer or artist.

LEDs also provide more color temperature, color rendering, better human factors, solid state, longer lifespan and flexibility in digital control. A lighting designer therefore has more tools to work and play with to make things more engaging and interactive. The game of lighting design has stepped up to another level where the rules are all changing.

The efficacy of lighting is getting into a theoretical threshold. In the coming years, lighting technology development will enter an era that simply hasn't been imagined before. I am particularly anxious to see how this plays out in the near future.

SOL: The Constant series

**ART**
-
**Teddy Lo**

**You claim that you are influenced by artists like Monet, Dali and Warhol…**
-

Because I came to the lighting "game" comparatively late in my early career and artistic development, these influences come from my art school days. But how those painters are connected to my work with LEDs these days is because of my father, Paul Lo. He is someone who strays from the traditional.

Even though he is foremost a businessman, he always comes up with unexpected solutions and unorthodox ideas. My father has been in the technology industry ever since he was 14 years old, so that has had a big influence on me. A big part of my inspiration is from him. It just makes it much easier and natural to integrate my artistic knowledge with technology.

So despite my love of artistic movements like surrealism, minimalism and contemporary arts, the fact that my father is a business visionary and inventor means that I get much of my passion from him.

Alarm of Hue

**What were the primary reasons for you publishing this book, PLANET LED?**
-

I feel that I'm very lucky to be in the position that I am — my company's knee-deep in the LED industry. With my background in art, technology and advertising I feel that I'm at the crossroads of the development of this exciting product.

My understanding of LED's influence is quite eclectic and I think that I have a particular insight as to where this technology is heading. I have found that many people with more limited knowledge have misunderstandings about LEDs so I think creating a book like this will inspire them. I also hope that the publication will speed up the LED revolution.

So many industries are, or could be, affected by LEDs and so many people want to find out more about the technology, either from a business, artistic or general interest point of view.

The LED industry at the moment is a "blue ocean" market. There is so much potential for growth, understanding and acceptance. I hope that this book will provide inspiration about where LED development is going and how it is evolving.

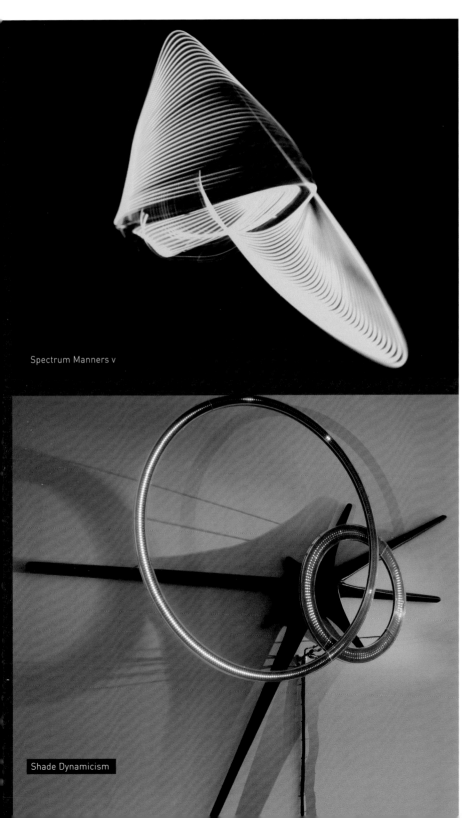

Spectrum Manners v

Shade Dynamicism

## Why LED?

-

I'm an environmentalist at heart and I want to be an artistic spokesperson for LED development. I'm promoting it by actually creating "the work" — I evolve my process each day to create LED-based intriguing and dynamic creative lighting or information solutions.

I devoted myself to the LED path because I realized I have stepped into something that has a huge market with creative potential. And yet all these endeavours can also have a much-needed positive impact on the world.

It is what the planet needs right now. LEDs can save the environment and I want to be a part of that force. In addition, the world has become a more visually compelling world.

My training in advertising design at the Art Center College of Design has helped me tremendously to strive to promote this disruptive technology and I love the challenge.

Besides the potential for a wide spectrum of applications, my work can also help reduce power consumption and build a greener world — and for me, that's a true calling. When I think about my responsibilities in this world, these are the things that keep me going.

**ART**

Erwin Redl
Leo Villareal
Ingo Maurer
Teddy Lo

# Swarovski

Nadja Swarovski
Vice-President
International Communications VP International Communications
-

*photo by Daniel King*

**SWAROVSKI** CRYSTAL PALACE
-
Anakin Koenig
Martin Richman
Louis M. Brill
Burning Man

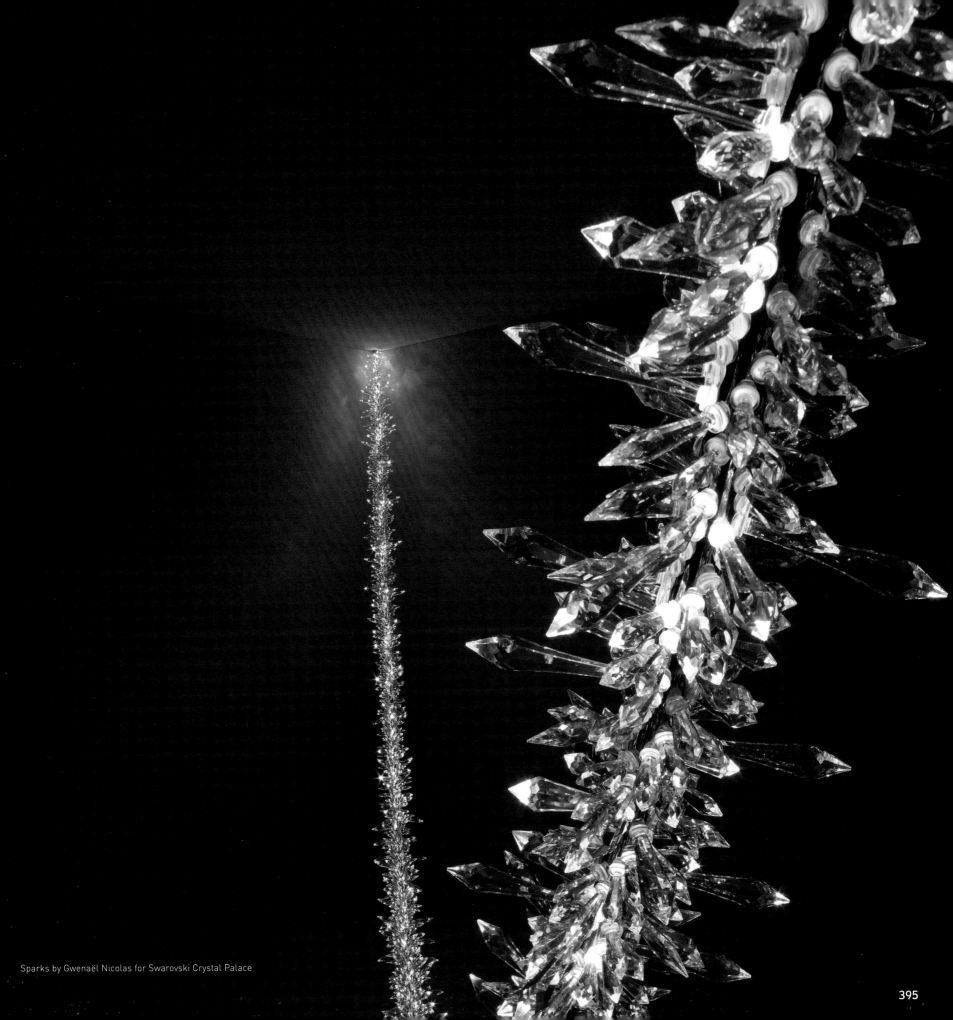

Sparks by Gwenaël Nicolas for Swarovski Crystal Palace

ART
-
Swarovski

SWAROVSKI IS A LEADING MANUFACTURER OF PRECISION CUT CRYSTAL AND IS THE FIRST BRAND TO USE LEDS AS PART OF ITS CRYSTAL-COMPONENT PRODUCT RANGE. SWAROVSKI CRYSTAL PALACE WORKS WITH SOME OF THE MOST FAMOUS DESIGNERS AND ARTISTS ACROSS THE GLOBE. SINCE 2002, THE COMPANY HAS CREATED FASCINATING INTERPRETATIONS OF LIGHTING FIXTURES WITH CRYSTALS AND LEDS FOR DECORATIVE LIGHTING SOLUTIONS. SWAROVSKI PROVIDES SPARKLING INSPIRATIONS FOR ARCHITECTS, INTERIOR AND LIGHTING DESIGNERS AND CUSTOMERS AROUND THE GLOBE.

Stellar by Tokujin Yoshioka

ART
-
Swarovski

**Why does Swarovski use LED technology?**
-

We want to provide new, innovative and the most energy-efficient solutions in lighting so we use LED technology extensively across a whole range of products.

**What do you see are the benefits of LEDs?**
-

Energy efficiency and longer lamp life. As well as greater color choices and better reliability, and the ability to instant switch the product on and off.

**What else can you tell us about Swarovski Crystal Palace?**
-

Every year Swarovski Crystal Palace invites a diverse group of emerging and established talent from the worlds of architecture, art, fashion and interior design to create signature interpretations of light and design using the emotive medium of cut crystal and the latest technology.

The designers we work with, such as Zaha Hadid, Tord Boontje, Ron Arad and Tom Dixon — to name just a few — push the boundaries of crystal to create contemporary interpretations of lighting and design.

**Over the years, what have been your signature pieces?**
-

Cascade by Vincent van Duysen; Lolita by Ron Arad; Blossom by Tord Boontje; Glitterbox by Georg Baldele; Ball by Tom Dixon; Morpheus by Yves Béhar; Amplify by Yves Behar; Stellar by Tokujin Yoshioka; and Sparks by Gwenaël Nicolas.

**At the moment, what are your most interesting projects?**
-

In 2010, Swarovski Crystal Palace presented exclusive selections of design collaborations at Salone Internazionale del Mobile, the International Furniture Fair of Milan, the largest decoration trade fair in the world. These included Amplify, Sparks, Stellar and Frost.

### "Amplify" by Yves Béhar

Yves Béhar combines the possibilities of technology with the inherent qualities of Swarovski crystal to create an understated low-energy and affordable chandelier called Amplify.

It consists of a series of deceptively simple sustainable paper lanterns shaped like crystals within which light is refracted from a real crystal, casting its patterns on the surface of the paper.

Béhar states: "We designed six shapes for the chandelier; each one carefully crafted to maximize the light output from the LED source and to beautifully reflect the effect of the light shining through the crystal. This effect can be seen on the faceted shade material, thus emulating the cut and reflective nature of the crystal inside. Each chandelier becomes its own large glowing crystal."

### "Sparks" by Gwenaël Nicolas

"I wanted to imagine a space with no gravity," explains Gwenaël Nicolas whose project consists of two separate designs. The first installation is almost "not an object anymore" where "crystal and light become life."

Nicolas has created a large, free-floating, transparent balloon filled with helium, in which floats a small crystal sculpture lit from within by a battery-powered LED. The balloon draws on NASA technology to enable it to be as thin and transparent as possible.

The LED light, emanating through the crystal, sets off a series of "sparks" which move as the balloon and crystal float. A separate design consists of a 12-meter crystal string, incorporating LED lighting, along which computer-programed light appears to dance. This is an eloquent work equally about the movement of light and the intrinsic beauty of the crystal: an elegant, minimal crystal necklace.

"Amplify" by Yves Béhar

### "Stellar" by Tokujin Yoshioka

Tokujin Yoshioka's 2010 work for Swarovski Crystal Palace is a one-meter diameter globe encrusted with Swarovski crystals and lit from within by powerful LEDs.

The globe is suspended in a stark, white, smoke-filled space in which it appears to float, casting bright beams of light which are caught in the smoke, creating a luminous star.

Stellar is set alongside a tank in which natural crystals grow into a twinned globe, an evolution of Yoshioka's 2008 work "Venus – Natural Crystal Chair" in which the chair – like Venus emerges from the water as crystals naturally grow on its frame.

"What is important to me is not just designing another new chandelier with crystals, but to incorporate the element of beauty born of coincidence and this was technically challenging because the unpredictable element found in nature had to be accurately re-expressed by human design," says Yoshioka.

### "Frost" by Vincent Van Duysen

Here, the designer has created a Swarovski crystal-encrusted forest of glowing beams. By using multiple elements, a wide variety of spatial compositions and dramatic architectural shapes can be created.

The installation for the 2010 Salone del Mobile in Milan is staged as a simple, mirrored field, with the refined single element multiplied in a never-ending series of reflections within a mirrored space.

The outer "crust" of randomly assorted, different sized crystals set into resin have a temptingly tactile quality while actually being quite rough to the touch. A thin glass panel is secured between the crystal exteriors, giving the "beams" their structure and rigidity while also acting as a vehicle for the LED lighting within.

As Van Duysen notes, "Crystals remind you of natural elements like water and ice, and allow you to bring in more poetic and emotional aspects to lighting design."

**ART**

Erwin Redl
Leo Villareal
Ingo Maurer
Teddy Lo
Swarovski

# Anakin Koenig

Anakin Koenig Airways
Artist and Founder
-

Martin Richman
Louis M. Brill
Burning Man

"Bracelet 2.0" - Collection of Richard and Lisa Baker. At Rupert
Ravens Gallery, New Jersey, United States

ART
-
Anakin Koenig

ANAKIN KOENIG IS A PERFORMANCE-SCULPTURE ARTIST WHO CREATES LARGE-SCALE INFLATABLE STRUCTURES. HIS TRANSFORMATIVE INSTALLATIONS ENGAGE ARCHITECTURAL SPACE AND CHALLENGE THE SOCIAL AND PSYCHOLOGICAL HORIZONS OF THE AUDIENCE.

HE FOUNDED ANAKIN KOENIG AIRWAYS IN 2001 (AKAIRWAYS) AND HIS WORK HAS BEEN PRESENTED IN A VARIETY OF CONTEXTS, FROM THE MUSEUM OF MODERN ART TO UNDERGROUND RAVES, FROM NASA TO THE WHITNEY BIENNALE. THE GROUP IS PREDOMINANTLY INTERESTED IN KINESIS, COLLABORATION, DIY, MODULARITY AND OPEN-SOURCE.

"Drop" at Burning Man, Black Rock Desert, Nevada, United States

## ART
-
**Anakin Koenig**

**Why do you choose inflatables as a medium?**
-

Both the economy and ecology of inflation fascinate me. Being able to generate a volume by controlling pressure — transferring air from one space to another —has an appealing simplicity.

Additionally, the primary material of my sculptures is available in quasi infinite quantity. That means that wherever I find myself I do not require anything to be manufactured or purchased, and that makes it very special to me. Some inflatables are not about the material that the membrane is made of, they are about air and how to visualize it.

**What sort of modern icons or movements influence your artistic endeavours?**
-

I find processes and methods of software development, open source in particular, inspiring. AKAirways strives to incorporate the collaborative aspect of open source development in its creations and in the way it thinks installation art.

Modularity, particularly that which places an emphasis on object-orientated software programing, is another source of inspiration. Questions of resilience are at the forefront of inflatable art practice, especially for outdoor presentations. Being able to replace a failing part can make huge difference.

Combining modularity with redundancy usually answers questions of resilience. Technical and conceptual concerns are intertwined here as finding such answers can make the difference between being and not being.

**How do these materials affect the style of your work?**
-

Atmosphere and presence more than style are at the core of our concerns. The choice of material is often dictated by the technique chosen to build a piece such as heat sealing, stitching or gluing.

**How does LED technology fit into your creations?**
-

I love LEDs! Cold light technology allows AKAirways to incorporate the light elements tightly on or inside the skin of our sculptures.

The precision of LEDs, the fact that this technology is mostly about dots rather than planes, allows us to surgically insert light in precise locations, sometimes using them sparingly, other times, creating low-resolution video screens.

LEDs are also an opportunity for us to collaborate with and learn from light artists. Several have become my friends over the years.

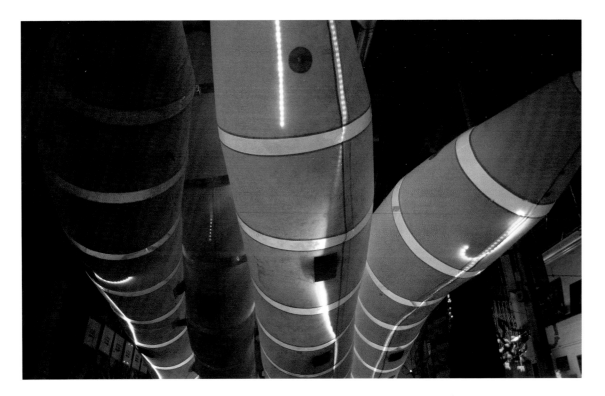

Cuddlefish is an array of inflatable tubes. Tubes are orange with rings of clear vinyl. Sequenced strings of light are installed inside each tube.

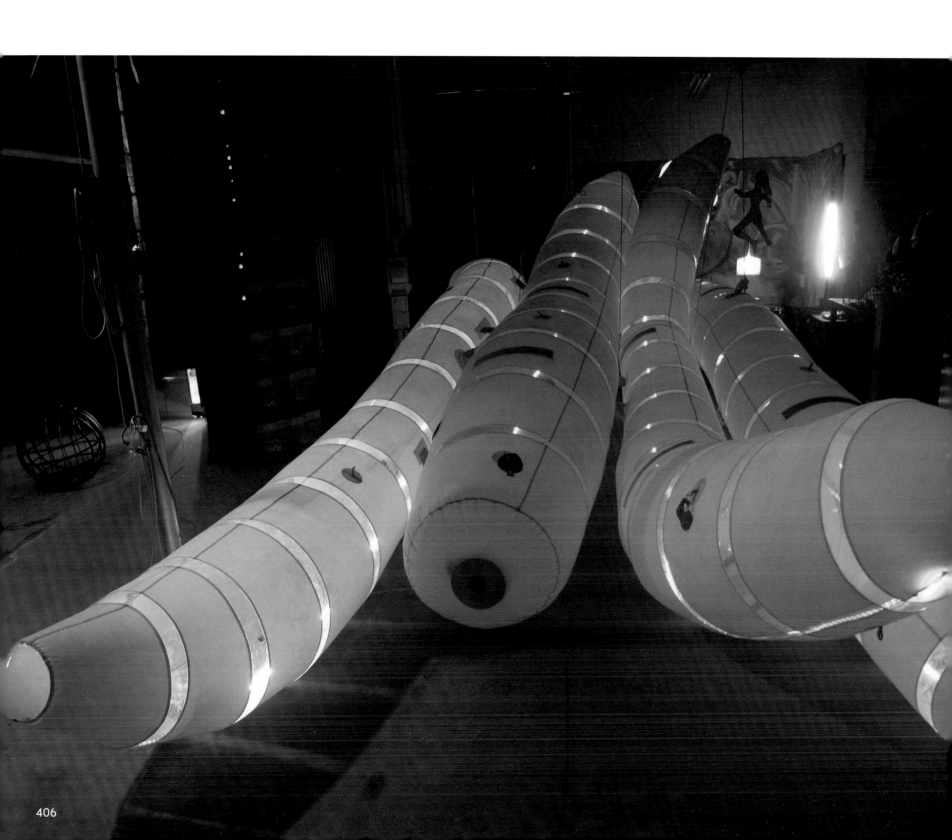

**Do you think LEDs have changed our creative landscapes?**
-

For several decades, I've wondered why more available public building walls and pavements (public), vehicle bodies and clothing (semi-public), and indoor walls and furniture surfaces (private) were not used as displays.

They have historically been used to display objects, banners, stickers and paintings, for instance, but they were not displays themselves.

LED technology is helping change that and adds intelligence to our worlds — public and private.

A future challenge, on the macro level of a city for instance, is going to be able to make informed decisions regarding the negative space, space voluntarily left without LEDs, that will hopefully be established so we can take a break from the light when we need or want to.

**What is the role of sculpture as it inhabits our 3D world?**
-
The role of sculpture is the same as the role of art. To open the mind.

**Traditionally, installation work inhabits our space and redefines it in new and exciting ways — how do you feel your work has achieved this?**
-

Large-scale pieces, on the verge between objects and architectures have the power to transform a space. Negative Shrink-Wraps is the name that we give to the most transformative pieces that AKAirways creates.

They are large indoor volumes made of polyethylene sheeting usually slightly smaller than the room in which they are inflated. The result is a womb-like space that vaguely inherits the proportions and details of the room.

The audience is invited to enter these sculptures that literally transform the physical space in which they are presented. Once inside, members of the audience find themselves surrounded by only one material: the polyethylene. At that moment, no other material can be seen by the participant. This is a unique situation, with no equivalent in our daily life. That leads to an array of reactions, sensations, feelings and questions. It is a simple gesture that instantly and abruptly takes the audience into an equivoque, stand-alone, world.

# Martin Richman

ART
-
Martin Richman

BRITISH-BORN ARTIST MARTIN RICHMAN HAS REALIZED LIGHTING PROJECTS IN A VARIETY OF LOCATIONS FROM THE UNDERSIDE OF BRIDGES IN HACKNEY TO THE TOWN CENTER IN BRISTOL TO A POWER STATION IN BIRMINGHAM. HE MAINTAINS A STRONG GALLERY PRACTICE EXHIBITING IN LONDON, BRUSSELS, NEW YORK AND VENICE.

WHAT UNIFIES HIS WORK IS HIS EMPATHETIC UNDERSTANDING OF HOW TO ENHANCE OUR EXPERIENCE OF THE SPACE THAT WE OCCUPY. EVEN WHEN HIS LIGHT PIECES ARE VERY COMPLEX TO REALIZE, HE HAS A SUBTLE ADEPTNESS, WHICH GIVES A SENSE OF EXQUISITE SIMPLICITY AND RIGHTNESS TO THE FINISHED WORK.

Photo credits: Martin Richman

Photo credits: Martin Richman

Private House, St John's Wood, London
Photo credits: Mark Bayley

ART
-
Martin Richman

Photo credits: Martin Richman

Inspired by the banded wrapping of the freight containers on
The River Liffey in Dublin, the sparkling sequins of "Flow" reflect the
light and pattern on the glazed surface of the structure
*Photo credits: Martin Richman*

**What kind of message do you hope to convey to the public and younger aspiring artists?**

-

I am interested in conveying how light is a powerful tool in the manipulation and perception of space.

**Your choice of experiments questions our sense of architectural installations. How do you feel your mediums, and your manipulation of them, reach out to contemporary society?**

-

I hope my installations encourage people to reconsider sites and spaces they may have been familiar with. But the work helps us to see nuances or elements we may have overlooked before, so I think my work can refresh the spirit and allow us all to see anew, which is always important within any society.

**What sort of modern icons or movements inform your artistic endeavours?**

-

My endeavours are informed by the sum of my experience. Places like beaches or woods, or city streets and buildings, are at least as powerful inspirations as any art or design movement, and actually more important to me.

**What was your first experience with LEDs?**

-

When I watched amplifiers and other electrical equipment glow with the red from LEDs when they were powered up.

**How do you feel about LEDs as a tool to create art and design installation?**

-

I think LEDs are a powerful tool for innovative lighting as they are often very compact, energy efficient, controllable and have long lives.

**Can you tell us your concept about your artworks with these technologies?**

-

I do not have a "concept" regarding LEDs. I use them as I would any other light sources and am interested in the quality of light rather than the technology behind it. The appealing elements of LEDs are their efficiency, size, availability and flexibility.

**How has technology affected your artistic expression through the years?**

-

I have always been interested in the light emitted more than the fitting or fixture. I use light sources according to their suitability for my aspirations.

*Photo credits: Martin Richman*

ART
-
Martin Richman

**Your sculptures and installations are known to have a subtle adeptness to the special environment. Is it something intentional?**
-

I am always interested in how light occupies space and configures our perception of that space. I am particularly interested in how a space can be made to appear perceptually ambivalent so that it is spatially uncertain. This encourages a loss of self and blurring of boundaries between the perceiver and the space.

**Traditionally, installation work inhabits our space and redefines it in new and exciting ways — how do you feel your work has achieved this?**

I mix colors and sources to partially confound expectations of perception of a given space. Generally I am more interested in the light occupying the space and surfaces than in the sources and production.

**How do you think LEDs have changed the creative landscape?**
-

They allow longer lasting, more flexible and potentially more nuanced lighting installations than were previously available.

I enjoy the variety of increasingly small and powerful luminaires that are possible with the development of better efficiency. This should allow a richer palette of illuminating possibilities.

**What do you think is the ultimate potential of this technology?**
-

I can envisage that organic LED technology (OLED) will make profound changes to our perception of light sources and possibilities of usage. I hope light schemes will be more subtle and carefully designed as a result of the possibilities of the new technology.

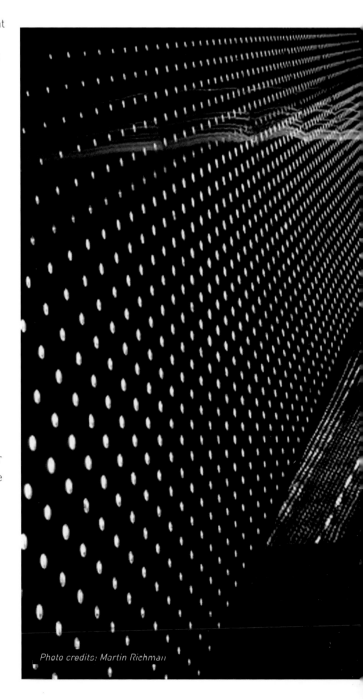

Photo credits: Martin Richman

Photo credits: Martin Richman

Photo credits: Martin Richman

ART

Erwin Redl
Leo Villareal
Ingo Maurer
Teddy Lo
Swarovski
Anakin Koenig
Martin Richman

# Louis M. Brill

Burning Man

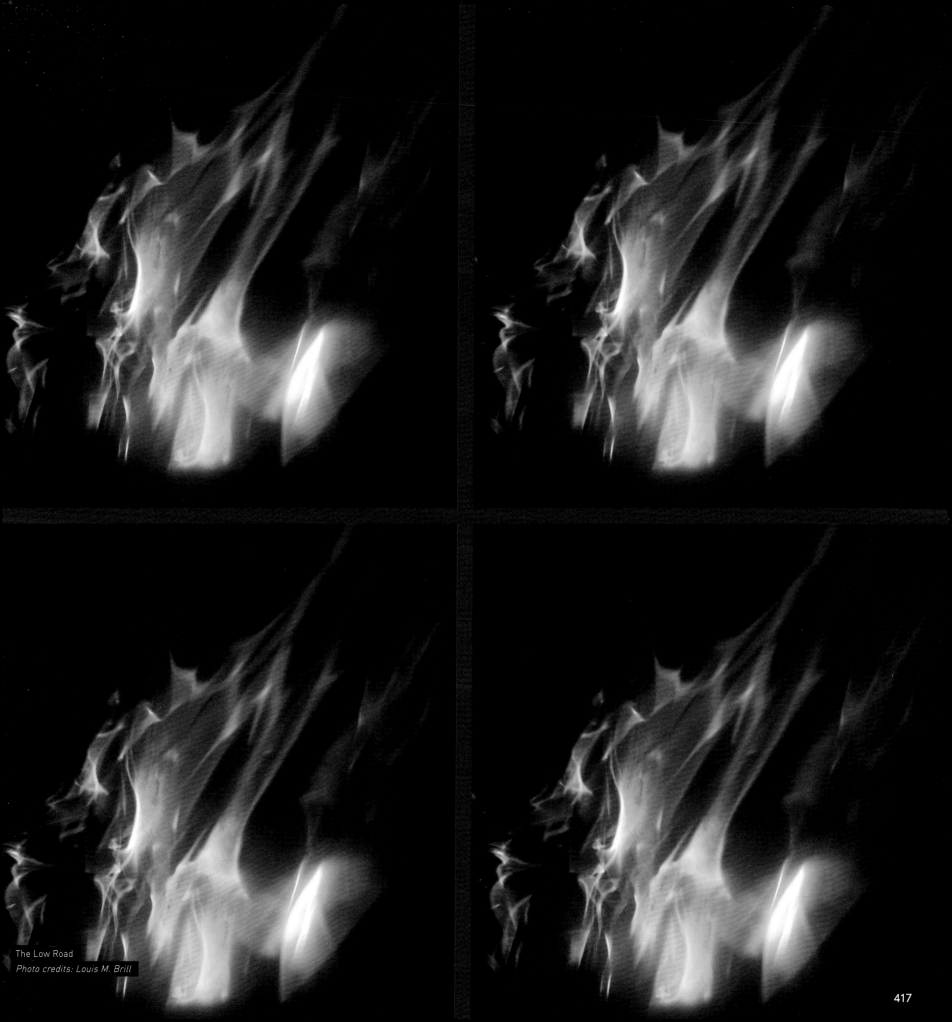

The Low Road
Photo credits: Louis M. Brill

417

# ART
-
**Louis M. Brill**

LOUIE'S PREFERRED ART MEDIUM IS SCULPTURED LIGHT THAT IS PROJECTED ONTO WALL SCREENS OR PRESENTED IN SMALL, STANDALONE CABINET DISPLAY SCREENS. THE ILLUMINATION SOURCE INCLUDE LASERS, CHRISTMAS-TREE LIGHTS, INCANDESCENT LIGHTS AND, IN MOST CASES, LEDS.

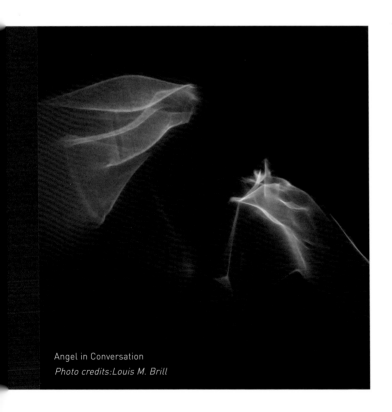

Angel in Conversation
*Photo credits:Louis M. Brill*

LIGHT HAS BECOME THE PAINT AND PAINTBRUSH OF HIS CREATIVE IMPULSES, REPRESENTED THROUGH VARIOUS CUSTOM-BUILT LIGHT PROJECTORS THAT DISPLAY ANIMATED ILLUMINATED LANDSCAPE OF PLAYFUL VISUAL IMAGERY THAT SLOWLY MOVE ACROSS A PROJECTION SCREEN.

ONE EXAMPLE OF HIS ARTWORKS IS AN EXPLORATION OF A LIGHT FORM KNOWN AS LUMIA, OF WHICH HE DEVELOPED AS ANY NUMBER OF LUMIA PROJECTORS OVER THE YEARS TO PRESENT AN ARCANE MYSTICAL ILLUMINATION.

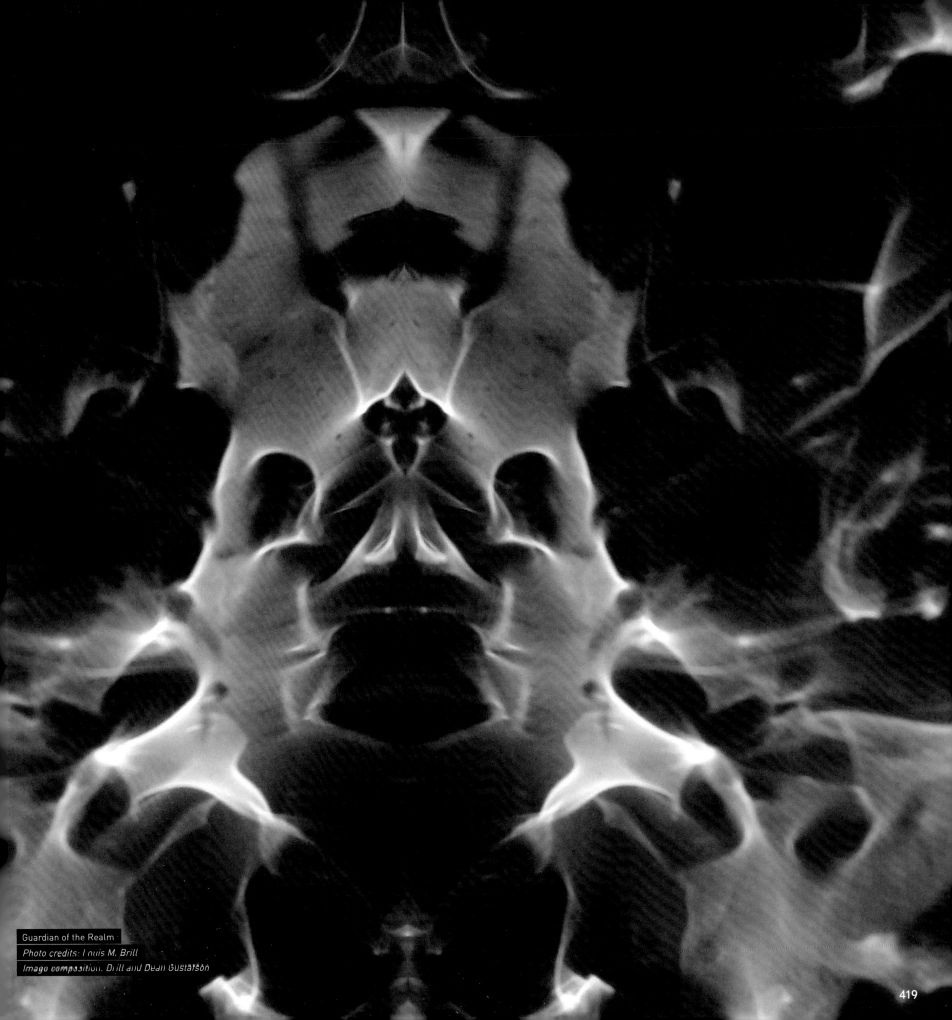

Guardian of the Realm
Photo credits: Louis M. Brill
Image composition: Brill and Dean Gustafson

419

## ART
-
**Louis M. Brill**

**TELL US MORE ABOUT LUMIA, WHICH YOU'VE DESCRIBED AS THE "ULTIMATE RORSCHACH."**
-

My fascination with Lumia light emerges from its amorphous shape, which I refer to as smoke-like "textured light" or what looks like a representation of the Aurora Borealis (nature's own Lumia show). My preference as a Lumia artist is to create animated Lumias that are in synchronization with music, where the music generates the color and shape of the Lumia landscape.

As I watch the Lumias unfold, they always present a visual narration of semi-abstract iconic imagery. Each Lumia image becomes a momentary picture of a somewhat familiar tangible object or animal-like form that floats across my mind as some entertaining Rorschach image.

Each moment of viewing a Lumia is a free-form narration of whatever your mind conjures up to "understand it." And like most things, the moment you understand it, it becomes something else.

**WHAT ARE THE ORIGINS OF LUMIA?**
-

As to Lumia's origins, it was created by Denmark light artist, Thomas Wilfred (1889-1968), who began his exploration of light, color and motion in 1905. In 1913, he built his first light instrument and in 1920 gave one of his first light recital performances in his South Huntington, Long Island, light studio.

My quest to build the ultimate Lumia projector began in 1999. After fits and starts, various versions of my Lumia projector, which I refer to as "El Grande" (The Big One), were started and aborted. Each project led to a dead-end of one kind or another.

In early 2006, I had an epiphany and saw a "vision" of the exact type of light projector I wanted, which would have a light engine using state-of-the-art high-brightness LEDs. The light engine would be computer controlled and sound activated, and display beautiful Lumia images.

Having built at least 15 other analogue-type Lumia projectors (between 1974 and the late 1980s), I envisioned designing and building a digital Lumia projector that would present high-brightness Lumia imagery in an auditorium setting.

**HOW WAS "EL GRANDE" BORN?**
-

"El Grande" took its final journey to creation in 2006 once I settled on the detailed design of an RGB, LED light engine. To maximize its color-changing capabilities, I used three 3W Luxeon LEDs (red, green and blue) which were heat-sinked and directed into a dichroic mirror mixing chamber (known as a light engine) that was managed by a micro-processor and allowed the RGB to be mixed into a multitude of blended colorized Lumia images.

The light engine was placed in a black box that projected a light beam through various collimating optics (two collimating lenses and a mirror). It directed the final image through a focusing lens to project a large animated Lumia display on a white projection screen.

## MUSIC IS ALSO A KEY COMPONENT TO ANY LUMIA. HOW CAN MUSICAL ELEMENTS INFLUENCE "EL GRANDE?"
-

An interesting factoid about Lumia is that just about every Lumia artist understands that Lumia is an expression of music, and lends itself to various synesthetic music compositions that are illustrated through the morphs and movements of Lumia's screen presence. Not only is its shape important in relation to the music, but so is its relationship of color to music.

To extend the capabilities of "El Grande" in that area, I collaborated with an art engineer, Jon Foote, who created for me an audio reactive software package, which I called "RotorBryte," that samples music from "El Grande" music and translates it via a color-sound matrix that acts to drive the LED light engine that presents the Lumia images (think of it as a Lumia color organ).

**So what's next for your Lumia journey?**
-

Currently "El Grande" is being refined into an operator-based "presentation" light projector that would enable a greater degree of personal control over the color, shape and texture of the Lumia imagery. This "light control" would allow the operator to harmonize the Lumia imagery more closely with its musical counter-part.

The combination of music and Lumia is often magical in its visual presentation and follows a tradition begun by Wilfred in the 1920s and onwards as he toured the United States and Europe giving Lumia recitals in concert halls and auditoriums.

Most people who witness Lumia concerts are in awe of the process as an unusual form of visual display. To see Lumia up-close-and-personal is a visual treat as its Imagery can be likened to what I call "visual quicksand."

The more you look at Lumia visuals, the more compelling they become and the more evocative its imagery is. It draws you deeper into its scenic landscapes, defined only by your imagination.

Confronting an Angel
*Photo credits: Louis M. Brill*

Erwin Redl
Leo Villareal
Ingo Maurer
Teddy Lo
Swarovski
Anakin Koenig
Martin Richman
Louis M. Brill

# Burning Man

Louis M. Brill and Christine Kristen
aka Louie Lights and Lady Bee, Art Curator

ᛉ Burning Man

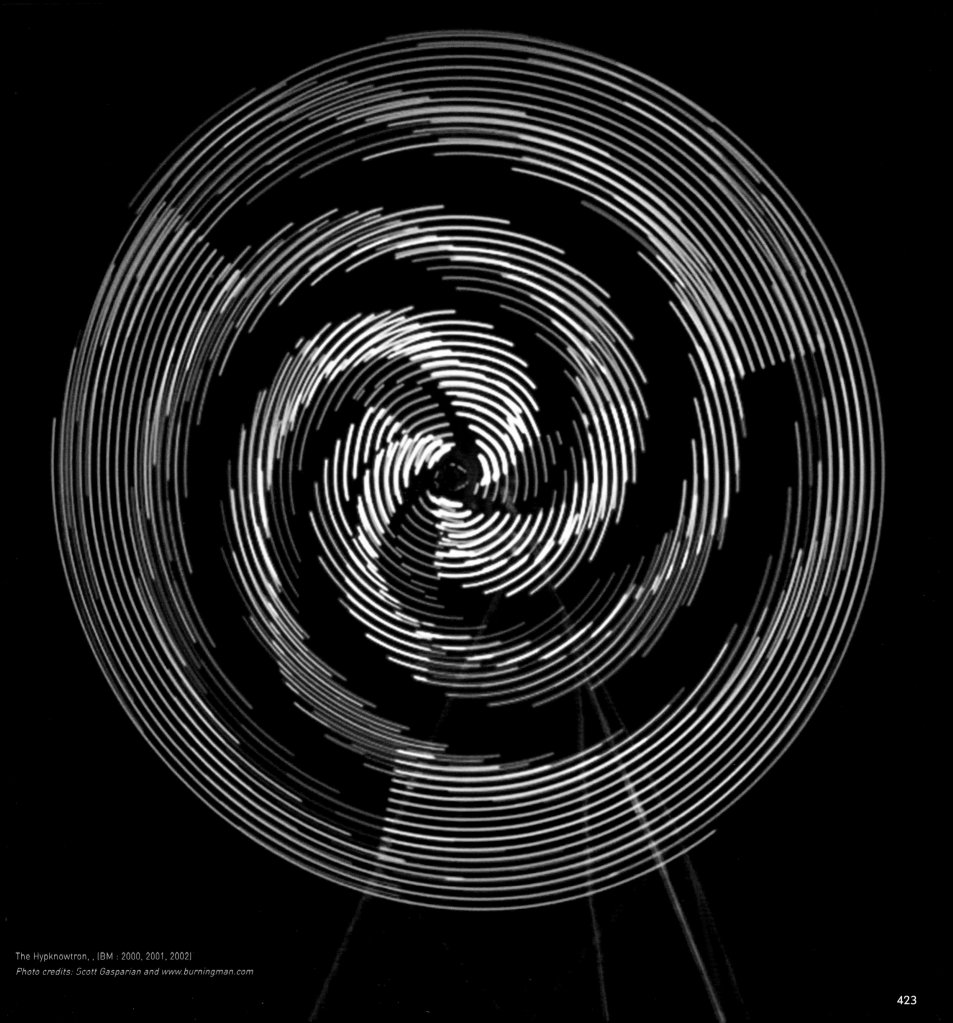

The Hypknowtron, , (BM : 2000, 2001, 2002)
*Photo credits: Scott Gasparian and www.burningman.com*

ART
-
Burning Man

BURNING MAN IS THE MOST INSPIRING AND LARGEST OUTDOOR COUNTER-CULTURE ART EVENT IN NORTH AMERICA. IT IS AN ANNUAL GATHERING OF CAMPERS, VOLUNTEERS, DESERT LOVERS, PERFORMERS AND ARTISTS, WHO ALL COME TOGETHER TO CREATE A GIGANTIC, TEMPORARY URBAN SPACE KNOWN AS BLACK ROCK CITY.

THE WEEK OF THE EVENT DRAWS UP TO 60,000 PEOPLE WHO COME TO LIVE AND CELEBRATE ITS ENERGY. BURNING MAN GENERATES EVERY KIND OF ART INCLUDING LARGE-SCALE SCULPTURE, ART CARS, TRADITIONAL SCULPTURE, MULTIMEDIA INSTALLATIONS, KINETIC SCULPTURE, INTERACTIVE AND PERFORMANCE ART.

**What kind of light art is typically on show?**

-

One of the many forms of art that appears at Burning Man is light art, which is represented in every imaginable light medium including incandescent, fluorescent, neon, black light, light wire and, of course, LEDs.

The various lighting pieces are developed into artworks that are presented as either an illumination, a projection or an interactive light display which allows its viewers to have some control over its final look.

Because Burning Man is held in a large, flat, open, desolate desert it provides a perfect exhibition area for light art. First, the surrounding land is so large (13 square kilometers) that for the light artists who participate, there are almost no restrictions in the size of an artwork — at least one light installation was 91 meters in diameter.

**Is the middle desert a good place to display these kinds of works?**

-

The isolation from nearby cities, and lack of light pollution, allows these works to be exhibited in their full splendor against the night sky. It presents their light as a pure art medium in interesting and compelling displays.

**But there must also be difficulties?**

-

While the dense, inky blackness of Nevada's Black Rock Desert is a stunning backdrop for these installations, it also presents significant challenges. The daytime heat isintense with an average temperature of 43 degrees celsius, which puts a strain on some electronic circuits. Proper cool-air circulation designs are needed in order to protect them.

A bigger challenge, however, is protecting sensitive mechanical devices such as motors, rotors and spinning gears from sudden ferocious dust storms. Deadly alkaline playa dust can quickly shut down rotating LED displays and ruin an art piece. This incredibly fine particulate matter seeps into the tiniest structural crevices, damaging spinning LED devices.

Some of the many LED artworks that have been presented in the Black Rock desert have suffered greatly within the harsh environment. In those instances, the affected LED artists presented on these pages have discussed their efforts to "desert-proof" their electronic and mechanical art for optimal performance and further visits to Burning Man.

**Black Rock is famous for inspiring creativity. Do you believe that?**

-

While the desert environment is very hard on light art, its vast space and darkness provides an unparalleled setting for illuminated creative inspirations.

Burning Man has popularized the light art-making process by allowing electronic engineers who may never have considered their creative tinkering to be art to be thrust into the public eye as artists, and rightfully so.

**What makes the displays at the festival so special?**

-

Because Burning Man is very democratic in its art selection, it allows artists and engineers to show their creations in a setting where anything goes, and where one is guaranteed an audience of thousands. For this reason, extremely sophisticated light art, often completely original in concept and execution, is standard. It is difficult to think of another venue which offers this opportunity.

The installations presented here are notable for their grand scale, unique conceptualization or specialized interactive operation. They allow thousands of Burning Man visitors to interact with them in compelling and entertaining ways.

The next few pages were selected as some of our favorites.

ART
-
**Burning Man**

### THE AMAZING JELLYFISH FROM THE YEAR 12,000
*by Jared Gallardo and the Jellycrew*
-

The Amazing Jellyfish comes from a future in which jellyfish have taken over. They are the dominant life form and they are huge, hyper-intelligent and have fused with computers.

**But what about us humans?**
-

Longing for companionship, the jellyfish have sent an emissary back to our time to spread a message that just might give us a shot at a Year 12,000 in which people and jellyfish live in harmony together.

Evolving at a fantastic pace, the jellyfish of the future are over 15 feet across, unimaginably intelligent and have incorporated robotics and computers into their biology.

This particular creature (pictured) appeared on the playa in 2007, made of 9,500 pounds of welded steel and vehicle chassis, containing two computers, one microcontroller, over 4,800 LEDs, 623 hand-assembled circuit boards and 650 feet of ethernet cable.

At 12' 6" high, 18-feet-long and 15-feet-wide, including its outer dome, the jellyfish can transport up to 14 passengers in the lower level and six more in its upper level.

The jellyfish is disguised as an art car with an eight-foot dome covered in thousands of animated LEDs, floating eight feet above ground at its base. The dome is accessible to visitors, allowing them to view the animations from the inside out.

Photo credits: Sallie Dean Shatz and www.burningman.com

Burning Man is famous for its large-scale light installations, such as this giant alien jellyfish
*Photo credits: Sallie Dean Shatz and www.burningman.com*

**The jellyfish brain is interactive with different modalities that allow it to communicate with its human friends:**

-

### • AUDIO INTERACTIVITY

The jellyfish can listen and respond to any audio source such as voice or music. Information received through its microphone is analyzed using a fast Fourier transform to extract frequency information. This information is passed to the brain in real time where it is incorporated in the animation design, allowing the LEDs to react to the auditory inputs.

### • TOUCH SCREEN RESPONSES

The jellyfish has an LCD screen with a representation of all the LEDs on the dome which allows participants to interact with it in real time by touching the screen. There are a variety of brush types and sizes, effects and colors the participant can utilize when interacting with the screen and the dome. What the participant sees on the LCD screen is mimicked by the jellyfish's dome LED lighting.

### • SONAR RESPONSES

The jellyfish utilizes narrow-beam ultrasonic range finders allowing it to get a fix on the distance and location of people near it. This information can also be utilized to modify the animations on the dome.

### • NON-INTERACTIVE LED COLOR DISPLAYS

This is a default mode that displays colors and visual animations and shapes while it is waiting for people to interact with it. These animations are widely varied in type, drawing inspirations from the *Game of Life* and an early artifice intelligence exploration into programmatic expressions of complexity. These are devised from simple rules and processes found in nature such as phyllotaxis, the patterns of leaf arrangements found on plants, which can be described algorythimatically.

Very commonly during a demonstration, a small group of people quickly grows as other people join in the interactive fun.

Burning Man reactions to the Amazing Jellyfish were amazing. Everybody who saw it, loved it. Some people would even chase after it or follow the jellyfish with their bicycles. Wherever we stopped it was an instant hit as we would be completely surrounded by Burners who'd come over to check us out and discover how they could play with it.

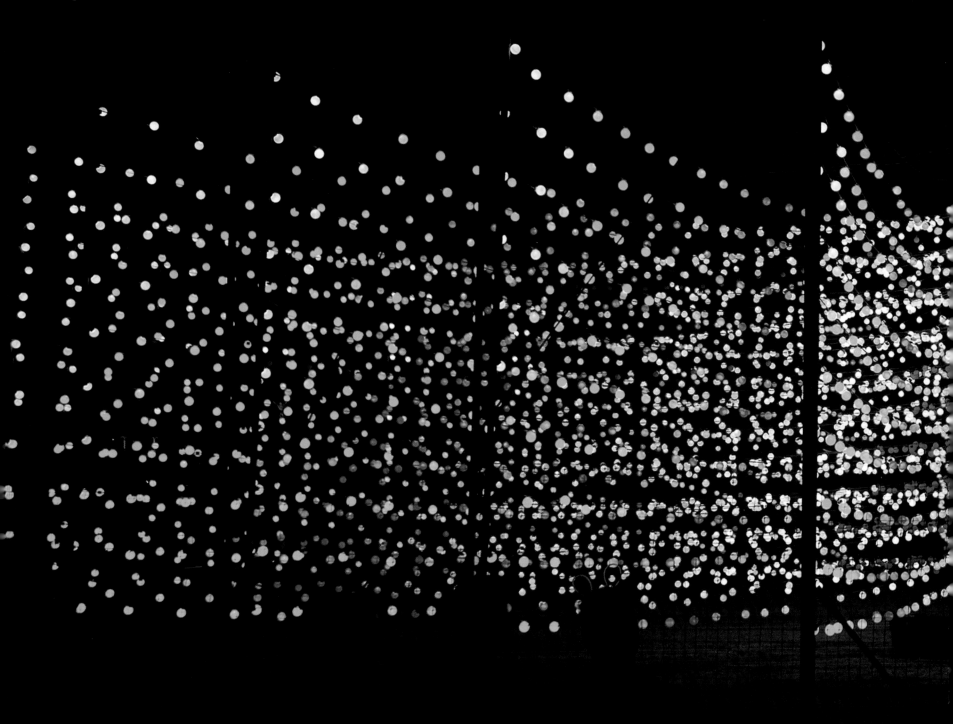

The Cubatron (BM 2005)
Photo credits: Gabe Kirchheimer and www.burningman.com

ART
-
**Burning Man**

## THE BIG ROUND CUBATRON
*by Mark Lottor*
-

At Burning Man 2005, Mark Lottor presented the Cubatron, a 10-foot-squared cube made up of small round lights which flashed in intricate patterns and colors.

In 2006, he returned with the Big Round Cubatron, a much bigger and more elaborate arrangement of strings of LED lights radiating out from a central point, forming constantly changing patterns, breathtaking in their scope and complexity.

From a distance, gradated color changes are visible, as well as rapidly circling lights, flashing patterns, the illusion of rain falling, and images which appear to move. These compelling illusions were mesmerizing, and the Cubatron was extremely popular; people would lie underneath the installation to view the light patterns closely.

The Big Round Cubatron v2.0, presented at Burning Man 2007, is the world's largest three-dimensional full-color dynamic light sculpture. It is an array of lights 40 feet in diameter and 10 feet high. It consists of 28 spokes, each of which is 24 lights wide by 10 lights high. Each light is independently controllable to display any color and brightness level and the entire display can be updated 50 times per second. There are 6,720 total lights made of 20,160 LEDs.

The physical structure that holds up the lights consists of two pieces, a central mast, and a circular wall of poles. The lights are strung horizontally and from the central mast to the outer posts. The central mast is a 10-foot, 4x4-inch wooden pole standing vertically in the center. It is supported by 1/8" steel cables that run from the top of the mast to the top of each outer pole.

The poles around the circumference are 1-3/8" diameter pipe and 10 feet high. They are pre-assembled into 14 "squares" along with some 3/4" EMT pipe to keep the squares together. The squares are held to the ground in each corner by rebar stakes. The tops of the squares are pulled tight and held down with rope and rebar stakes.

The light string wires are attached to the poles at 10-inch height intervals using plastic wire ties and paper clips. The bottom string of lights starts about three feet off the ground.

A small viewing tower was located to one side of the sculpture. It was built from some scaffolding two tiers high (10 feet), allowing people to view the sculpture from an eye level of around 15 feet high.

### ELECTRONICS
The light strings are based on an improved version of the design used in the Cubatron Jr. They are a slightly customized version of Triklits. The controller consists of five parallel microcontrollers which read pre-programed patterns from SD memory cards and send them to the lights. The controllers are synchronized over an rs-485 connection. Each light consists of an RGB LED that can be set to a 24-bit color value and changed 50 times per second.

### SOFTWARE
The software and effects are written in C and testing is done using a custom 3D graphics simulator that runs on a PC. There are currently about 40 different effects lasting about a minute each, and the show loops continuously.

### POWER
The total power required if everything is set to maximum brightness is around 4500W. A 240v/30A circuit is required to operate the BRC. This is converted to 10vdc at 400A by four power supplies.

At some installations the BRC was solar powered by Energy Efficiency Inc. An array of panels charges a large battery bank during the day, and the BRC runs off the 12vdc from the batteries at night.

The Cubatron (BM 2005)
Photo credits: Gabe Kirchheimer and www.burningman.com

ART
-

**Burning Man**

## THE HYPKNOWTRON
### *By Tim Black and Scott Gasparian, Burning Man 2000-2002*
-

The HypKnowTron was first displayed at Burning Man in 2000 and was presented as an interactive LED "pattern generator." In its original incarnation, the first HypKnowTron was placed on a pyramid stand and built with three three-foot aluminium blades (or propellers) upon which 70 single-color LEDs were attached per blade.

The pattern of lights on the blades were driven by a microphone where an audience gathered each night to visually affect the HypKnowTron's look by singing, cheering or clapping their hands. Unfortunately, the HypKnowTron lasted only two days before it became mechanically unstable and was shut down.

In the following year, a second more advanced HypKnowTron was also built and brought to Burning Man thus providing double the visual HypKnowTron entertainment for its audiences. The advanced unit again consisted of three propellers, but each one being five-foot long and having 40 RGB clusters of LED units attached per blade.

As the propellers spun, the end result was that it appeared as a completely circular pulsing Mandela of light, and whose illumination level was programed to pulse and change colors as it rotated.

The changing of its colors and patterns was influenced by nearby ambient sounds which increased and decreased its visual patterns. In later years, to comfortably appreciate the effect, a series of couches encircled the HypKnowTron allowing its audience to sit for prolonged periods and enjoy its morphing sound-active color patterns. Altogether over the years, at least five similar HypKnowTron devices were presented at Burning Man.

The HypKnowTron, (BM : 2000, 2001, 2002)
*Photo credits: Scott Gasparian and www.burningman.com*

**ART**

-

**Burning Man**

## THE L2K PROJECT
### by Tim Black

-

L2K or Lights 2000 is an interactive installation first exhibited at Burning Man in 1999. Evoking a "wheel of time," the effect appears as a series of patterns of light that race around a circular track, creating a feeling that something is moving at a great speed.

The project consists of 2,000 orange LEDs mounted on the ground in a huge 500-foot circle that surrounds the Burning Man sculpture.

Light patterns start as pre-programed sequences and are modified via 200 interactive control panels holding a total of 2,000 pushbuttons, which are contained inside a small participation pavilion. Access to the pavilion, know as the Pattern Buffer Lounge invites "live participation" by allowing Burner visitors to directly control the L2K patterns.

People pushing the 2,000 small buttons in the lounge could look out the door and see the effect of their actions written across the horizon. People anywhere nearby could see the huge ring of LED lights, racing wildly in circles, but could only wonder who or what was controlling them. It was the microcosm and the macrocosm illustrated on the dirt of an empty desert.

L2K's biggest effort involved building its ring display from scratch. There were five separate categories of components that made up the final form: the individual LED light pods (all 2,000 of them), the micro computers that ran the light pods (200 of those), and the wire harnesses that the light pods attached to (each being 40-50 feet long).

A second part of the 1999 installation was the creation of the Pattern Buffer Lounge, the command center for L2K. This site was a small, wooden framed tent-like pavilion and became a public gathering area. Event attendees were able to enter and immediately access a series of "button boards" (there were 2,000 keys on the button boards — one for every LED pod). Visitors were able to tap out changes to the light patterns and see them immediately illuminate the LEDs. These patterns then began racing around the ring to create amazing circular pattern effects.

The L2K Fabrication team was a volunteer group of San Francisco Bay Area artists and engineers who worked continuously on the L2K ring components for approximately three months leading up to the 1999 Burning Man event. That group also maintained the L2K ring as a continuing light display during its time in the desert.

Over 38,000 feet of wire were used to connect all the parts. I worked for about six months on designing and programing, giving up my "normal job" in the last month to make sure the project would finish on time. Installing the ring components into the L2K display required a shallow trench that would be dug with a 500-foot diameter.

Hundreds of people helped on site to lay out and connect the 2,000 feet of wiring harness and plug in the 4,000 wires from the LED light pods to the harness.

The L2K project explores many limits of human perception as it defines our sense of place and space as if it was a physical boundary. L2K also played with people's sense of scale.

Close up, viewers could see segments of the ring with its racing light patterns. From a distance most of the L2K ring was visible, and it appeared almost alive as the light patterns continuously raced around, changing every few minutes.

From a distance it became apparent there were two playa spaces: the inner ring and the outside of the ring space, in some ways creating a contrast between public and private space, and which was which could only be defined by the viewers watching the lights chase themselves endlessly. Despite the separation of space, from the darkness it became obvious that L2K was a beacon of awareness to our presence in the Black Rock desert.

L2K (BM 2000)
Photo credits: Steve Fritz and www.burningman.com

435

ART
-
Burning Man

The Lily Pond: (BM: 2002) an experiential adventure
*Photo credits: Jeremy Lutes and www.burningman.com*

# *THE LILY POND: *
## /an experiential adventure/
### by Jeremy Lutes

-

The Lily Pond project was installed as a literal representation of a pond with lily pads on the playa at Burning Man 2002. The piece incorporated just under 300 individual lily pads on two-foot stalks which sat in a 3,500-square-foot "pond."

Each lily pad had a solar array on top and a blue LED mounted underneath, and a chosen few had resident dragon flies and lotus blossoms. Several ceramic koi fish could also be seen swimming in the calm blue waters.

As with many creative works, The Lily Pond was born out of a desire to create a large scale interactive environment. The pond was originally conceived as a large array of electronic devices that would respond both visually and audibly to people passing near them.

Function quickly gave way to form, upon the realization that there was no reason these devices could not be sculptural as well as functional. Prior experience with botanical sculpture led us to the idea of each device becoming a plant, and from there it was a short leap to the concept of The Lily Pond.

On an individual level, each frond was actually a green circuit board, fabricated in the shape of a lily pad, and home to the various electronic circuits that give life to the pond. The pads are arrayed in a hexagonal grid on four-foot centers. This arrangement allowed participants to walk amongst the pads, with the illusion that one is wading into a knee-deep pond.

The illusion of wading into a pond is greatly enhanced at night, when each lily pad projects a diffused blue glow onto the ground beneath it. As one walks amongst the pads, they individually modulate their light levels, in effect simulating the movement of ripples on water. These ripples of light propagate out into the pond, where they collide and combine with other illuminated ripples travelling in the pond.

Breathing life, motion, and light into the pond requires the collision of several different technologies. The light sources used to illuminate the ground are some of the latest generation of LEDs. In order to produce the rippling water effect, the lily pads "talk" to one another, using infrared technology similar to that found in television remote controls.

The ripple effect itself is based upon a relatively new branch of science known as Cellular Automata, or CA. And finally, each lily pad contains its own power source, which is recharged every day by a set of photovoltaic solar cells. Thus the entire pond is wireless and self-sustaining, powered by the sun.

The Lily Pond represents a variety of techniques, technologies, materials, and creative visions. Collaborators include the Sunbrothers (lotus blossoms and solar cells), Kathleen Fernald (ceramic fish), Michael Christian (shore sculpture), Lee Kobus and Jay Kravitz (glass fish).

Though we did not strive to achieve strict realism in the depiction of a pond, it succeeded in transcending its technology to create a real, vibrant, and inviting space in which people could immerse themselves.

ART
-
**Burning Man**

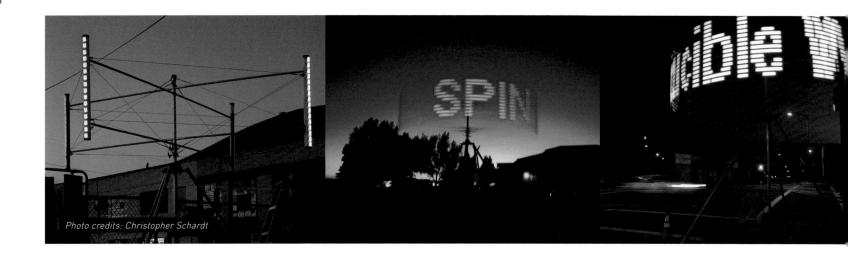

Photo credits: Christopher Schardt

## SPIN
### by Christopher Schardt
-

SPIN is a large interactive kinetic LED light sculpture, that first appeared at Burning Man in 2000. It was devised as a two-part display, with the first part appearing as a 12-foot diameter cylinder of light, a round digital display, projecting text and pictures in the air.

It is actually a set of four spinning columns of LEDs that change color at just the right time, creating the illusion of a solid display with the assistance of a retinal phenomenon known as persistence-of-vision.

The second part of the display is a special complementary software that allowed interested participants to create original text and image files that could be forwarded to SPIN for presentation on its rotating display on-site at Burning Man.

The images displayed are determined by a piece of software running on a laptop computer. Viewers can type in text and see it appear live. Or they can download the software and create animated sequences of text and simple graphics that can be later displayed. In the months preceding the 2000 Burning Man Festival, nearly 100 such sequences were emailed in by Burning Man participants. The scope of what people came up with surprised SPIN's creator.

Its columns move at approximately 60 miles per hour. Its 2,880 LEDs are turned on and off by a computer in precise synchronization with the rotation of the columns. SPIN has a vertical resolution of 16 pixels (picture elements), each of which can display one of 8 colors. The horizontal resolution is 360 pixels around the cylinder. The main shaft is powered by a lawnmower engine through a two-stage gear-reduction.

SPIN was first installed at Burning Man 2000. It stood tall through the dust storms that would be its eventual undoing. When the weather was finally calm enough, it ran beautifully for a few minutes. The second time it was started, it moved in a jerky fashion. The main shaft cracked in a spiral path, and that was that. It turned out that dust had gotten into the drive mechanism. Ah, the challenges of techy art on the playa!

SPIN was rebuilt to better survive the elements and successfully ran for hours at the Burning Man Decompression party that October. Since then, it has performed at Burning Man 2005, several of The Crucible's Fire Arts Festivals, and other events around the San Francisco Bay Area.

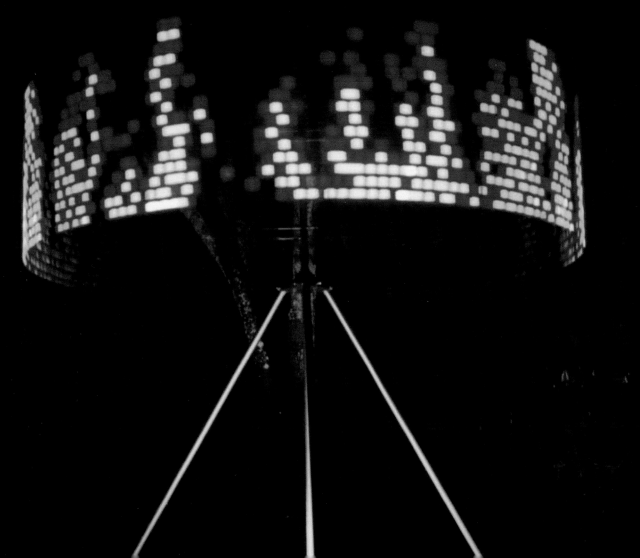

Photo credits: Christopher Schardt

ART
-

**Burning Man**

## THE BEANSTALK
### (An Experiment in Perceptive Disorder)
*Burning Man 2000-2006,*
*by Michael Light and David Rattray*
-

The Beanstalk uses LEDs to create a mobile vertical line of light that floats up to 180 feet into the sky. It debuted at Burning Man in 2001, and was improved upon every year until 2006, the last time it was brought to Burning Man. It could be seen from almost any part of Black Rock City.

The piece is elegantly simple. The vertical line of LEDs is composed of multiple strands of industrial-quality white Christmas lights plugged end-to-end. These are attached to a helium airfoil that lifts the illuminated line directly upwards.

This 11-foot "SkyDoc" balloon has been used by the military and is capable of 10-15 pounds of lift. It has also been tested in winds up to 90 miles an hour. Unlike unshaped balloons fixed to a point on the ground, this lift source generates more lift the stronger the winds blow, which is a key aspect of its success.

The airfoil is connected to a reelable line mounted to a small mobile pull-cart, from which its height can be adjusted. The cart also carries a small and quiet 1,000W gasoline generator, which provides power to the light line.

The Beanstalk requires a crew of three: one person to gently and slowly pull the cart in a desired direction, one person to orchestrate the bottom of the light line and its electrical connection on the ground through the throng of interested admirers and possible ground obstacles. The third person helps with the large, delicate helium airfoil during launch and landing.

One of the beauties of The Beanstalk is that while a viewer can see the piece even from extreme distances, it is not clear exactly what it is, or how it is suspended in space. That is until one is directly underneath it and sees the large dark balloon floating above.

The work has an enigmatic quality of "just being there," floating in the sky, coming from nowhere and going off into the cosmos amidst the surrounding starlight.

Another wonderful layer is its disorientating movement. As the tallest thing on the night time playa, it is a landmark and a vertical reference point within the vast blackness. Over time, though, its persistent migration tends to pull a viewer's larger perceptual navigational coordinates with it.

Another aspect of its beauty is the audience interactivity. Viewers at the bottom of the line are able to gently shake the light line, setting up wave-form oscillations from the ground to the airfoil high above, and back down again.

Lastly, because LEDs run on standard alternating electric current cycle and turn on and off many times a second, The Beanstalk's light has an exceptionally sparkly effect. Viewed in long-exposure photographs as a series of dots in the night, to the naked eye it is something even more celestially "charged."

The Beanstalk (BM: 2005)
(An experiment in perceptive disorder)
Photo credits: Michael Light and Tristan Savaier and www.burningman.com

World at Night

*Photo credits: Nasa*

# TECHNICAL
# REFERENCE

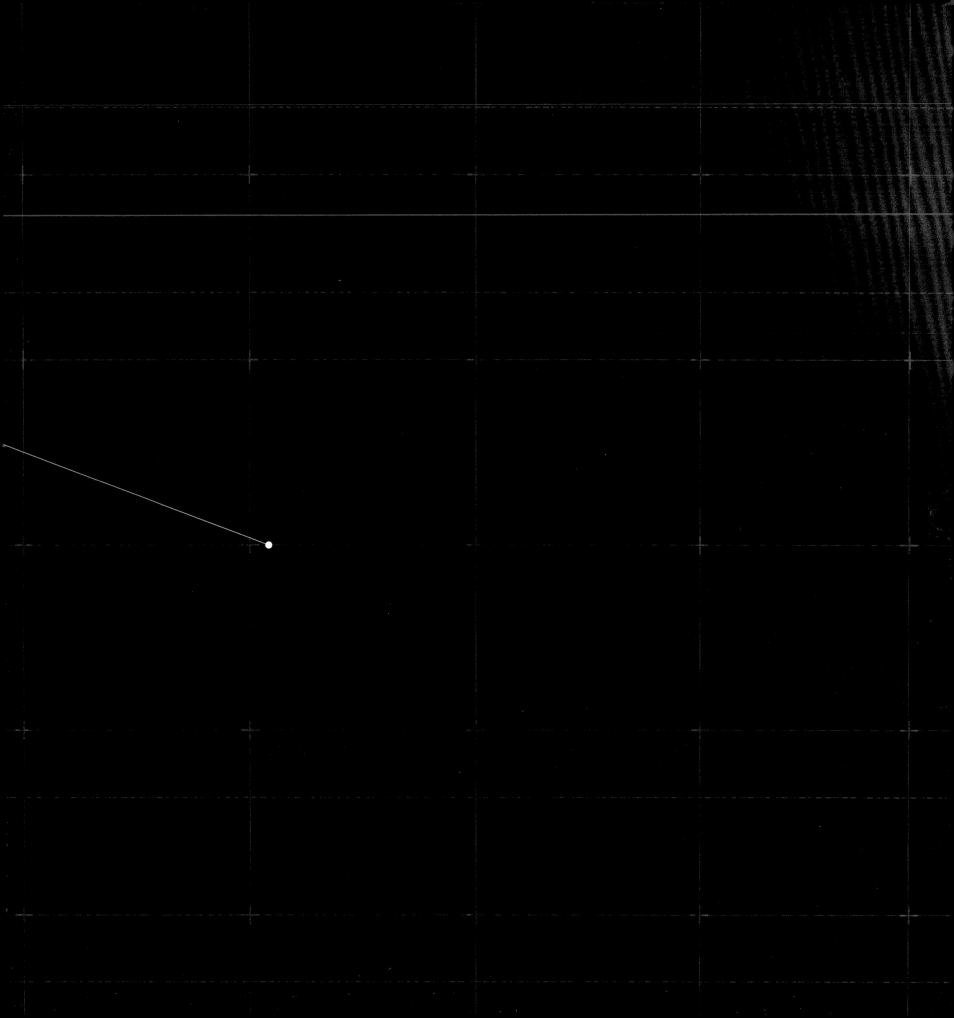

# LIGHTING INVENTION TIMELINE

**Lighting Invention Timeline**

-

Most people recognize LED technology as the initiator of the fourth generation of lighting technology in human history. Lighting technology has certainly progressed since our ancestors discovered the use of fire as nighttime's light source. Even though LED development has been explored for a mere sixty years, the advancements since discovery have been monumental, bringing a new paradigm to the lighting and information world. Here is a chronological timeline of the major milestones and breakthroughs in the discoveries and developments of Light-Emitting Diodes (LEDs).

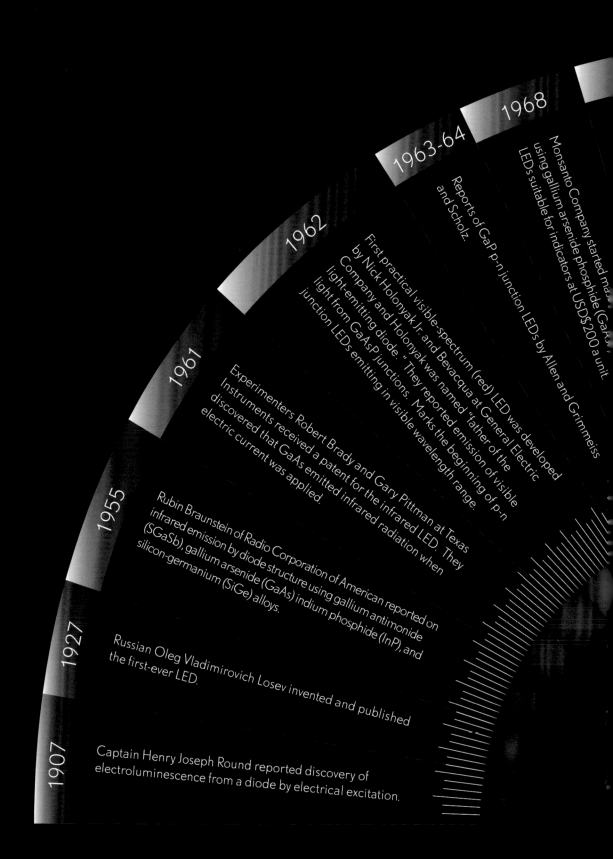

**1968** — Monsanto Company started ma_____ using gallium arsenide phosphide (GaP___) LEDs suitable for indicators at USD$200 a unit.

**1963-64** — Reports of GaP p-n junction LEDs by Allen and Grimmeiss and Scholz.

**1962** — First practical visible-spectrum (red) LED was developed by Nick Holonyak Jr. and Bevacqua at General Electric Company and Holonyak was named "father of the light-emitting diode." They reported emission of visible light from GaAsP junctions. Marks the beginning of p-n junction LEDs emitting in visible wavelength range.

**1961** — Experimenters Robert Brady and Gary Pittman at Texas Instruments received a patent for the infrared LED. They discovered that GaAs emitted infrared radiation when electric current was applied.

**1955** — Rubin Braunstein of Radio Corporation of American reported on infrared emission by diode structure using gallium antimonide (SGaSb), gallium arsenide (GaAs) indium phosphide (InP), and silicon-germanium (SiGe) alloys.

**1927** — Russian Oleg Vladimirovich Losev invented and published the first-ever LED.

**1907** — Captain Henry Joseph Round reported discovery of electroluminescence from a diode by electrical excitation.

1972

M. George Crafcrd demonstrated first yellow LED and improved brightness of red and red-orange LEDs by factor of ten.

...o by Jacques Pankove at RCA

1976

T. P. Pearsall created the first high-brightness and high-efficiency LEDs for optical fiber telecommunications by inventing new semiconductor materials specifically adapted to transmission wavelengths.

1989

Cree Inc. introduced the first commercially available blue LED based on silicon carbide (SiC), an indirect band gap semiconductor.

1993

High-brightness blue LEDs using wide band gap semiconductor Gallium Nitride (GaN) were invented by Shuji Nakamura at Nichia Corporation and revolutionized high-power and full-spectrum LED lighting.

1999

Lumileds introduced one-watt power LEDs.

2002

Philips Lumileds made five-watt LEDs available with luminous efficacy of 18-22 lumens per watt (lm/W)

2006

Cree demonstrated prototype with record white LED luminous efficacy of 131 lm/W at 20 mA.

2006-07

Professor Taguchi invented RGB phosphor-conversion white LED by n-UV LED excitation and invented a high CRI type of white LED consists of GaN-based LED and visible phosphor material combination.

2011

Osram Sylvania achieved 107 lumens per watt in 100 watt incandescent lamp replacement and record of 142 lm/W efficacy for a warm white LED in laboratory.

Bridgelux reached 160 lm/W in lab using GaN on silcon.

2012

Cree advanced to barrier-breaking 254 Lumen per watt white power LED, which breaks the LED efficacy records.

# ELECTRO
# MAGNETIC
# SPECTRUM

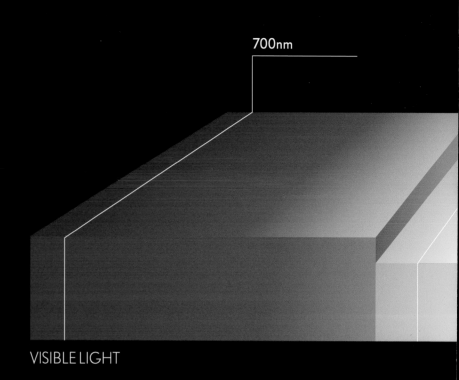

700nm

VISIBLE LIGHT

### Electromagnetic spectrum

-

The electromagnetic spectrum has been with us since
the beginning of time and it has been an ongoing quest
figuring out how to utilize and mimic its properties
for our needs. The spectrum covers a vast range
of wavelengths, frequencies and photon energies
of electromagnetic radiation distribution. Most
interestingly, the visible spectrum is only a tiny fraction
of the whole spectrum, but it is what makes this a
compelling world and it is the most important stimuli to
our senses. Don't you agree?

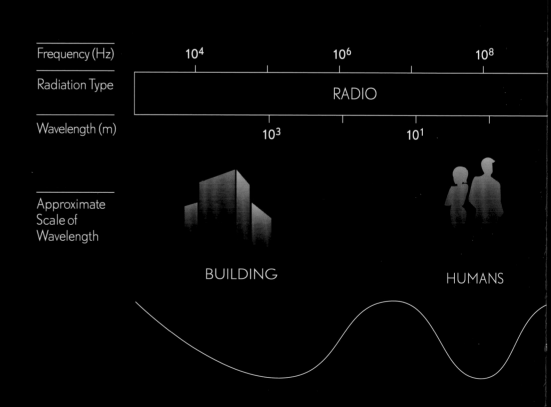

| Frequency (Hz) | $10^4$ | | $10^6$ | | $10^8$ |
|---|---|---|---|---|---|
| Radiation Type | | | RADIO | | |
| Wavelength (m) | | $10^3$ | | $10^1$ | |

Approximate
Scale of
Wavelength

BUILDING                    HUMANS

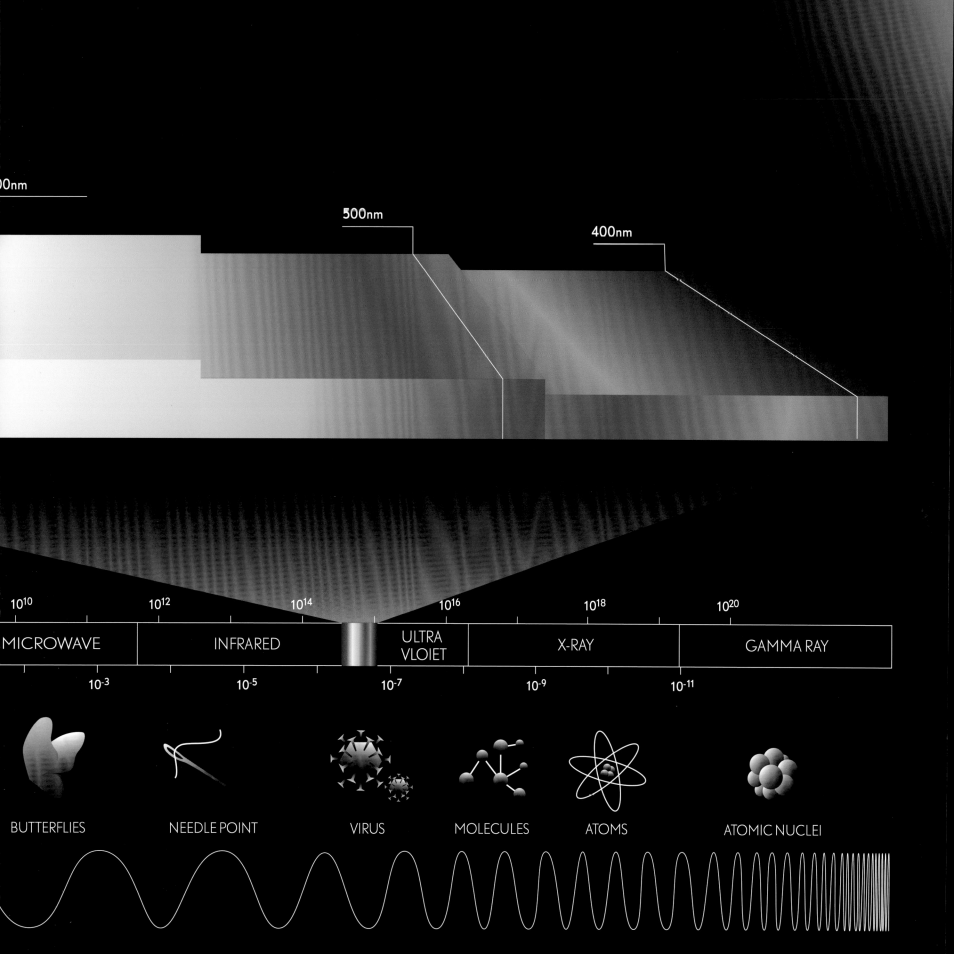

# LED
# CONSTRUCTION

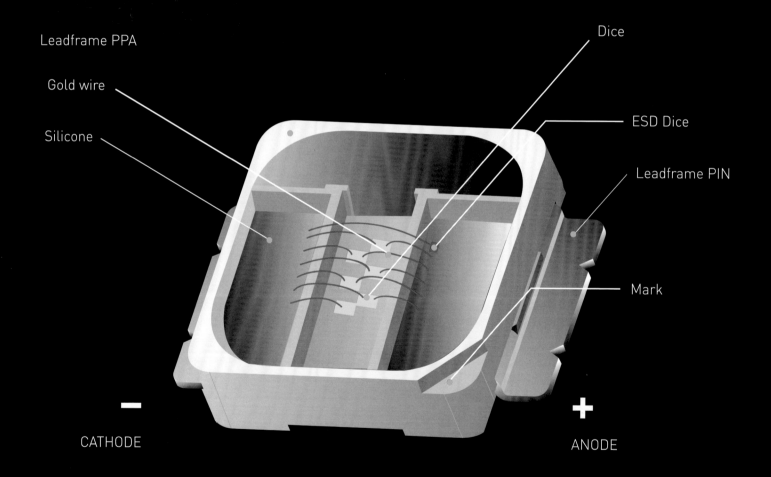

Leadframe PPA

Gold wire

Silicone

Dice

ESD Dice

Leadframe PIN

Mark

**—**

CATHODE

**+**

ANODE

**LED Construction**

-

Here are the anatomies of generic types of 5mm Light-Emitting Diodes (LEDs), and
SMD (Surface Mount Diode) type of white and RGBW LEDs. They are designed to be
compact and allow the electrons to combine with the electron holes in order to release
energy in the form of photons. This process is called electroluminescence.

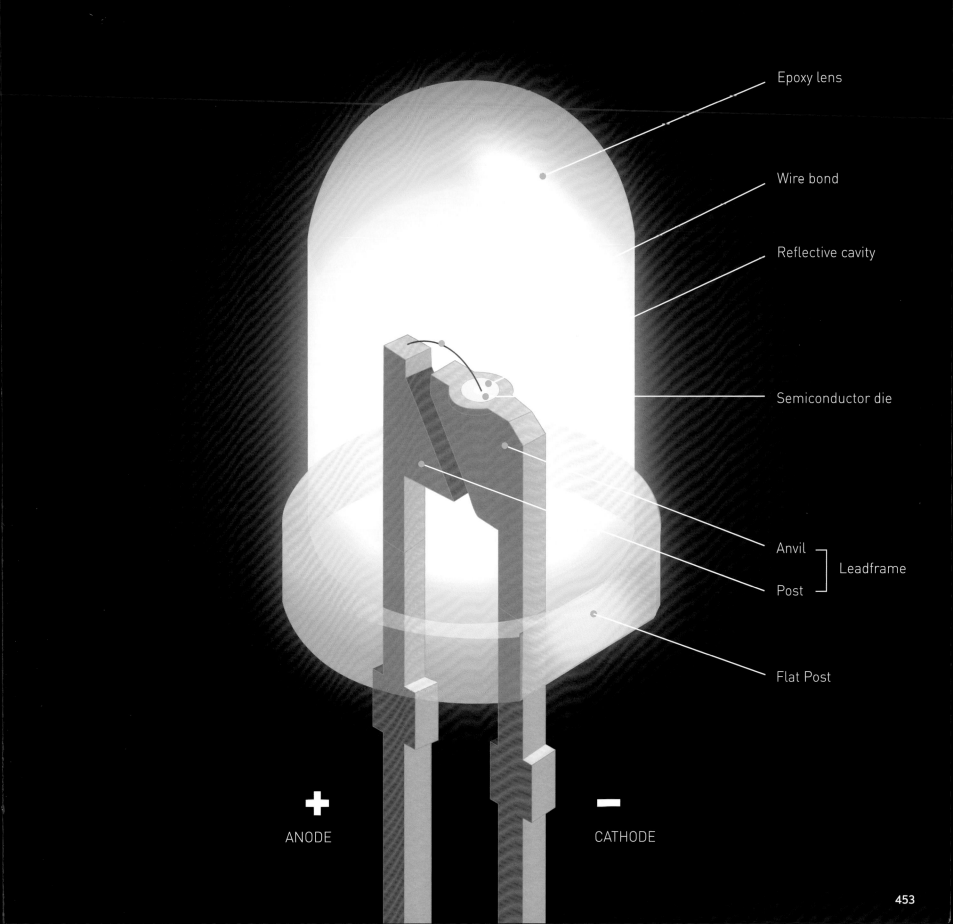

Epoxy lens

Wire bond

Reflective cavity

Semiconductor die

Anvil ⎤
      ⎬ Leadframe
Post  ⎦

Flat Post

**+**

ANODE

**—**

CATHODE

# CREE'S ARRAYS
## MC-E

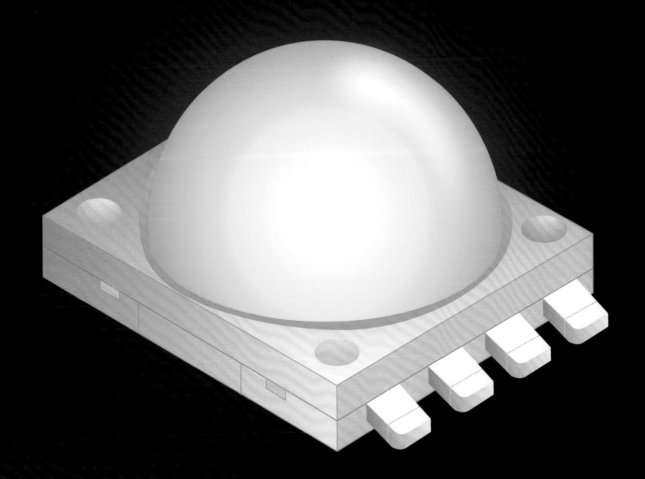

# MCE

All measurements are ±.1 mm unless otherwise indicated.

Top View

Color/
D1- Red
D2- Green
D3- Blue
D4- White

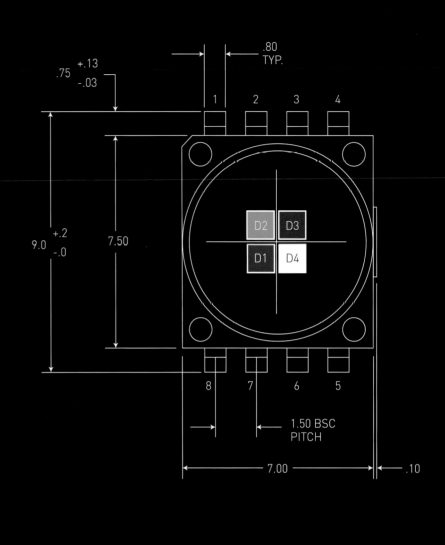

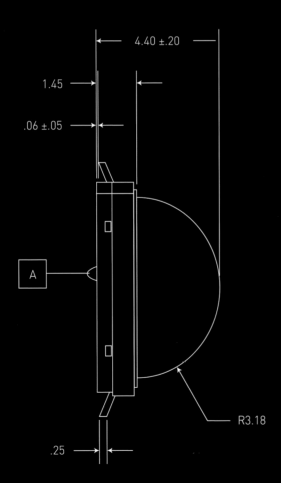

Side View

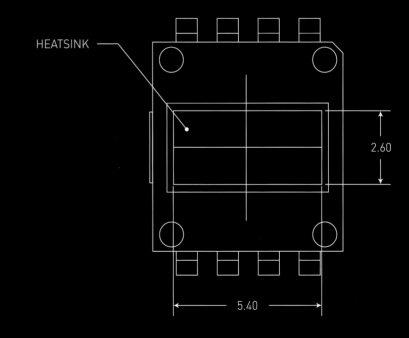

Bottom View

# LED CHEMICAL SUBSTRATE

| | |
|---|---|
| Infrared | Gallium arsenide (GaAs)<br>Aluminium gallium arsenide (AlGaAs) |
| Red | Aluminium gallium arsenide (AlGaAs), Gallium arsenide phosphide (GaAsP),Aluminium gallium indium phosphide (AlGaInP), Gallium(III) phosphide (GaP) |
| Orange | Gallium arsenide phosphide (GaAsP), Aluminium gallium indium phosphide (AlGaInP), Gallium(III) phosphide (GaP) |
| Yellow | Gallium arsenide phosphide (GaAsP), Aluminium gallium indium phosphide (AlGaInP), Gallium(III) phosphide (GaP) |
| Green | Indium gallium nitride (InGaN) /Gallium(III) nitride (GaN), Gallium(III) phosphide (GaP), Aluminium gallium indium phosphide (AlGaInP), Aluminium gallium phosphide (AlGaP) |
| Blue | Zinc selenide (ZnSe), Indium gallium nitride (InGaN), Silicon carbide (SiC) as substrate, Silicon (Si) as substrate — (under development) |
| Violet | Indium gallium nitride (InGaN) |
| Purple | Dual blue/red LEDs, blue with red phosphor, or white with purple plastic |
| Ultra-violet | diamond (235 nm) , Boron nitride (215 nm), Aluminium nitride (AlN) (210 nm), Aluminium gallium nitride (AlGaN), Aluminium gallium indium nitride (AlGaInN) - (down to 210 nm) |
| White | Blue/UV diode with yellow phosphor |

## LED Chemical Substrate

-

Light-Emitting Diodes are made from a wide range of inorganic semiconductor materials.  In material science terms, these band gap insulators can be doped with impurities with the goal to control its electronic properties.  As you can see in this table and diagram on the available colors with wavelength range, material names with acronyms and voltage drop are used for various type of LEDs.

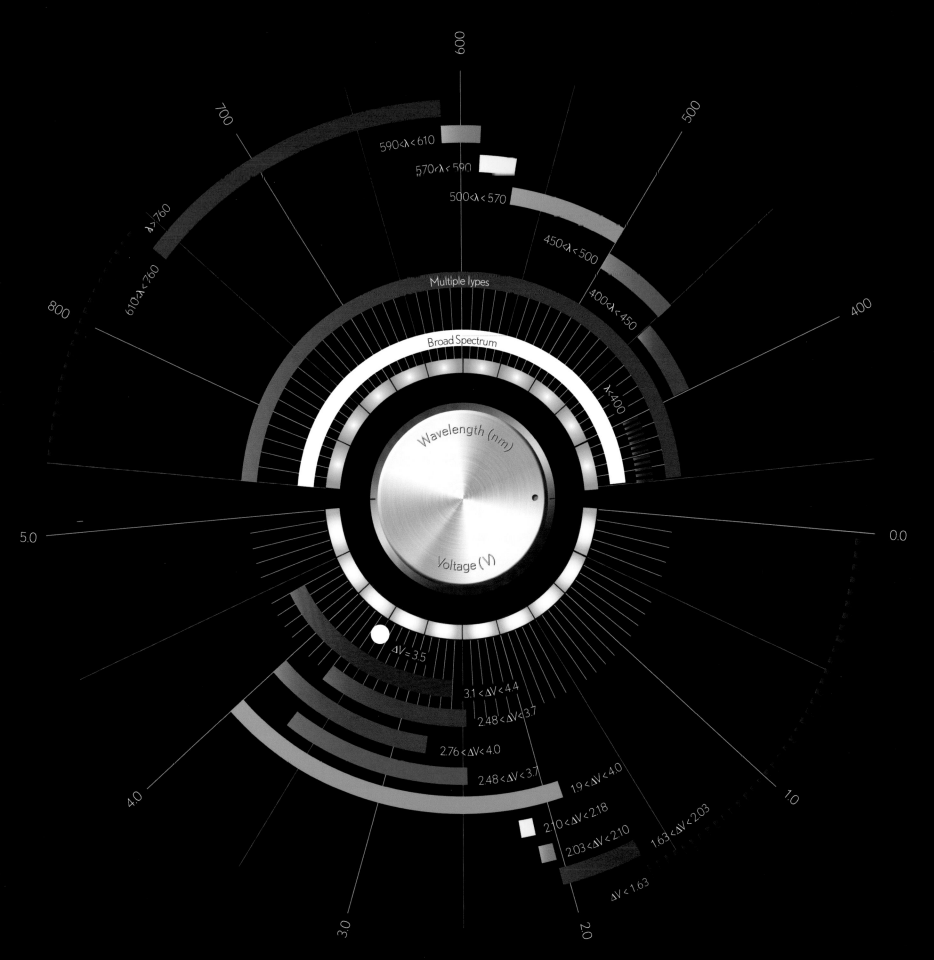

600

700

500

590<λ<610

570<λ<590

500<λ<570

450<λ<500

800

400<λ<450

400

λ>760

610<λ<760

Multiple Types

Broad Spectrum

λ<400

Wavelength (nm)

5.0

0.0

Voltage (V)

ΔV = 3.5

3.1<ΔV<4.4

2.48<ΔV<3.7

2.76<ΔV<4.0

2.48<ΔV<3.7

1.9<ΔV<4.0

4.0

1.0

2.10<ΔV<2.18

1.63<ΔV<2.03

2.03<ΔV<2.10

ΔV<1.63

3.0

2.0

457

# COLOR
# TEMPERATURE

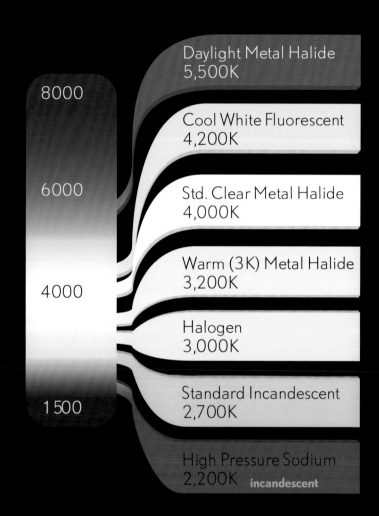

## Color Temperature
-

Color temperature is a measuring method of visible light's chromaticity with an ideal black body radiator that radiates a comparable hue of the light source. Its absolute temperature is measured in kelvin (K).

A cool color has a higher color temperature or cool color (ie: 5,000K or more) while a warm color has a lower color temperature (ie: 2,700-3,000K). These measurements have great applications in lighting, photography, videography, publishing, manufacturing, astrophysics, horticulture, filmmaking and other fields that involve natural or artificial lighting.

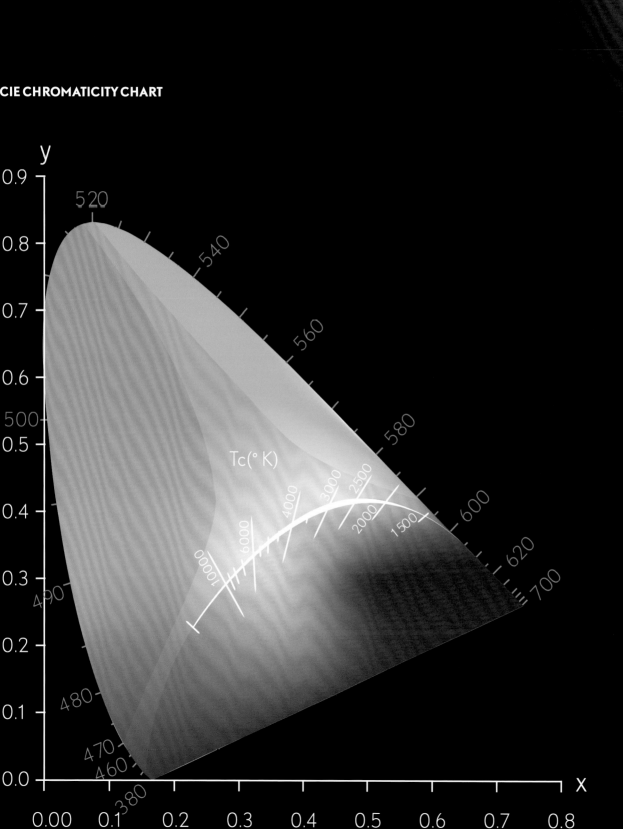
CIE CHROMATICITY CHART

# COLOR RENDERING INDEX

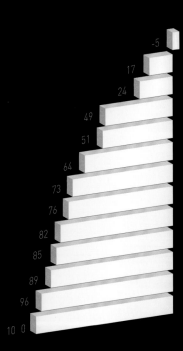
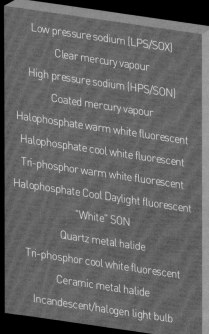

| Light Source | CCT [K] | CRI |
|---|---|---|

Low pressure sodium (LPS/SOX)
Clear mercury vapour
High pressure sodium (HPS/SON)
Coated mercury vapour
Halophosphate warm white fluorescent
Halophosphate cool white fluorescent
Tri-phosphor warm white fluorescent
Halophosphate Cool Daylight fluorescent
"White" SON
Quartz metal halide
Tri-phosphor cool white fluorescent
Ceramic metal halide
Incandescent/halogen light bulb

CRI values: -5, 17, 24, 49, 51, 64, 73, 76, 82, 85, 89, 96, 100

CCT values: 1800, 6410, 2100, 3600, 2940, 4230, 2940, 6430, 2700, 4200, 4080, 5400, 3200

## Color Rendering

-

The Color Rendering Index (CRI) is a quantitative measure of the effects of a light source to reproduce the colors of various objects, in comparison with natural light source. Light sources with high CRI are desirable for colors-critical situations as in cosmetic shops, high-end fashion boutique, cinematography and photography.

**Light-Emitting Diodes**

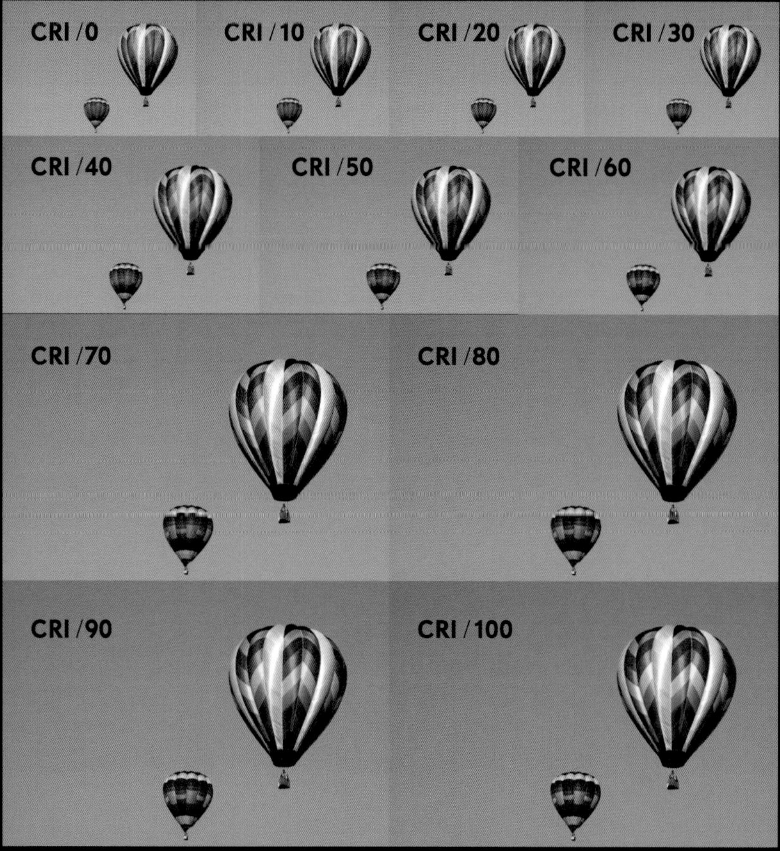

CRI /0
CRI / 10
CRI /20
CRI /30
CRI /40
CRI /50
CRI /60
CRI /70
CRI /80
CRI /90
CRI / 100


**FAIR**

50-60 CRI

Standard Warm White Fluorescent

Standard Cool White Fluorescent

60-70 CRI

Premium High-Pressure Sodium

Conventional Metal Halide

---

**BETTER**

70-80 CRI

Thin Coat Tri-Phosphor Fluorescent

---

**BEST**

80-90

White High-Pressure Sodium

Warm Metal Halide

Thick Coat Tri-Phosphor Fluorescent

90-100

High CRI Fluorescents

Incandescent and Tungsten-Halogen

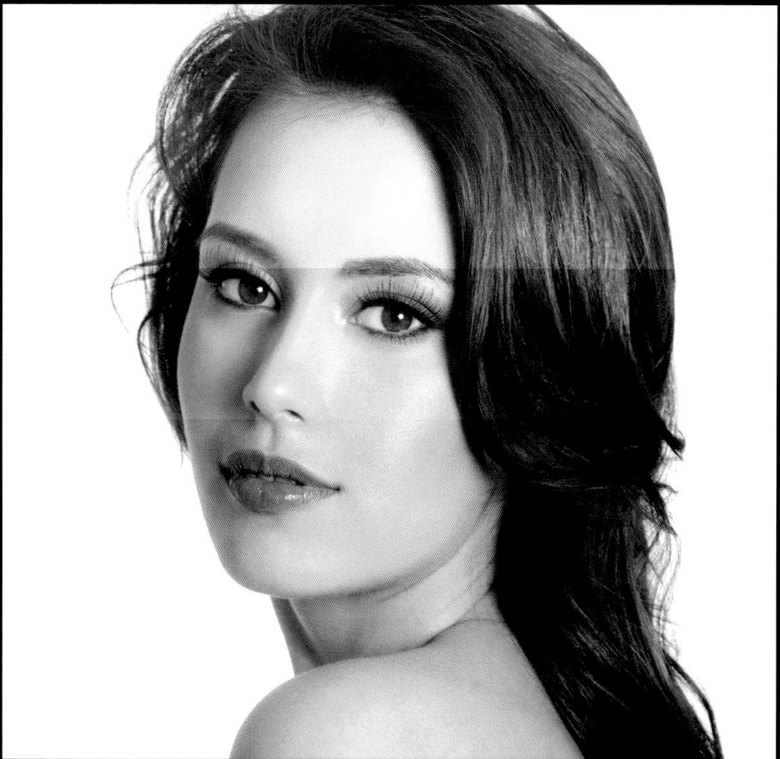

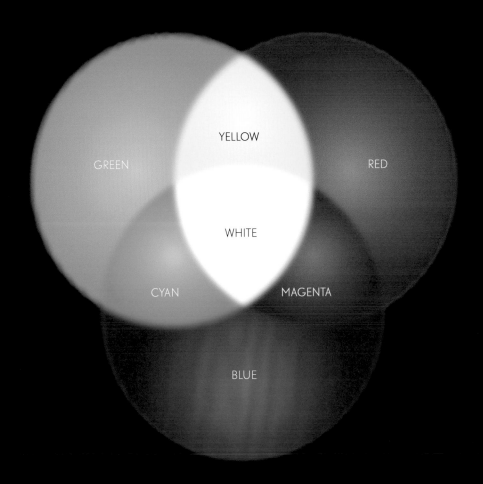

Additive color mixing: adding red to green yields yellow; adding all three primary colors together yields white.

## CIE CHART

-

The CIE XYZ color space was created by the International Commission on
Illumination (CIE) in 1931. It is the mathematically defined color space in the study
of the color perception.

The Tristimulus value of a color is conceptualized as the quantity of the primary
colors Red, Green and Blue (RGB) in a tri-chromatic additive color model with
luminance of the color as its third dimension. This mathematical constructs which is
indistinguishable in chromaticity or color saturation to the human eye.

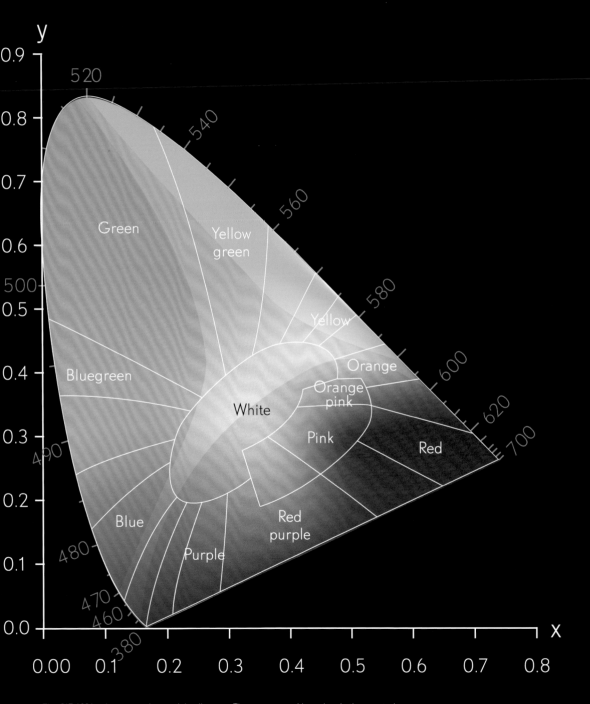

The CIE 1931 color space chromaticity diagram. The outer curved boundary is the spectral

## Luminous Efficacy

-

Luminous efficacy is a unit of efficiency for lighting. It is a ratio of power to luminous flux. The two are usually measured in watts and lumens, respectively. The fraction of luminous flux ($\Phi v$) to total input power (Watts) is called the efficacy of the lamp.

It is formally called the luminous efficacy of a source (LES) or luminous coefficient in a percentage. The LES is a measure of the efficiency with the source produces visible light.

For example a 8.7W LED lamp produces around 809 lm and therefore has an efficacy of 809/8.7 = 93 lm/W.

464

Here are more examples of different lamps' efficacy:

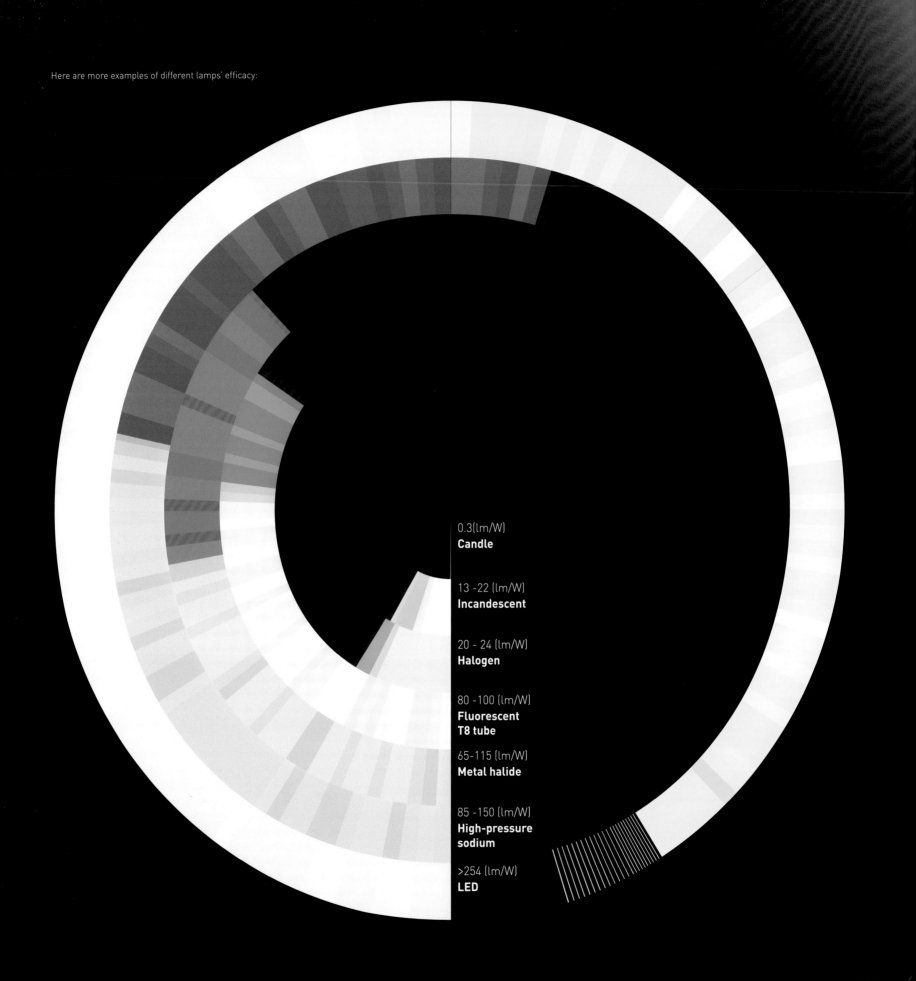

0.3 (lm/W)
**Candle**

13 -22 (lm/W)
**Incandescent**

20 - 24 (lm/W)
**Halogen**

80 -100 (lm/W)
**Fluorescent
T8 tube**

65-115 (lm/W)
**Metal halide**

85 -150 (lm/W)
**High-pressure
sodium**

>254 (lm/W)
**LED**

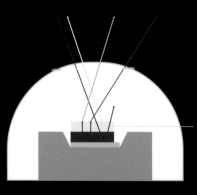

Chip Level conversion:
Conformal phosphor
close to Blue InGan Chip

LEDs produce light in a chip, or die, which is a small semiconductor device about 0.1 mm thick. From top to bottom a voltage is applied that injects charge carriers into the active region, which is a planar region within the semiconductor crystal.

Depending on the material used, most light is emitted through the top surface of the chip, although some light may come through the side surfaces as well. LED chip sizes are usually small, from 0.1 mm for low light applications to 1 mm for typical high brightness LEDs and even larger for special applications.

An LED chip always produces single-color light. Although LED light doesn't have as narrow a bandwidth as lasers, it is almost pure and highly saturated. This makes the light source very attractive for colored lighting. It makes LED lighting in such applications very efficient, too, because the LED produces only the desired color, unlike incandescent lamps, that needs to be filtered — at very low efficiency.

## TYPICAL EMISSION SPECTRUM OF A WHITE LED
## WITH PHOSPHOR CONVERSION

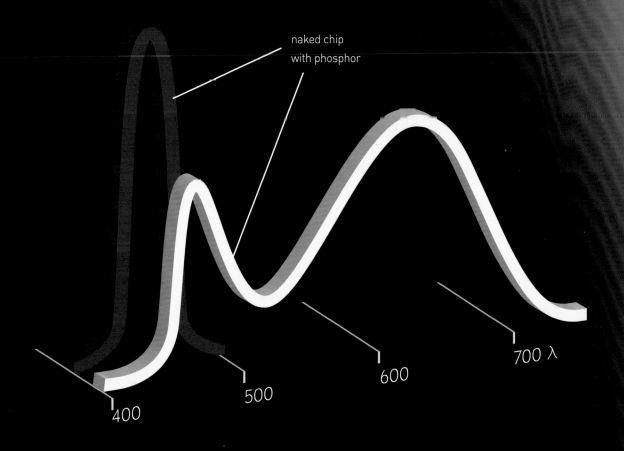

naked chip

with phosphor

700 λ

600

500

400

In applications where white light is needed, light from three or more LEDs can be mixed. When the right amount of red, green, and blue are overlapped, the resulting light appears as white. The same can be achieved by applying a phosphor or a mix of phosphors on top of a blue LED. Part of the blue light of the LED is converted into yellow and green light, while some blue light is left to leak out, so that the mixture of light becomes white, too.

There are different approaches currently found in phosphor-converted LEDs. Some use large phosphor "globs" over a chip. Such LEDs are cheap to make, but this makes the source look larger and there are issues with color non-uniformities. Some LEDs produce bluish and yellowish fringes. If the conversion is done on the blue LED chip with a small "conformal" phosphor, the light quality is better and such LEDs can be

Different phosphors or phosphor mixes can be used to change the color temperature from LEDs from cold white to warm white. However, the spectrum of many white LEDs lacks blue-green and red light. This sometimes leads to color-rendering problems.

For example skin tones often don't look natural under LED light. The LED makers are aware of this and start to come out with higher CRI (color rendering index) LEDs. However, such LEDs always produce less luminous flux than their low CRI counterparts.

Virtually all LED chips are covered with some kind of a clear encapsulant to protect the chip from the elements. A clear dome also increases the light output of the LED substantially because it helps to extract the light from LED chip that may otherwise be trapped in it.

## Optics

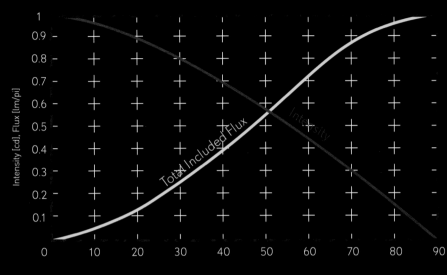

Lambertian intensity emission pattern and total included flux

Today's LEDs are starting to be very bright. A few decades ago they were merely dim telltales but now their small surfaces emit substantial amounts of light. When measured as luminance (as opposed to flux), modern LEDs reach up to 20 cd/mm^2, which is comparable to the brightness of the filament of a good incandescent bulb (25 cd/mm^2).

However, LEDs are involving rapidly, so not only their efficiency will be much higher than incandescent lighting, but also their brightness. It may actually be possible that LEDs will compete with the brightest commercially available white sources, which are short arc lamps.

### Why optics?
-

In almost all cases the emission of the bare LED does not suit the purpose. Only few LEDs come with primary optics, which normally consists of shaping the package to pre-focus the light. This can be sufficient in some applications like LED displays. However, such LED domes work well only with very small chips so such pre-focusing works only for relatively low flux LEDs.

High-efficiency LEDs need high-efficiency secondary optics. Topics like energy efficiency, light pollution and ever more stringent specifications make lighting applications more complex. Such specifications, legal or customer defined, consist of light intensities at certain points in space, or light illuminance, and color specifications. Color mixing optics can provide uniform color in the far fields, so very far away from the lighting fixture.

However, this doesn't mean that when you look back into the light source, you will see white light. You may still see red, green and blue section of the emitting surface. Where this is an issue, RGB mixing must provide white light in the near field, too, which adds considerable complexity to the mixing optics.

Some applications in which very specialized light shaping by the secondary optics is necessary are:

♦ Create highly collimated light (think about a flashlight, or a car headlamp)
♦ Collimate light with good uniformity (office lighting, street lighting)
♦ Coupling the light into a thin plate to become a uniform surface emitting source
♦ Distribute the light to make a luminaire less blinding
♦ Make a LED light bulb that emits like an incandescent bulb

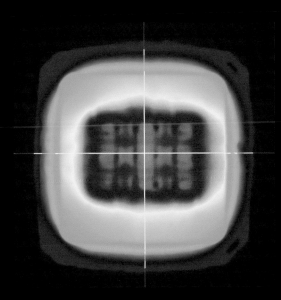

### How to shape light

-

Nature provides several possibilities to change the course of light rays. There is reflection, which can be either from metallic surfaces, or by total internal reflection (called TIR), which occurs when light hits this "inside" surface of a clear material under large angles. Other reflective mechanisms are interference effects, such as multilayer reflection, or dichroic coatings.

The efficiency of metallic reflection is usually in the range of about 80-90 percent. This can lead to substantial light loss, especially if the light undergoes several metallic reflections. TIR on the other hand is the only reflection in nature that is 100-percent efficient.

In practical cases, however, a little loss might occur if the optical surfaces are not perfectly smooth. Interference coatings can be made to extremely high reflectivities for specific wavelengths which is great for lasers. For general illumination dichroic coatings can be expensive, although there a numerous uses for such color selective filters.

A different technology is used for plastic foils that look metallic and can have extremely high reflectivities. Many

Diffusion is basically light scattering on small surface or volume features. Diffuse reflectors, like ordinary white paint or special diffuse-reflecting material, are widely available. Transmissive diffusers are basically flat plates or films that scatter the light to wider angles than the incident light.

Simpler diffusers are based only on roughened surfaces and have limited transmission efficiencies and beam control, while high-quality diffusers are holographic or diffusers consisting of microlens arrays on a flat surface that minimize back scattering and are available in precisely defined reflection angles. Diffusion is often used for color mixing and light smoothing.

Another class of optics is the diffractive optics that uses microscopic features on a surface to influence the light by interference. Such optics are sometimes combined with ordinary refractive optics to form powerful hybrids, for example to reduce color aberrations from a single optical lens.

Fresnel reflections always occur when light hits a surface of higher index of refraction. About four percent at normal incidence on a typical glass surface is "lost." Such reflected light can reduce system performance or created unwanted reflexes and artifacts. Coatings can be applied to reduce such reflections and are commonly used for high-end applications.

UFO-type lens with faceting for general illumination. This is a clear plastic lens with no metallization!

## Secondary optics types for LEDs
-
LEDs are often combined with mass producible inexpensive optics such as plastic optics or standard metal optics. Such elements can have different functions.

Collimation optics provide parallel beams of high intensity; Distribution optics do the opposite in creating broad areas of uniform illumination, guiding optics transport the light to where it is needed, coupling optics take the light from the source to a guide or another optical system, backlighting optics provide illumination for LCD panels, color mixing optics use the light from single color LEDs to provide white (or any other color) light. Many other types exist and often optics comply with several of such functions simultaneously.

In each of these fields, specialized optics are designed to meet the specific needs. However, most common are collimators that pick up the light from the LED emitting into a 180-degree cone to produce a more or less narrow beam. It is important to keep in mind that the larger the aperture of a collimator, the smaller the collimation angle of the light.

## AN OVERVIEW OF COMMON LENS TYPES:

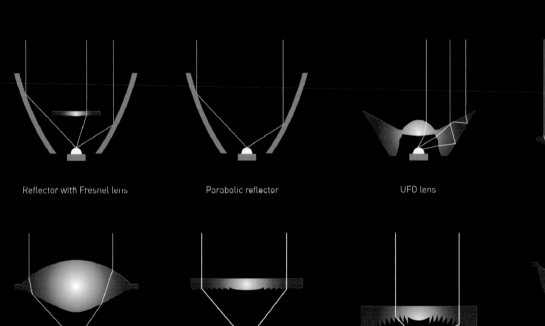

Reflector with Fresnel lens

Parabolic reflector

UFO lens

RXI lens

Aspheric refractive lens.

Fresnel lens

TIR lens

Photon funnel

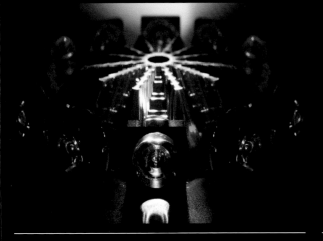

LED refractive/reflective optic for general illumination

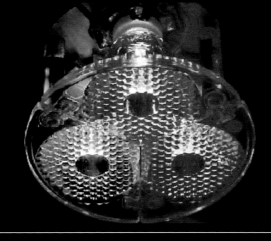

RGB collimation optics

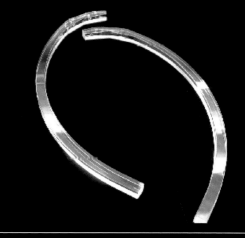

Specialized light guide for a medical application

Each collimator has certain advantages and disadvantages. Beside aesthetics, which can be very important for illumination applications and price, some key issues are:

• A refractive lens collects only a small portion of the emitted light but can create a highly focused beam. Such lenses tend to be very thick for large collection angles.

• Fresnel lenses are much thinner but do the same as refracting lenses, although the focusing isn't quite as good. Small Fresnel teeth can be placed on the inside or outside of the lens, or both.

• TIR lenses use teeth, too, but they work by total internal reflection instead of refraction. This makes it possible to collect all the light emitted from the LED and can be quite efficient, if carefully designed and manufactured. Such collimators are very compact.

• Photon funnels are basically TIR lenses but only with a single tooth. The simplicity and efficiency of such lenses has made this lens to be the standard collimator used in numerous LED applications. However, large photon funnels become impractical to manufacture, so for large LEDs or large collimator apertures, other concepts are preferred.

• Parabolic mirror are simple but not very compact and large amounts of light from the LED is not collimated and escapes as a wide cone of light. This problem can be partially solved with a reflector combined with a Fresnel lens.

• The UFO optic is an optic that is much more compact than the photon funnel but besides it is comparable. It can be made for larger exterior apertures.

• The RXI is a specialized lens that is the most compact collimator available and provides very tight collimation but at the expense of higher cost due to the metallization needed.

Some collimators are imaging devices, which mean one will find an image of the LED (with often undesired detail like the shape of the chip, bond wires, etc.) in the far field, while other collimators are "non-imaging," so the far field is to some degree mixed or blurred.

Imaging collimators are the refractive lens, the Fresnel lens and the RXI optic while all others, at least partially, are not image forming. The UFO and the RXI optic are patented by LPI.

All collimators shown here produce basically "spot" patterns. However, this is a good starting point, because such light can be easily be distributed by other elements or within the collimator itself to form other shapes like smooth Gaussian-type wide distributions or sharply defined radiation patterns of different types.

Microlenses or small mirror facets are often a powerful and very diverse tool to create different lighting effects that at the same time create a sparkling look of the collimator itself.

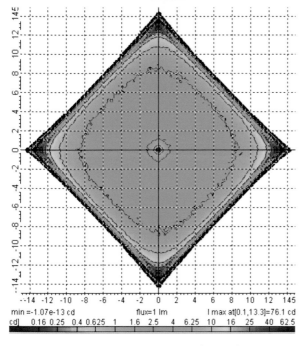

min =-1.07e-13 cd   flux=1 lm   I max at[0.1,13.3]=76.1 cd

cd] 0.16 0.25 0.4 0.625 1 1.6 2.5 4 6.25 10 16 25 40 62.5

Simulated intensity pattern of a faceted diffuser, (log scale)

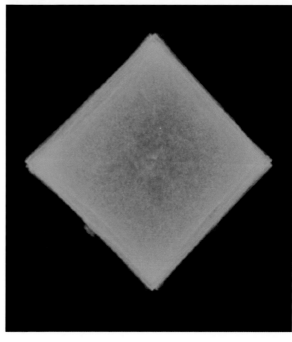

Picture of the intensity pattern of a prototype of the optics

Optical designers use different design tools to create optics. Those can be either analytic calculations from the laws of refraction and reflection or commercial or proprietary design tools based on numerical methods. Often optimization tools are used to find best solutions of certain mechanical shape parameters to make the light output meet specifications best. In almost all cases, before prototypes are built, the optical designs are checked with so-called raytracers.

These are sophisticated simulation programs into which the optical geometry and all surface and material definitions are loaded. Many "rays" are launched from a virtual light source and their path traced through the optical system. This allows the designer to predict with ever-increasing accuracy the output of the optical system.

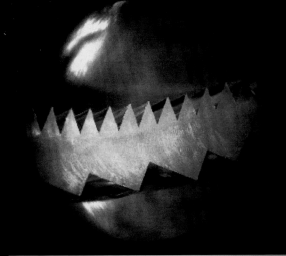

Cut through a complex TIR lens

High-quality facetted collimator

Virtual filament LED optic for incandescent
bulb replacements
*Patented by LPI*

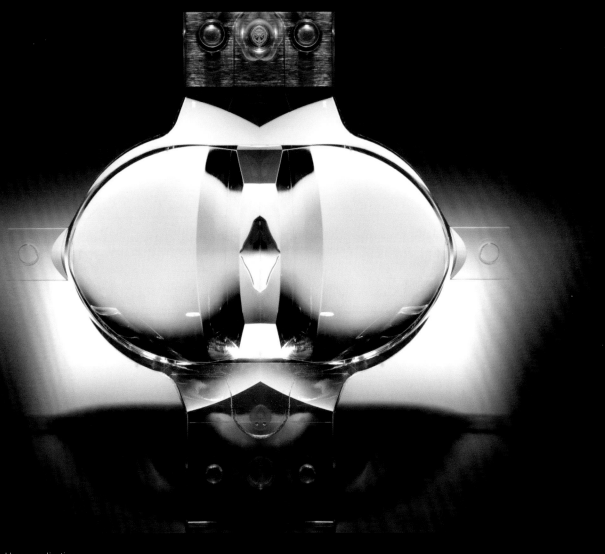

A freeform collimator made for automotive head lamp applications
*Design and patent: LPI.*
*Manufacturing: Bayer Material Sciences*

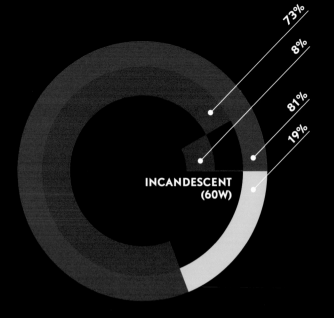

73%

8%

81%

19%

**INCANDESCENT**
**(60W)**

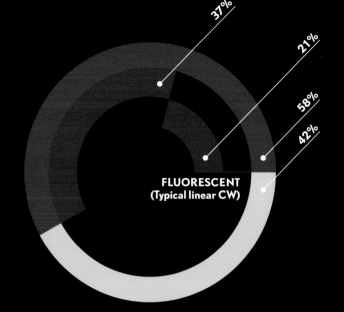

37%

21%

58%

42%

**FLUORESCENT**
**(Typical linear CW)**

For every luminaire, it consists of two major parts:

A. Light source

B. Light fixture

As a new kind of light source, LEDs' efficacy has surppassed the traditional light source as a result of technology breakthrough in these few years. The following pie charts show the trend.

LED has such a good performance, one should think that we have already reached a point replacing all traditional lower efficacy luminaires. In fact, this is not the case and this is because light source's efficacy is not being converted all into luminaires' efficacy when they are put into use.

By decomposing a luminaire, we can see there are 3 sub-systems; each of them will consume part of the input energy to enable its function. The overall luminaire efficacy will be the product of efficacies of the sub-systems.

| | |
|---|---|
| Input power: | 100% |
| Optical system efficiency: | x% |
| Electrical system efficiency: | y% |
| Thermal system: | z% |
| Luminaire efficacy: | x * y * z% |

Of the 3 sub-systems, there are respective experts focusing on obtaining highest possible efficiency. Thermal sub-system is more important to LED luminaire than other light source; the following paragraph debriefs the reason.

By analyzing the spectrum of a few important light sources against LED, as shown in the pie charts, one can see with all power going into different light sources; LED is the special one that generates nearly no infrared nor ultraviolet energy.

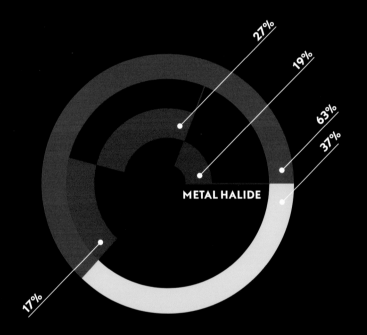

27%

19%

63%

37%

17%

METAL HALIDE

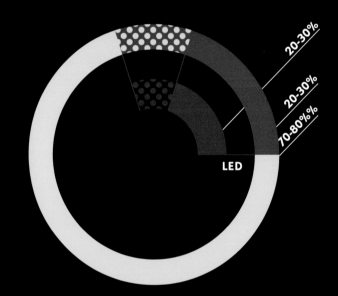

20-30%

20-30%

70-80%%

LED

"Thermal Management of White LEDs", DOE of US, Jun 2009

The advantage of generating no IR or UV light is that LED will not damage the objects being lit up; the disadvantage is that 70~80% of its input power has to be dissipated through convection or by conduction, which in terms of percentage is almost 5 times of an incandescent lamp.

Here details the differences between LED and other light sources:

A. Other light sources are usually made of material that can withstand very high temperature; therefore, there is no need to extract heat energy from them to reduce their body temperatures. For instance, an incandescent lamp actually produces light when its filament is heated up to a temperature up to a few thousand degrees. LED conversely should be kept operating at low temperatures.

B. A big portion of energy is extracted from a light source by radiation; where LED does not have this heat dissipation path.

C. LED is a semi-conductor device. Light output is obtained by generating photons in PN junction. If the PN junction is heated up, the performance of generating photons will drop, result ing in decreased efficacy and degraded chromaticity.

D. LED semi-conductor material needs encapsulation in packaging material which cannot withstand high temperature, otherwise the packaging material will degrade or even de-composite quickly.

With the advance of packaging and semi-conductor technology; LED nowadays can withstand up to 150 deg C without problem. However, its efficacy will drop from 10% to 30% while operating in high temperature, its color and lumen maintenance is significantly affected, which make its advantage over other light source diminished.

Thus the way of doing thermal management for LED light source is very important and very different compared to other light sources.

In fact, thermal management has to be more important in integrated or self ballast lamps, where the ballast is located by the side of the LED light source. The reason is that the LED thermal characteristic has been improved a lot; however, some electronic components for making ballast are still required to work in much lower temperature especially the electrolytic capacitors. Another concerning material is lens which are made of plastic. When both LED and ballast are lit up and heat is generated, the heat sink of the luminaire has to be capable of dissipating heat to maintain low operating temperature. In some extreme cases, separate heat conduction paths are required to isolate the thermal effect of LED and ballast.Therefore, designer of LED luminaire has put a lot of attention to the thermal management, new material or new device for enhancing the conduction and heat dissipation; whether it is passive or active cooling are tried out in the history of LED lighting.

Thermal characteristics of LED light source have also put a fundamental design difference in luminaire as compared to traditional light sources. It is the thermal sub-system has tight coupling between the light source and the housing of the luminaire. The housing has to be a high efficiency heat sink for LED light source. This makes the housing design a complicated thermal engineering task instead of cosmetic and structural only design. Many traditional approaches of housing design thus need to be re-considered; thicker metallic part are used more often.

**Thermal analysis of heat sink design**
-
With computational simulation, software such as Flotherm, FloWork, and Ansys etc, one can put in solid models; set up input conditions of real situations; obtain the thermal performance of luminaire with considerations of radiation, convection and conduction. Thus, the thermal path, the overall temperature profile and the critical area can be located; engineers can focus on solving the heat-sink design problem.

 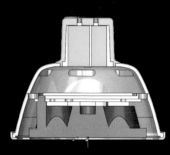 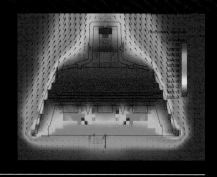

**MR-16 G5.3**

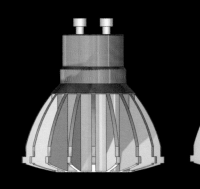 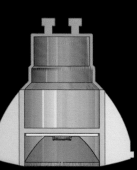 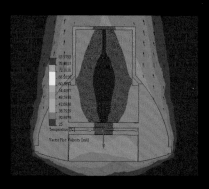

**MR-16 GU10**

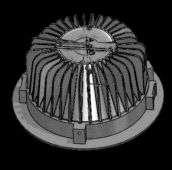 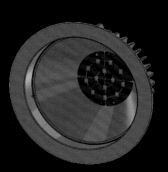 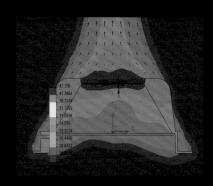

**DOWNLIGHT**

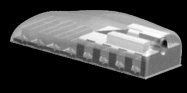  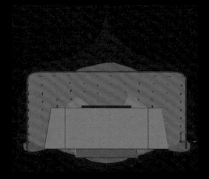

**STREET LAMP**

## BOOKS:

*1000 Lights* by editors Charlotte and Peter Fiell

*AD – 4dspace: Interactive Architecture*
by Lucy Bullivant

*Architectural Lighting Design* by Gary Steffy

*BRIGHT* – architectural illumination and light installations by FRAME

*Designing with Light and Shadow* by Kaoru Mende and Lighting Planners Associates Inc.

*Geometre des Lichts* (Geometry of Light)
by James Turrell

*Human Factors in Lighting* by Peter R. Boyce

*Light for Art's Sake – Lighting for Artworks and Museum Display* by Christopher Cuttle

*Light Revealing Architecture* by Mariella S. Millet

*Lighting Design – Principles Implementation Case Studies* by Birkhauser

*Lighting Design for Architecture* by Licht Kunst Licht 2

*Lighting by Design* by Christopher Cuttle

*Lighting by Design* by Sally Storey

*Lighting Spaces – The Art & Science of Architectural Lighting* by Roger Yee

*Made of Light – The Art of Light and Architecture* by Mark Major, Jonathan Speirs and Anthony Tischhauser

*Residential Lighting – A practical Guide* by Randall Whitehead

*Ultimate Lighting Design* projects by Herve Descottes/ L'Observatoire International

## REPORTS:

"China LED industry Downstream Application Research Report" by gg-led.com

"Energy Savings Estimates of Light Emitting Diodes in Niche Lighting Applications" from the US Department of Energy, Office of Energy Efficiency and Renewable Energy, Washington: Building Technologies Program. Navigant Consulting Inc (2008)

"The Market for High-Brightness LEDs in Lighting - Application Analysis and Forecast 2010" by strategies unlimited

Extra information (for Heat Sink sections):
Reference by W.H Leung, Director of Engineering, Light Engine. October 18, 2010

"Thermal Management of White LEDs", US Department of Energy June 2009

"Solid-State Lighting Research and Development, Multi-Year Program Plan FY'09-FY'15", US Department of Energy, March 2009

**INTERNET:**

http://www.brand.swarovski.com/Content.Node/presscentre/
news/news-architectureartdesign/lbindianmarket.en.html#/
en/presscentre/news/news-architectureartdesign/
lbindianmarket

http://thecleanrevolution.org/_assets/files/LED_report
_web1.pdf

http://www.goldwynled.com/Content/Timeline.aspx

http://web.mit.edu/newsoffice/2004/lemelson-0428.html

http://www.doubulb.com/led-history.html

http://hyperphysics.phy-astr.gsu.edu/hbase/vision/cie.html

http://dba.med.sc.edu/price/irf/Adobe_tg/models/
ciexyz.html

http://www.convert-measurement-units.com/convert+Terawatt+
hour+to+Kilowatt+hour.php

http://zfxxgk.nea.gov.cn/

http://www.reuters.com/article/2012/05/14/china-power-
consumption-idUSL4E8GE7BJ20120514

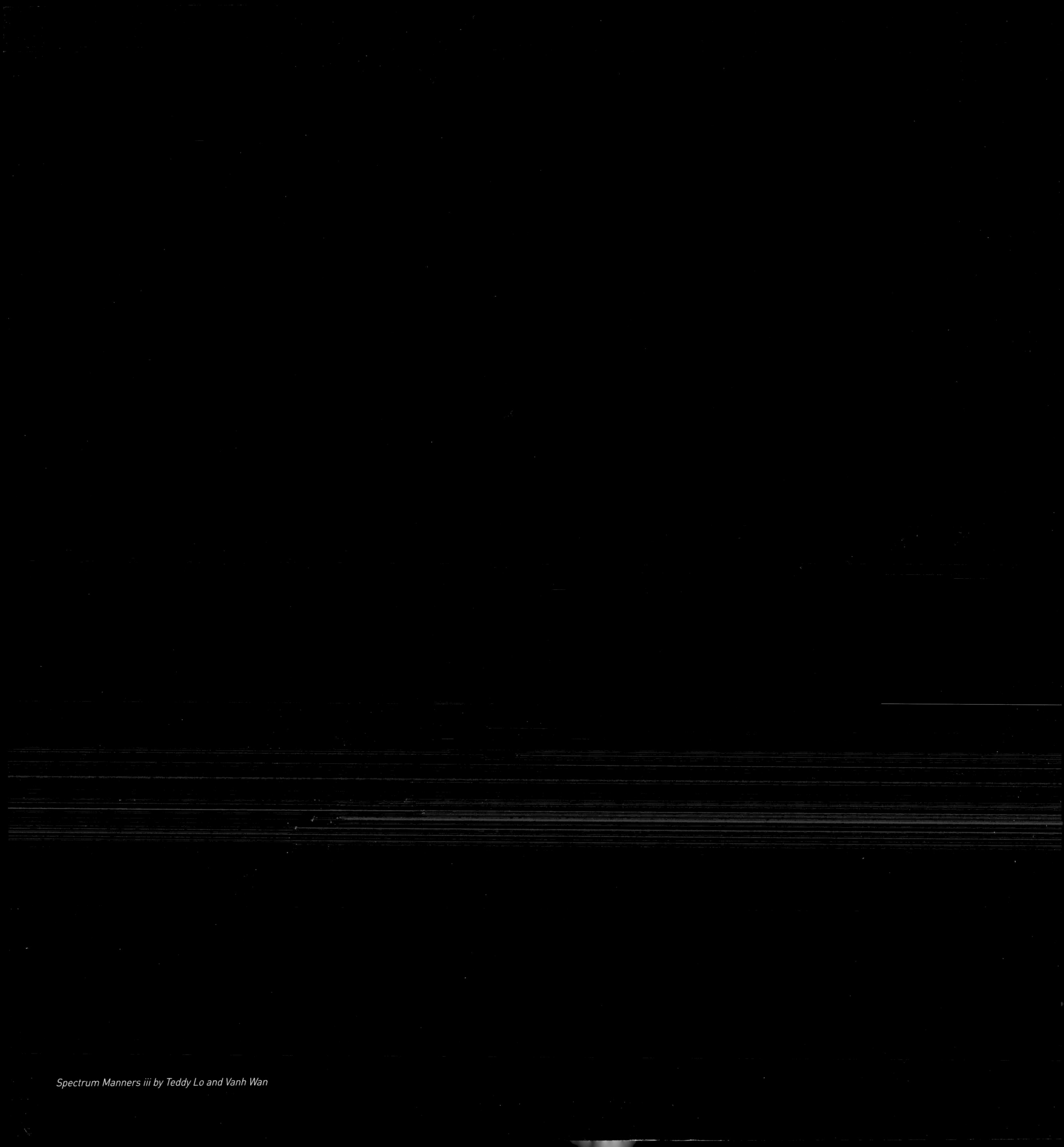

*Spectrum Manners iii by Teddy Lo and Vanh Wan*